A TEXT BOOK OF

SYSTEMS APPROACH IN CIVIL ENGINEERING

(Elective-I)
For
(Semester-I)
FINAL YEAR (B.E.) DEGREE COURSE IN CIVIL ENGINEERING

ACCORDING TO NEW REVISED SYLLABUS OF
SAVITRIBAI PHULE PUNE UNIVERSITY, PUNE.
(2012 PATTERN)

H.K. Gite
M.E. (Const. Mgt.), M.B.A. (H.R.D.)
Assistant Engineer Grade - 1
Water Resource Department, Govt. of Maharashtra
Formally Rajarshi Shahu College of Engineering
Tathwade, PUNE

K.M. Bagwan
M.E. Civil (Const., Mgt)
Assistant Professor,
Civil Engg. Deptt.
KJ College of Engg. & Mgt. Research
Pisoli, PUNE

Ms. M.A. Lulla (Pawar)
M.E. (Strutural), PGDCM (NICMAR)
Assistant Professor, Civil Engg. Deptt.
JSPM's Rajarshi Shahu College of Engineering
Tathwade, PUNE

N3689

SYSTEMS APPROACH IN CIVIL ENGG. **ISBN 978-93-5164-691-4**

First Edition : July 2015
© : **Authors**

The text of this publication, or any part thereof, should not be reproduced or transmitted in any form or stored in any computer storage system or device for distribution including photocopy, recording, taping or information retrieval system or reproduced on any disc, tape, perforated media or other information storage device etc., without the written permission of Authors with whom the rights are reserved. Breach of this condition is liable for legal action.

Every effort has been made to avoid errors or omissions in this publication. In spite of this, errors may have crept in. Any mistake, error or discrepancy so noted and shall be brought to our notice shall be taken care of in the next edition. It is notified that neither the publisher nor the authors or seller shall be responsible for any damage or loss of action to any one, of any kind, in any manner, therefrom.

Published By : **Printed By :**
NIRALI PRAKASHAN **Repro Knowledgecast Limited**
Abhyudaya Pragati, 1312, Shivaji Nagar,
Off J.M. Road, Pune – 411005
Tel - (020) 25512336/37/39, Fax - (020) 25511379
Email : niralipune@pragationline.com

☞ **DISTRIBUTION CENTRES**

PUNE
Nirali Prakashan : 119, Budhwar Peth, Jogeshwari Mandir Lane, Pune 411002, Maharashtra
Tel : (020) 2445 2044, 66022708, Fax : (020) 2445 1538
Email : bookorder@pragationline.com, niralilocal@pragationline.com
Nirali Prakashan : S. No. 28/27, Dhyari, Near Pari Company, Pune 411041
Tel : (020) 24690204 Fax : (020) 24690316
Email : dhyari@pragationline.com, bookorder@pragationline.com

MUMBAI
Nirali Prakashan : 385, S.V.P. Road, Rasdhara Co-op. Hsg. Society Ltd.,
Girgaum, Mumbai 400004, Maharashtra
Tel : (022) 2385 6339 / 2386 9976, Fax : (022) 2386 9976
Email : niralimumbai@pragationline.com

☞ **DISTRIBUTION BRANCHES**

JALGAON
Nirali Prakashan : 34, V. V. Golani Market, Navi Peth, Jalgaon 425001,
Maharashtra, Tel : (0257) 222 0395, Mob : 94234 91860

KOLHAPUR
Nirali Prakashan : New Mahadvar Road, Kedar Plaza, 1st Floor Opp. IDBI Bank
Kolhapur 416 012, Maharashtra. Mob : 9850046155

NAGPUR
Pratibha Book Distributors : Above Maratha Mandir, Shop No. 3, First Floor,
Rani Jhanshi Square, Sitabuldi, Nagpur 440012, Maharashtra
Tel : (0712) 254 7129

DELHI
Nirali Prakashan : 4593/21, Basement, Aggarwal Lane 15, Ansari Road, Daryaganj
Near Times of India Building, New Delhi 110002
Mob : 08505972553

BENGALURU
Pragati Book House : House No. 1, Sanjeevappa Lane, Avenue Road Cross,
Opp. Rice Church, Bengaluru – 560002.
Tel : (080) 64513344, 64513355,Mob : 9880582331, 9845021552
Email:bharatsavla@yahoo.com

CHENNAI
Pragati Books : 9/1, Montieth Road, Behind Taas Mahal, Egmore,
Chennai 600008 Tamil Nadu, Tel : (044) 6518 3535,
Mob : 94440 01782 / 98450 21552 / 98805 82331,
Email : bharatsavla@yahoo.com

niralipune@pragationline.com | www.pragationline.com
Also find us on www.facebook.com/niralibooks

PREFACE

It gives us great pleasure in presenting the book on **"Systems Approach in Civil Engineering"**, which is written as per Savitribai Phule Pune University Revised Syllabus (2012 Pattern) and in most concised form. The book will also be very useful for Master of Civil Engineering Construction Management Course.

The book is as per New Revised Examination Scheme which has been implemented from this academic year. According to this, In-Semester Examination carries 30 Marks over first three units and End-Semester Examination carries 70 Marks over entire syllabus of which the first three units will carry 20 Marks and units 4, 5 and 6 will carry 50 Marks.

The subject matter is presented in simple and easy form so as to enable the students to understand the subject easily. Sufficient care is taken to present the subject matter in the point wise form in most of the chapters. **Sample Question Papers for the In-Semester and End-Semester University Examination are also included in this book for practice to students.**

Authors are extremely grateful to, **Shri Vijay Pandare**, Chief Engineer, META Nashik, **Shri R. D. Pantankar**, Superintending Engineer, **Shri S. M. Sangle**, Executive Engineer, PH-Division 4, CDO Nashik, **Dr. P. P. Vitkar**, Director JSPM's Pune. **Dr. D. S. Bormane**, Principal RSCOE, Pune. **Prof. Dr. S. J. Wagh** Principal KJE's KJCOE&MR, Pune, **Prof. M. E. Dhanak**, HOD, Civil Engg. Dept., KJCOE&MR Pune and all staff of for providing conclusive environment and facilities for completing this book.

We are sincerely thankful to **Shri Dineshbhai K. Furia, Shri. Jignesh C. Furia, Mrs. Nirali Verma, Shri. M. P. Munde** and the entire team of Nirali Prakashan who really have taken keen interest and untiring efforts in publishing this text. We are also thankful to Mrs. Deepali Lachake (Co-ordinator) Mr. Akbar Shaikh, Miss. Mandakini Jadhwar for their kind co-operation throughout the work.

Also, it is important to mention invaluable moral support of our beloved family members, who consistently encouraged us for better work.

Despite the best efforts taken by authors, it is possible that some unintentional errors might have taken place. Authors would gratefully acknowledge if any of these is pointed out. Suggestions and comments for further improvement of this book will be gratefully received and acknowledged from the students, teachers and others to our following Emails.

hkgitein@rediffmail.com, kha_bag @yahoo.com, and monica-lulla@rediffmaii.com

Pune **Authors**

SYLLABUS

Unit 1: Introduction of Systems Approach (06 Hours)

Introduction to System Approach, Operations Research and Optimization Techniques, Use of Systems Approach in Civil Engineering, Methods, Introduction to Linear and Non-linear Programming Methods (with reference to objective function, constraints), Local and Global Optima, Unimodal Function, Convex and Concave Function.

Unit 2: Non-Linear Programming (06 Hours)

Single Variable Unconstrained Optimization: Sequential Search Techniques - Dichotomous, Fibonacci, Golden Section.

Multivariable Optimization without Constraints: The Gradient Vector and Hessian Matrix, Gradient Techniques, Steepest Ascent/Decent Technique, Newton's Method Multivariable Optimization with Equality Constraints - Lagrange Multiplier Technique.

Unit 3: Stochastic Programming (06 Hours)

Sequencing - n jobs through 2, 3 and M machines.

Queuing Theory: Elements of Queuing System and its Operating Characteristics, Waiting Time and Ideal Time Costs, Kendall's Notation, Classification of Queuing Models, Single Channel Queuing Theory: Model I (Single Channel Poisson Arrival with Exponential Services Times, Infinite Population (M/M/I) : (FCFS/∞/∞).

Simulation : Monte Carlo Simulation.

Unit 4: Dynamic Programming (06 Hours)

Multi Stage Decision Processes, Principle of Optimality, Recursive Equation, Applications of D.P.

Unit 5: Linear Programming (A) (06 Hours)

Formulation of Linear Optimization Models for Civil Engineering Applications. The simplex Method, Model of Big M, Two Phase Method, Duality.

Unit 6: Linear Programming (B) (06 Hours)

The Transportation Model and its variants, Assignment Model and its variants.

■■■

CONTENTS

Unit 1: Introduction of Systems Approach — 1.1 – 1.18
- 1.1 Introduction — 1.1
- 1.2 Introduction to Optimization and Operation Research — 1.2
- 1.3 Use of System Approach in Civil Engineering — 1.2
- 1.4 Various Models which are used in System Approach — 1.3
- 1.5 Objective Function — 1.4
- 1.6 Constraint — 1.4
- 1.7 Convex and Concave Set — 1.4
- 1.8 Convex and Concave Functions — 1.5
- 1.9 Linear Programming — 1.6
- 1.10 Non-Linear Programming — 1.7
    - 1.10.1 Introduction — 1.7
    - 1.10.2 Non-Linear Programming Problems — 1.8
    - 1.10.3 Local and Global Optimum — 1.11

Unit 2: Non-linear Programming — 2.1 – 2.40
- 2.1 One Dimensional Minimization Methods — 2.1
    - 2.1.1 Unimodal Function — 2.1
- 2.2 Dichotomous Search Method — 2.1
- 2.3 Fibonacci Method — 2.3
- 2.4 Golden Section Method — 2.5
- 2.5 Unconstrained Multidimensional Methods — 2.17
    - 2.5.1 Steepest Ascent/Descent Method (Wchy's Method) — 2.17
    - 2.5.2 Newton's Modified Method — 2.23
- 2.6 Constrained External Problems — 2.26
    - 2.6.1 Problem with all Equality Constraints — 2.26
    - 2.6.2 Necessary and Sufficient Conditions for a General NLPP — 2.27
    - 2.6.3 Constrained External Problem with more than One Equality Constraint — 2.32
    - 2.6.4 Non–Linear Programming Problem with Inequality Constraints — 2.36
    - • Theoretical Questions — 2.38
    - • Numerical Problems — 2.39

Unit 3: Stochastic Programming — 3.1 – 3.44
- 3.1 Sequencing Model — 3.1
    - 3.1.1 Introduction — 3.1
    - 3.1.2 Notations and Terminology — 3.1
    - 3.1.3 Analytical Methods have been Developed for Solving only Five Simple Cases — 3.2
    - 3.1.4 Assumptions in Sequencing Problem — 3.2
    - 3.1.5 Processing 'n' Jobs Through Two Machines — 3.2
    - 3.1.6 Processing n Jobs Through Three Machines — 3.6
    - 3.1.7 Processing n Jobs Through m Machines — 3.10

3.2	Queuing Theory		3.14
	3.2.1	Introduction	3.14
	3.2.2	Applications of Queuing Models	3.15
	3.2.3	The basic Queuing Model Consist of	3.16
	3.2.4	Characteristic of Queuing Theory	3.16
	3.2.5	Operating Characteristics of a Queuing System	3.16
	3.2.6	Kendall's Notation for representing Queuing Models	3.17
	3.2.7	Classification of Queuing Models	3.18
	3.2.8	Model 1, Single Channel Poisson Arrivals with Exponential Service, Infinite Population Model [(M/M/1) : (FCFS/∞/∞)]	3.19
	3.2.9	Service Mechanism	3.28
	3.2.10	Assumptions of Queuing Model	3.29
	3.2.11	Limitations of Queuing Model	3.30
	3.2.12	Mathematical Symbols of Queuing Model	3.30
3.3	Simulation		3.33
	3.3.1	Introduction	3.33
	3.3.2	Advantages of the Simulation Technique	3.34
	3.3.3	Limitations of the Simulation Technique	3.34
	3.3.4	Applications of Simulation	3.34
	3.3.5	Monte Carlo Simulation	3.35
	•	Theoretical Questions	3.40

Unit 4: Dynamic Programming — 4.1 – 4.40

4.1	Introduction	4.1
4.2	Characteristics of Dynamic Programming Problems	4.2
4.3	Application of Dynamic Programming in Civil Engineering	4.2
4.4	Advantages of Dynamic Programming	4.3
4.5	Disadvantages of Dynamic Programming	4.3
4.6	Terminology of Dynamic Programming	4.3
4.7	Stages for Solution through Dynamic Programming	4.4
4.8	Bellman's Principal of Optimality	4.4
4.9	Representation of Dynamic Programming	4.5
	4.9.1 Single Stage Decision Process	4.5
	4.9.2 Multistage Decision Process	4.5
4.10	Computational Procedure in DP	4.7
4.11	Application of Dynamic Programming to LPP	4.33
	• Theoretical Questions	4.36

Unit 5: Queuing Theory and Sequencing Models — 5.1 – 5.48

5.1	Formulation of Linear Programming Model	5.1
5.2	Graphical Method	5.2
5.3	Simplex Method	5.11
5.4	Two Phase Method	5.22
5.5	Big M - Method	5.31
5.6	Duality in Linear Programming	5.43
	• Theoretical Questions	5.47

Unit 6: Network Models — 6.1 – 6.34

Transportation Problem

6.1	Introduction	6.1
6.2	Applications	6.1
6.3	Mathematical Representation of Problem	6.1
6.4	Basic Terminology	6.3
6.5	Methods of solution	6.4
	6.5.1 North-West Corner Method (NWCM)	6.4
	6.5.2 Least Cost Method (LCM)	6.5
	6.5.3 Vogel's Approximation Method (VAM)	6.6
6.6	Test for Optimality	6.8
	6.6.1 Modified Distribution Method or MODI Method	6.8
	6.6.2 Stepping Stone Method	6.11
6.7	Special cases in Transportation Problem	6.14
	6.7.1 Unbalanced Transportation Problems → Supply ≠ Demand	6.14
	6.7.2 Degenerate Solution	6.16
	6.7.3 Maximization Objective	6.19

Assignment Problem

6.8	Introduction	6.22
6.9	The Assignment Problem is used for Assignment of	6.22
6.10	Mathematical Representation of Assignment Problems	6.22
6.11	Solution Steps of Assignment problem	6.23
6.12	Special Cases in Assignment Problem	6.26
	6.12.1 Maximization Objective	6.26
	6.12.2 Unbalanced Assignment Problems	6.28
	6.12.3 Restrictions in Assignment	6.29
	6.12.4 Multiple Optimal Solutions	6.29
	• Theoretical Questions	6.30

- **Sample Question Paper for In Semester Examination (30 Marks)** — P.1 – P.2
- **Sample Question Papers for End-Semester Examination (70 Marks)** — P.3 – P.8

Unit 1

INTRODUCTION OF SYSTEMS APPROACH

1.1 INTRODUCTION

Now-a-days Civil Engineering projects complexity is increased, but the abilities of the engineers, planners, managers, decision makers remains limited. There are many conflicts between the complexity of the limited no. of ides that can be included in considerations of decisions. So system approach provides a general decision making scheme that makes involvement in broadly based decisions accessible.

System approach is nothing but a line of thought in the management which stresses the interactive nature and interdependence of external and internal factors in an organisation. A system approach is commonly used to evaluate market elements which affect the profitability of a business.

System approach is the systematic application of quantitative methods, techniques and tools to the analysis of problem involving operation of system.

This new decision making field has been characterized by the use of scientific knowledge through inter disciplinary team effort for the purpose of determining the best utilization of limited resources.

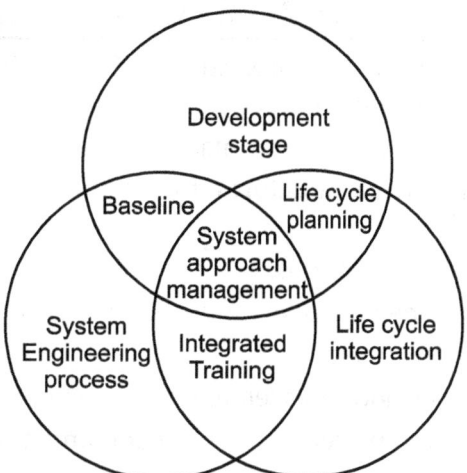

Fig. 1.1: The scope of system approach.

1.2 INTRODUCTION TO OPTIMIZATION AND OPERATION RESERACH

Optimization (maximization or minimization) is an art of obtaining the best result under a given situation. In design, construction and planning of any engineering system, engineers have to make many technical and managerial decisions at several stages. The final goal to be achieved from all such decisions is either to minimize the efforts required or to maximize the desired benefit.

Operation research is a branch of mathematics concerned with the application of scientific methods and techniques to decision making problems and with establishing the best optimal solutions. The table given below list down the various mathematical programming techniques;

Table 1.1

Mathematics Programming Techniques	Stochastic Process Techniques	Statistical Methods
• Non-linear programming • Linear programming • Dynamic programming • Network methods – **CPM OR PERT** • Game theory	• Queuing theory • Simulation methods	• Regression analysis • Design of experiments

1.3 USE OF SYSTEM APPROACH IN CIVIL ENGINEERING

- Design of civil engineering structures such as frames, foundations, bridges, towers, chimneys and dam for minimum cost.
- Design of water resources systems for maximum benefit.
- Minimum weight design of structures for earthquake, wind and other types of random loading.
- Optimal plastic design of structures.
- Design of optimal pipeline networks for process industries.
- Selection of a site for an industry.
- Planning of maintenance and replacement of equipment to reduce operating costs.
- Planning of maintenance and replacement of equipment to reduce operating costs.
- Inventory control.
- Allocation of resources or services among several activities to maximize the benefit.

1.4 VARIOUS MODELS WHICH ARE USED IN SYSTEM APPROACH

1. **Linear Programming:** Linear programming is an optimization method applicable for the solution of problems in which the objective function and the constraints appear as linear functions of the decision variables. The constraints equations in a linear programming problem may be in the form of equalities or inequalities. Linear programming is considered as a revolutionary development that permits us to make optimal decisions in complex situations.

2. **Non-Linear Programming:** A key assumption of linear programming is that all its functions are linear. Although this assumption does not hold for all problems. As a result the objective function of / or one or more of the constraints will have non-linear relationship among decision variables.

   If the problem is to optimize the objective function without any constraints then they are unconstrained optimization problem.

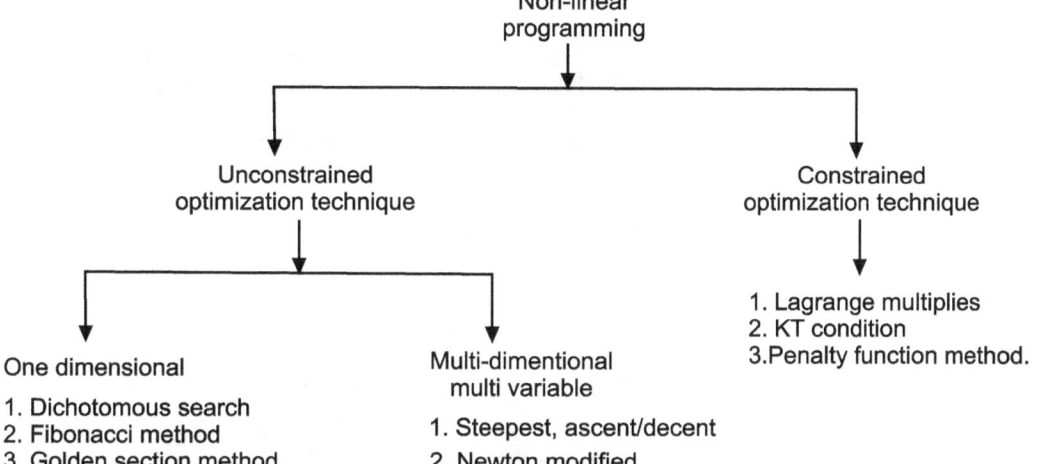

3. **Dynamic Programming:** Dynamic programming is a mathematical technique well suited for the optimization of multistage decision problems. The dynamic programming technique, when applicable, represents or decomposes a multistage decision problem as a sequence of single stage decision problems.

4. **Sequencing Model**
5. **Simulation**
6. **Queuing Theory**
7. **Game Theory**
8. **Replacement Model**

1.5 OBJECTIVE FUNCTION

In general there will be more than one acceptable design, of the purpose of optimization is to choose the best one of the many acceptable design available. Thus a criterion has to be chosen for comparing the different alternative acceptable designs and for selecting the best one. The criterion with respect to which the design is optimized, when expressed as a function of the design variables, is known as the criterion or objective function. The choice of objective function is governed by the nature of problem. In civil engineering structural design, the objective is usually taken as the minimization of cost.

1.6 CONSTRAINT

Constraints is the element factors or a subsystem that works as a bottle neck. It restricts an entity, project, or system from achieving its potential with reference to its goal. The constraints represent uncontrollable variables. They define system boundary.

1.7 CONVEX AND CONCAVE SET

A convex set is a collection of points such that if x_1 of x_2 are the two points in a collection and line segment joining them is also in the collection.

On the other hand, it is not possible to find two points a and b in the set such that not all the points on the line joining them belong to the set, and this set is called as non convex or concave set.

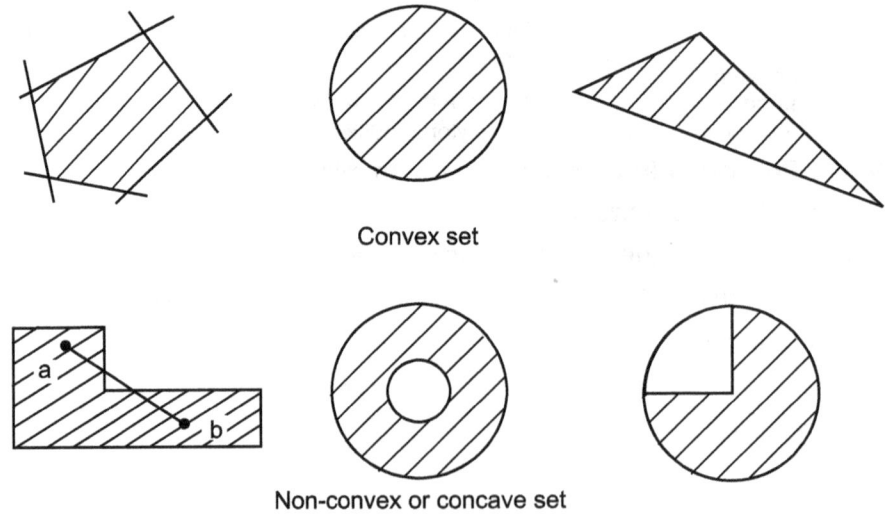

Convex set

Non-convex or concave set

Fig. 1.2

1.8 CONVEX AND CONCAVE FUNCTIONS

A function f (x) is said to be convex if for any pair of points.

$$x_1 = \begin{Bmatrix} x_1^{(1)} \\ x_2^{(1)} \\ \vdots \\ x_n^{(1)} \end{Bmatrix} \text{ and } x_2 = \begin{Bmatrix} x_1^{(2)} \\ x_2^{(2)} \\ \vdots \\ x_n^{(1)} \end{Bmatrix}$$

And all λ) o $\leq \lambda \leq 1$

$$f [\lambda x_2 + (1-\lambda) x_1] \leq \lambda f(x_2) + (1-\lambda) f(x_1)$$

That is, if the segment joining the two points lies entirely above or on the graph of f (x).

The following fig. Shows the convex function of single variable.

So let λ = ½

$$f\left[\frac{1}{2}x_2 + \left(1 - \frac{1}{2}\right)x_1\right] \leq \frac{1}{2}f(x_2) + \left(1 - \frac{1}{2}\right)f(x_1)$$

$$f\frac{1}{2}[x_2 + x_1] \leq \frac{1}{2}[f(x_2) + f(x_1)]$$

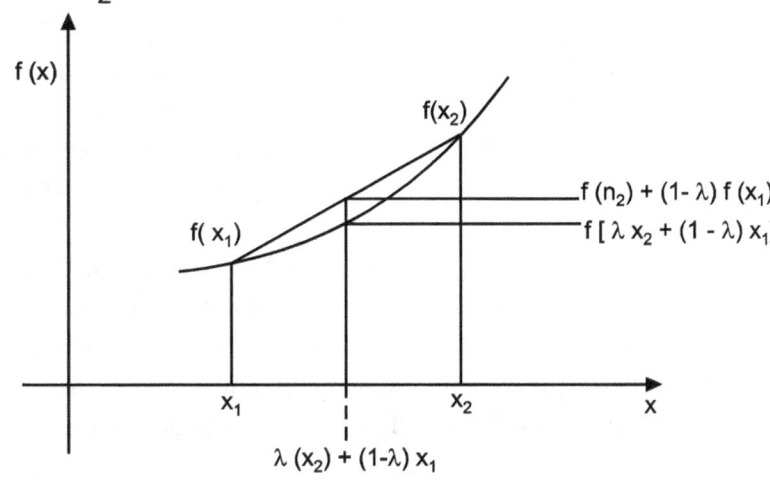

Fig. 1.3

It is can be seen that a convex function is always bending upward and hence it is apparent that the local minimum of a convex function is also a global minimum.

A function f (x) is called a concave function if for any two points x_1 and x_2 and for all $0 \leq 1 \leq 1$

$$F [\lambda x_2 + (1 - \lambda) x_1] \geq \lambda f(x_2) + (1 - \lambda) f(x_1)$$

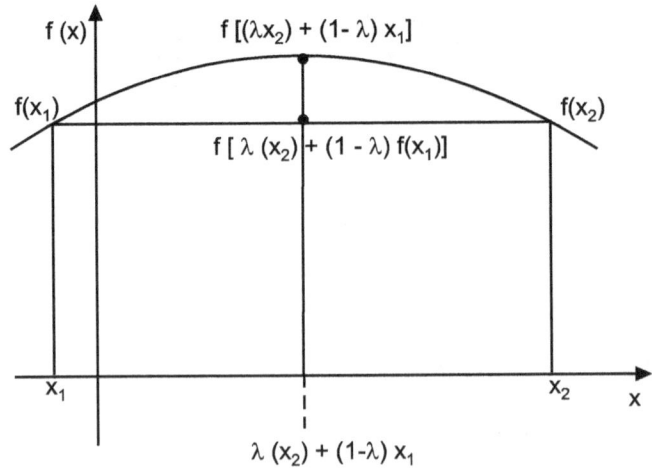

Fig. 1.4

That is, if the line segment joining the two points lies entirely below or on the graph of f(x).

It can be seen that a concave function bends downward and hence the local maximum will also be its global maximum. It is also seen that the negative of a convex function is a concave function and vice versa.

1.9 LINEAR PROGRAMMING

The word "Linear" is used to describe the proportionate relationship of two or more variables. The word "programming" is used to specify a sort of planning that involves economic allocation or strategy from various alternative strategies to achieve the desired objective.

Linear programming is a general technique which deals with the optimisation (maximization or minimization) of a function of variables known as objective function subject to a set of linear equalities and /or inequalities known as constraints. The objective function may be increment, cost, profit, production capacity or any other measure which is to be optimised. The constraints which are imposed are market condition, demand, requirement, production process, and equipments, machineries etc.

The objective function and constraints are linear to the decision variables. The variables which are directly under control of the manager who takes decision for the organization are known as decision variables.

Some Important Definitions in Linear Programming

1. **Decision Variable:** Decision variables are the unknowns to be determined from the solution to the model.

    Example, quantity of product to be produced, quantity of different foods, etc.

Assumptions:
- **Divisibility:** Fractional values are permitted in the solution.
- **Non-negativity:** Decision variables must either zero or positive values i.e. x ≥ 0, y ≥ 0.
- **Proportionality:** Direct proportional.

2. **Objective Function:** An objective function represents the mathematical equation of major goals of the system in terms of unknown called decision variables. The objective function may be maximization or minimizations.
3. **Constraints:** The constraint represents mathematical equation of the limitations imposed by the problem characteristics. The constraints define the limits within which a solution to a problem must be found.
4. **Feasible Solution:** In linear programming problem, any solution that satisfies the constraints is called a feasible solution.
5. **Basic Solution:** A basic solution is one in which n – m variables are set equal to zero. A basic solution is obtained by setting n–m variables to zero and solving the constraint simultaneously.
6. **Basic:** The collection of variables which are not set equal to zero to obtain basic solution is called the basis.
7. **Basic Feasible Solution:** This is a basic solution that satisfies the non-negativity condition.
8. **Non-Degenerate Basic Feasible Solution:** A basic feasible solution is called non-degenerate if all m basic variables are non-zero and positive.
9. **Degenerate Basic Feasible Solution:** A basic feasible solution is called degenerate if at least one basic variable is zero.
10. **Optimum Basic Feasible Solution:** The basic feasible solution, which optimises the objective function i.e. maximizes or minimizes, is the optimum basic feasible solution.
11. **Unbounded Solution:** The solution which increases or decreases the value of the objective function is unbounded solution.

A Linear Programming Problem (LPP) may be solved either by graphical method or by simple method.

1.10 NON-LINEAR PROGRAMMING

1.10.1 Introduction

The non-Linearity of the functions makes the solutions of the problem much more involved as compared to Linear programming problems and there is no single algorithm like simplex method, which can be employed for this purpose. A number of algorithms have been developed by the researchers each applicable to a specific type of NLPP only.

The problem in which objective function become non-linear or one or more of constraints inequalities have non-linear relationship or both is known as Non-Linear Programming Problem (NLPP).

The solution method of non-linear programming generally can be classified as either direct or indirect algorithms. Examples of direct methods are the gradient algorithms. Where the maximum of a problem is found by following the fastest rate of increases of the objective function and vice-versa.

In the direct methods the original problem is replaced by an auditory/auxiliary one from which the optimum is determined.

This chapter includes dichotomous and golden section i.e. direct search methods gradient method, Fibonacci method, network method and Lagrange multiplier technique of NLPP.

1.10.2 Non-Linear Programming Problems

A general optimization problem is to select n decision variables $x_1, x_2, ..., x_n$ from a given feasible region in such a way as to optimize (minimize or maximize) a given objective function.

$$f(x_1, x_2, ..., x_n)$$

of the decision variables. The problem is called a nonlinear programming (NLP) if the objective function is nonlinear and/or the feasible region is determined by nonlinear constraints. Thus, in maximization from, the general nonlinear program is stated as:

$$\text{Maximize } f(x_1, x_2, ...x_n)$$

Subject to:
$$g_1(x_1, x_2, ... x_n) \le b_1,$$
$$\vdots \qquad \vdots$$
$$g_m(x_1, x_2, ... x_n) \le b_m,$$

Where each of the constraint functions g_1 through g_m is given. A special case is the linear program that has been treated previously. The obvious association for this case is

$$f(x_1, x_2, ..., x_n) = \sum_{j=1}^{n} c_j x_j,$$

and
$$g_1(x_1, x_2 ...., x_n) = \sum_{j=1}^{n} a_{ij} x_j \ (i = 1, 2, ..., m).$$

Note that no negativity restrictions on variables can be included simply by appending the additional constraints:

$$g_{m+i}(x_1, x_2, ..., x_n) = -x_i \le 0 \qquad (i = 1, 2, ..., n).$$

Sometimes these constraints will be treated explicitly, just like any other problem constraint. At other times, it will be convenient to consider them implicitly in the same way that no negativity constraints are handled implicitly in the simplex method.

For notational convenience, we usually let x denote the vector of n decision variables $x_1, x_2, \ldots, x_n$ – that is, $x = (x_1, x_2, \ldots, x_n)$ and write the problem more concisely as,

$$\text{Maximize } f(x),$$

Subject to: $\quad g_i(x) \leq b_i \; (i = 1, 2, \ldots, m)$

As in linear programming, we are not restricted to this formulation. To minimize f(x), we can of course maximize – f(x). Equality constraints h(x) = b can be written as two inequality constraints h(x) ≤ b and – h(x) ≤ – b. In addition, if we introduce a slack variable, each inequality constraint is transformed to an equality constraint. Thus sometimes we will consider an alternative equality form:

$$\text{Maximize } f(x),$$

Subject to: $\quad h_i(x) = b_i \quad (i = 1, 2, \ldots m)$

$$x_j \geq 0 \quad (j = 1, 2, \ldots n)$$

Usually the problem context suggests either an equality or inequality formulation (or a formulation with both types of constraints), and we will not wish to force the problem into either form.

The following three simplified examples illustrate how nonlinear programs can arise, in practice.

Portfolio Selection

An investor has ₹ 10,000 and two potential investments. Let x_j for j = 1 and J = 2 denote his allocation to investment j in thousands of dollars. From historical data, investments 1 and 2 have an expected annual return of 10 and 06 percent, respectively. Also, the total risk involved with investments 1 and 2, as measured by the variance of total return, is given by $2x_1^2 + x_2^2 \; (x_1 + x_2)^2$, so that risk increases with total investment and with the amount of each individual investment. The investor would like to maximize his expected return and at the same time minimize his risk. Clearly, both of these objectives cannot in general, be satisfied simultaneously. There are several possible approaches. For example, he can minimize risk subject to a constraint imposing a lower bound on expected return. Alternatively, expected return and risk can be combined in an objective function, to give the model:

$$\text{Maximize } f(x) = 20x_1 + 16x_2 - \theta \, [2x_1^2 + x_2^2 + (x_1 + x_2)^2]$$

Subject to: $\quad g_1(x) = x_1 + x_2 \leq 5,$

$$x_1 \geq 0, \; x_2 > 0, \; (\text{that is, } g_2(x) = -x_1, \; g_3(x) = -x_2)$$

The nonnegative constant θ reflects his trade-off between risk and return. If θ = 0, the model is a linear program, and he will invest completely in the investment with greatest expected return. For very large θ, the objective contribution due to expected return becomes negligible and he is essentially minimizing his risk.

Water Resources Planning: In regional water planning, sources emitting pollutants might be required to remove waste from the water system. Let x_j be the pounds of Biological Oxygen Demand (an often-used measure of pollution) to be removed at source j.

One model might be to minimize total costs to the region to meet specified pollution standards:

$$\text{Minimize} \quad \sum_{j=1}^{n} f_j(x_j),$$

Subject to:

$$\sum_{j=1}^{n} a_{ij} x_j \geq b_i \quad (i = 1, 2, \ldots, m)$$

$$0 \leq x_j \leq u_j \quad (j = 1, 2, \ldots, n),$$

where

$f_j(x_j)$ = Cost of removing x_j pounds of Biological Oxygen Demand at source j,

b_i = Minimum desired improvement in water quality at point i in the system,

a_{ij} = Quality response, at point i in the water system, caused by removing one pound of Biological Oxygen Demand at source j

u_j = Maximum pounds of Biological Oxygen Demand that can be removed at source j

Constrained Regression: A university wishes to assess the job placements of its graduates. For simplicity, it assumes that each graduate accepts either a government, industrial, or academic position. Let

N_j = Number of graduates in year j (j = 1, 2,....n) and let G_j, I_j, and A_j denote the number entering government, industry, and academia, respectively, in year j ($G_j + I_j + A_j = N_j$).

One model being considered assumes that a given fraction of the student population joins each job category each year. If these fractions are denoted as λ_1, λ_2, and λ_3, then the predicted number entering the job categories in year j is given by the expressions.

$$\hat{G}_j = \lambda_1 N_j,$$
$$\hat{I}_j = \lambda_2 N_j$$
$$\hat{A}_j = \lambda_3 N_j$$

A reasonable performance measure of the model's validity might be the difference between the actual number of graduates G_j, I_j, and A_j entering the three job categories and the predicted numbers $\hat{G}_j$, $\hat{I}_j$, and $\hat{A}_j$, as in the least-squares estimate:

$$\text{Minimize} \sum_{j=1}^{n} [(G_j - \hat{G}_j)^2 + (I_j - \hat{I}_j)^2 + (A_j - \hat{A}_j)^2],$$

Subject to the constraint that all graduates are employed in one of the profession. In term; of the fractions entering each profession, the model can be written as:

$$\text{Minimize} \sum_{j=1}^{n} [(G_j - \lambda_1 N_j)^2 + (I_j - \lambda_1 N_j)^2 + (A_j - \lambda_3 N_j)^2],$$

$$\lambda_1 + \lambda_2 + \lambda_3 = 1$$
$$\lambda_1 \geq 0, \lambda_2 \geq 0, \lambda_3 \geq 0,$$

This is a non-linear program in three variables,

$$\lambda_1, \lambda_2, \lambda_3$$

1.10.3 Local and Global Optimum

In non-linear programming, a function may have more than one *maxima* or *minima* values. That is, when the function is plotted, it has more than one peak and more than one valley. Each of these is a local maximum or local minimum. A local *maximum* need not be a global maximum. A global *maximum* of a function is a value which is higher than all the values of the function. Similarly a global *minimum* of a function is a value which is the lowest of all the values of the function.

Consider the single variable function plotted in Fig. 1.5. Over the interval $x = a$ and $x = b$, this function has three local maxima at x_1, x_3 and x_6. The global maxima is at x_6.

$$\therefore \quad f(x)_{max} = \max \{ f(x_1), f(x_3), f(x_6) \} = f(x_6).$$

Similarly, there are three local minima at x_2, x_4 and x_7. The global minima is $f(x_7)$ at $x = x_7$. Point corresponding is $f(x_5)$, which has zero slopes is called *point of inflexion*. If a point with zero slopes is not a maximum or a minimum then it must automatically be an inflexion point or a *saddle point*.

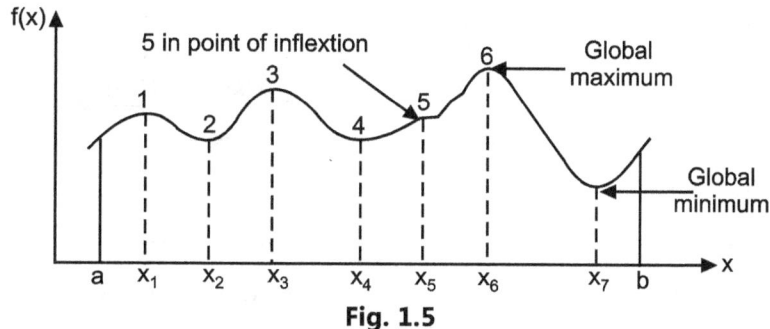

Fig. 1.5

Local minimum and Local maximum property

1. A local $\begin{Bmatrix} \text{Minimum} \\ \text{Maximaum} \end{Bmatrix}$ of a $\begin{Bmatrix} \text{Convex} \\ \text{Concave} \end{Bmatrix}$ function on a Convex feasible region is also global $\begin{Bmatrix} \text{Minimum} \\ \text{Maximum} \end{Bmatrix}$

2. A local $\begin{Bmatrix} \text{Minimum} \\ \text{Maximum} \end{Bmatrix}$ of a strictly $\begin{Bmatrix} \text{Convex} \\ \text{Concave} \end{Bmatrix}$

Function on a convex feasible region is the unique global $\begin{Bmatrix} \text{Minimum} \\ \text{Maximum} \end{Bmatrix}$

Concave and Convex Functions:

A single variable function, which when plotted, results in a curve, always curving downwards or not curving at all, is called a *concave function*. Fig. 1.6 (a) shows a single variable concave function. The shape of this function is such that for any two points on the curve, in, the feasible region S, the line joining the points is always below the function. It is clear from the figure that there is always a unique global maximum of such a function.

It can be shown for a concave function of several variables, that if it has a local maximum, the same is also its global maximum. A concave function can also be defined as: A function f(x) is said to be concave over a region S, if for any two points x and y in S.

$$f[\lambda x + (1-\lambda)y] \geq \lambda f(x) + (1-\lambda)f(y), \text{ where } 0 \leq \lambda \leq 1.$$

A function, which when plotted, results in a curve always curving upwards or not curving at all is called a *convex function*. Fig. 1.6 (b) shows a single variable convex function. A line joining any two points on the curve, in the feasible region S, is always above the function. There is always a unique global minimum of such a function.

For a convex function of several variables, if there exists a local minimum, it can be proved, that the same is also the global minimum.

In mathematical form,

A function f (x) is a convex function over a convex set S, if for any two points x and y is S,

$$f[\lambda x + (I-\lambda)y] \leq \lambda f(x) + (1-\lambda)f(y), \text{ where } 0 \leq \lambda \leq 1.$$

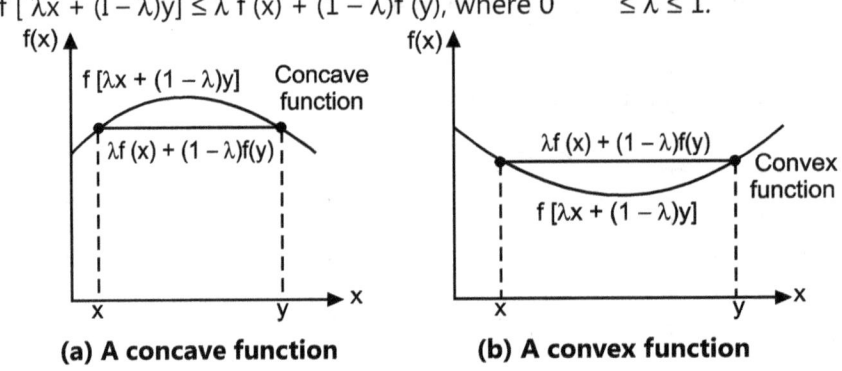

(a) A concave function   (b) A convex function

Fig. 1.6

It may be recalled from calculus that when an ordinary doubly differentiable function of a single variable f(x), without any constraints is maximized. Then for the local or relative maximum to be also the global maximum,

$$\frac{d^2f}{dx^2} \leq 0, \text{ for all } x.$$

Such a function is concave function. Similarly, if ≤ is replaced by ≥ sign, it is a convex function with local or relative minimum to be also the global minimum.

It can be shown that a function $f(x_1, x_2, \ldots x_n)$ is a convex function if and only if the matrix. of second derivatives or *Hessian matrix* is positive semi-definite and the principal minor determinants of this matrix are all non-negative.

For example, if

$$H(x) = \left[\frac{\partial^2 f}{\partial x_i \cdot \partial x_j}\right] = \begin{bmatrix} a_{11} & a_{12} & \cdots & a_{1n} \\ a_{21} & a_{22} & \cdots & a_{2n} \\ \vdots & \vdots & & \vdots \\ a_{m1} & a_{m2} & \cdots & a_{mn} \end{bmatrix}$$

$$i = 1, 2, \ldots n$$
$$j = 1, 2, \ldots m$$

Then the kth principal minor determinant is

$$\begin{vmatrix} a_{11} & a_{12} & \cdots & a_{1k} \\ a_{21} & a_{22} & \cdots & a_{2k} \\ \vdots & \vdots & & \vdots \\ a_{k1} & a_{k2} & \cdots & a_{kk} \end{vmatrix}, \text{ where } k \leq m \leq n.$$

The function $f(x_1, x_2, \ldots x_n)$ is a concave function if and only if $H(x)$ is negative semidefinite. i.e.

$$H(x) = \left[\frac{\partial^2 f}{\partial x_i \partial x_j}\right] \leq 0 \text{ for all } x \neq 0$$

And the principal minors have sigh of $(-1)k$ for $K = 1, 2, 3, \ldots$

Hessian Matrix

In mathematics, the *Hessian matrix* or *Hessian* is a square matrix of second-order partial derivatives of a function. It describes the local curvature of a function of many variables. The Hessian matrix was developed in the 19th century by the German mathematician Ludwig Otto Hesse and later named after him. Hesse originally used the term "functional determinants".

Given the real-valued function $f(x_1, x_2, \ldots, x_n)$, if all second partial derivatives of f exist and are continuous over the domain of the function, then the Hessian matrix of f is $H(f)_{ij}(x) = D_i D_j f(x)$, where $x = (x_1, x_2, \ldots x_n)$ and D_i is the differentiation operator with respect to the ith argument. Thus

$$H(f) = \begin{bmatrix} \dfrac{\partial^2 f}{\partial x_1^2} & \dfrac{\partial^2 f}{\partial x_1 \partial x_2} & \cdots & \dfrac{\partial^2 f}{\partial x_1 \partial x_n} \\ \dfrac{\partial^2 f}{\partial x_2 \partial x_1} & \dfrac{\partial^2 f}{\partial x_2^2} & \cdots & \dfrac{\partial^2 f}{\partial x_2 \partial x_n} \\ \vdots & \vdots & \ddots & \vdots \\ \dfrac{\partial^2 f}{\partial x_n \partial x_1} & \dfrac{\partial^2 f}{\partial x_n \partial x_2} & \cdots & \dfrac{\partial^2 f}{\partial x_n^2} \end{bmatrix}$$

Because f is often clear from context, H(f)(X) is frequently abbreviated to H(X). The Hessian matrix is related to the Jacobian matrix by $H(f)(x) = J(\nabla f)(x)$. The determinant of the above matrix is also sometimes referred to as the Hessian. Hessian matrices are used in large-scale optimization problems within Newton-type methods because they are the coefficient of the quadratic term of a local Taylor expansion of a function. That is,

$$y = f(X + \Delta x) \approx f(X) + J(X)\Delta x + \frac{1}{2}\Delta x^T H(X) \Delta X$$

SOLVED EXAMPLES

Example 1.1: *For each of the following function show whether it is convex, concave or neither,*

(a) $f(x) = 15 - x^2$

(b) $f(x) = x^4 + 6x^2 + 10x$

(c) $f(x) = x^3 + x^4$

(d) $f(x) = x_1^2 + x_2^2 - 2x_1 x_2$

(e) $f(x) = 2x_1 x_2 - 2x_1^2 - x_2^2$ [Nov. 2011]

(f) $f(x) = x_1^2 + 3x_1 x_2 + 3x_2^2$ [Nov. 2012]

(g) $f(x) = 3x_1 + 2x_1^2 + 4x_2 + x_2^2 - 2x_1 x_2$

Solution:

(a)
$$f(x) = 15 - x^2$$
$$f(x) = 15 - x^2$$
$$\frac{\partial f}{\partial x} = 0 - 2x$$

and $\dfrac{\partial^2 f}{\partial x^2} = -2$

Since $\dfrac{\partial^2 f}{\partial x^2}$ is always < 0 for all value of x, the function is concave.

(b) $f(x) = x^4 + 6x^2 + 10x$

$\dfrac{\partial f}{\partial x} = 4x^3 + 12x + 12$

and $\dfrac{\partial^2 f}{\partial x^2} = 12x^2 + 12$

Since $\dfrac{\partial^2 f}{\partial x^2} =$ is always > 0 for all values of x the function is convex

(c) $f(x) = x^3 + x^4$

$\dfrac{\partial f}{\partial x} = 3x^3 + 4x^3$

and $\dfrac{\partial^2 f}{\partial x^2} = 6x + 12x^2$

which is positive i.e. ≥ 0 for all value of $x \geq 0.5$. Thus the function is convex when x is ≥ -0.5.

(d) $f(x) = x_1^2 + x_2^2 - 2x_1 x_2$

$\dfrac{\partial f}{\partial x_1} = 2x_1 - 2x_2$

$\dfrac{\partial^2 f}{dx^2} = 2$ which is > 0

$\dfrac{\partial f}{\partial x_2} = 2x_2 - 2x_1$

$\dfrac{\partial^2 f}{\partial x_2^2} = 2$ which is > 0 $\dfrac{\partial^2 f}{\partial x_1 \partial x_2}$

$= -2$

$$\therefore \quad \frac{\partial^2 f}{\partial x^2} \cdot \frac{\partial^2 f}{\partial x_2^2} - \left[\frac{\partial^2 f}{\partial x_1 \partial x_2}\right]^2 = 2 \times 2 - (-2)^2 = 0$$

which is ≥ 0

$\therefore$ Function is convex but not strictly convex

(e) $\quad f(x) = 2x_1 x_2 - 2x_1^2 - x_2^2$

$$\frac{\partial f}{\partial x_1} = 2x_2 - 4x_1$$

$$\frac{\partial^2 f}{\partial x_1^2} = -4 \text{ which is } < 0$$

$$\frac{\partial f}{\partial x_2} = 2x_1 - 2x_2$$

$$\frac{\partial^2 f}{\partial x^2} = -2 \text{ which is } < 0 \quad \frac{\partial^2 f}{dx_1 dx} = 2$$

$$\therefore \quad \frac{\partial^2 f}{\partial x_1^2} \cdot \frac{\partial^2 f}{\partial x_2^2} - \left[\frac{\partial^2 f}{\partial x_1 \partial x_2}\right]^2 = (-4)(-2) - (2)^2$$

$$= 8 - 4$$

$$= 4 \text{ which is } > 0$$

$\therefore$ Function is strictly concave.

(f) $\quad f(x) = x_1^2 + 3x_1 x_2 + 3x_2^2$ [Nov. 2011]

$$\frac{\partial f}{\partial x_1} = 2x_1 + 3x_2$$

$$\frac{\partial^2 f}{\partial x_1^2} = 2 \text{ which is } > 0$$

$$\frac{\partial f}{\partial x_2} = 3x_2 + 6x_2 \quad \frac{\partial^2 f}{\partial x_2^2} = 6 \text{ which is } > 0 \quad \frac{\partial^2 f}{\partial x_1 \partial x_2} = 3$$

$$\therefore \quad \frac{\partial^2 f}{\partial x_1^2} \cdot \frac{\partial^2 f}{\partial x_2^2} - \left[\frac{\partial^2 f}{\partial x_1 \partial x_2}\right]^2 = 2 \times 6 - (-3)^2$$

$$= 12 - 9$$

$$= 3 \text{ which is } > 0$$

∴ Function is strictly convex.

(g)
$$f(x) = 3x_1 + 2x_1^2 + 4x_2 + x_2^2 - 2x_1 x_2$$

$$\frac{\partial f}{\partial x_1} = 3 + 4x_1 - x_2$$

$$\frac{\partial^2 f}{\partial x_1^2} = 4 \text{ which is } > 0$$

$$\frac{\partial f}{\partial x_2} = 4 + 2x_1 - 2x$$

$$\frac{\partial^2 f}{\partial x_2^2} = 2$$

∴ $$\frac{\partial^2 f}{\partial x_1^2} \cdot \frac{\partial^2 f}{\partial x_2^2} - \left[\frac{\partial^2 f}{\partial x_1 \partial x_2}\right] = 4 \times 2 - (-2)^2 = 4 \text{ which is } > 0$$

∴ Function is strictly convex.

Methods of Non-Linear programming

The different method of solving NLP problems are as below:

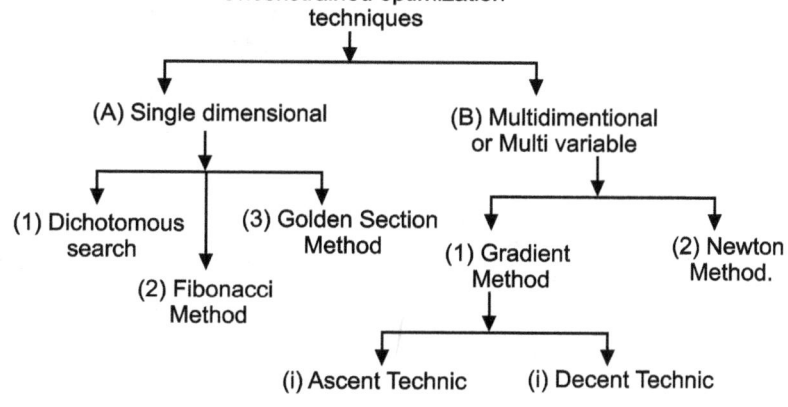

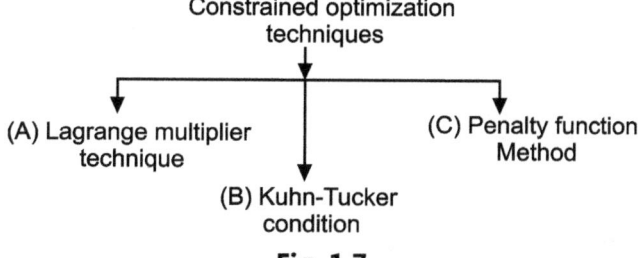

Fig. 1.7

The basic produce of most of the methods of NLP optima ion is as:
- Always start with an initial value.
- Find a suitable direction d_i (i = 1 to start with) which gives the general direction the minimum.
- Find an appropriate step length t_1^* for movement along the direction d_i.
- Obtain the new approximation $x_i + 1 = x_i + t_i^* \, d_i$.
- Check whether $x_i + 1$ is optimum or not. If it is optimum, stop the process. Otherwise i = i + 1 repeat the procedure from step (ii).

■■■

Unit 2

NON–LINEAR PROGRAMMING

2.1 ONE DIMENSIONAL MINIMIZATION METHODS

If $f(x)$ is the objective function to be minimized, the problem of finding step length $t_i = t_i^*$ which minimizes.

$f(x_i + 1) = f(x_i + t_i d_i) = f(t_i)$ for fixed values of x_i and d_i.

Since 'f' becomes a function of one variable t_i only, the methods of finding t_i^* are called one dimensional minimization methods. All one dimensional minimization methods applicable for unimodal function with known interval of uncertainty.

2.1.1 Unimodal Function

Unimodal function is one that has only one pack (maximum or minimum) in a given interval. A function of one variable is said to be unimodal if given that the two values of the variable are on the same side of the optimum. The one nearer the optimum given the better functional value. This can be started mathematically as follows:

A function $f(x)$ is unimodal function of

(i) $x_1 < x_2 < x^*$ implies that $f(x_2) < f(x_1)$ and

(ii) $x_2 > x_1 > x^*$ implies that $f(x_1) < f(x_2)$ where x^* is the minimum point.

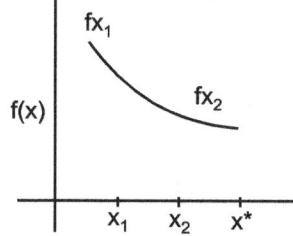

Fig. 2.1

2.2 DICHOTOMOUS SEARCH METHOD

It is a sequential search method in which the result of any experiment influences the location of the subsequent experiment.

In this method, two experiments are placed as close as possible to the centre of the interval of uncertainty. Based on the relative's values of the objective function at the two points, almost, half of the interval of uncertainty is eliminated.

Let the position of the experiments are:

$$x_1 = \frac{L_0}{2} - \frac{\delta}{2}, \quad x_2 = \frac{L_0}{2} + \frac{\delta}{2}$$

where, δ is a small positive number.

Then, find the functional values or the values of the objective function at these two points. Then based on the relative values of the objective function (whether maximization or minimization problem). Find the new interval of uncertainty given as $\left(\dfrac{L_o}{2} + \dfrac{\delta}{2}\right)$ by eliminating the interval where the optimal value is not going to lie on the basis of unimodality.

The dichotomous search method consists of conducting a pair experiments at the centre of the current interval of uncertainty. The next paring experiment's is conducted at the centre the remaining interval of uncertainty. This results in the reduction of the interval of uncertainty. The intervals of uncertainty at the end of different pairs' of experiments are as follows:

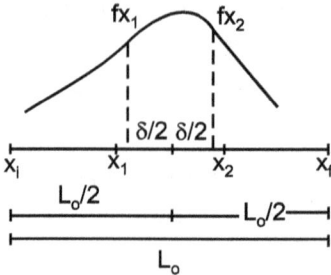

Fig. 2.2

Number of Experiments	Find Interval of Uncertainty
2	$\dfrac{L_o}{2} + \dfrac{\delta}{2}$
4	$\dfrac{1}{2}\left(\dfrac{L_o+\delta}{2}\right) + \dfrac{\delta}{2}$
6	$\dfrac{1}{2}\left[\dfrac{L_o+\delta}{4} + \dfrac{\delta}{2}\right] + \dfrac{\delta}{2}$
⋮	⋮
n	$L_n = \dfrac{L_o}{2^n/2} + d\left(\dfrac{1}{2^n/2}\right)$

If L_n final interval of uncertainty after conducting n experiments then,

$$\dfrac{1}{2}\dfrac{L_n}{L_o} \leq \alpha$$

Where, α is the accuracy (say within 10% of the exact value).
Using this, the number of experiments to be conducted can be find out.

2.3 FIBONACCI METHOD

The method is used to find the minimum of a function of one variable even if the function is not continuous but it has limitations as follows:
- The initial interval of uncertainty, in which optimum lies has to be known.
- The function must be unimodal in the initial interval of uncertainty.
- No exact value can be obtained but result is very close to the optimal value (within a specified degree of accuracy).
- The number of times, the function is to be evaluated must be specified. The method makes use of the sequence of Fibonacci numbers F_n for the placing the experiments.

$$F_0 = F_1 = 1$$
$$F_n = F_{n-1} + F_{n-2} \text{ where, } n = 2, 3, 4, \ldots\ldots$$

which gives the sequence.

The first 21 Fibonacci number F_n for $n = 0, 1, 2, \ldots Z_0$ are

List of Fibonacci Numbers: The first 21 Fibonacci numbers F_n for $n = 0, 1, 2, \ldots, 20$ are:

F_0	F_1	F_2	F_3	F_4	F_5	F_6	F_7	F_8	F_9	F_{10}	F_{11}	F_{12}	F_{13}	F_{14}	F_{15}	F_{16}	F_{17}	F_{18}	F_{19}	F_{20}
0	1	1	2	3	5	8	13	21	34	55	89	144	233	377	610	987	1597	2584	411	6765

The sequence can also be extended to negative index n using the re-arranged recurrence relation $F_{n-2} = F_n - F_n - 1$.

Which yields the sequence of "negafibonacci" numbers satisfying.

$$F_{-n} = (-1)^{n+1} F_n.$$

Thus the bidirectional sequence is

F_{-8}	F_{-7}	F_{-6}	F_{-5}	F_{-4}	F_{-3}	F_{-2}	F_{-1}	F_0	F_1	F_2	F_3	F_4	F_5	F_6	F_7	F_8
−21	13	−8	5	−3	2	−1	1	0	1	1	2	3	5	8	13	21

Procedure:

(i) Let L_0 – initial interval of uncertainty defined by $a \le x \le b$, n – total number of experiments to be conducted.

(ii) Define $L_2^* = \dfrac{F_n - 2}{F_n} F_0$ and place the first two experiments at points x and x_2, which are located at a distance of L_2. From each end of L_0.

This gives, $x_1 = a + L_2^* = a + \dfrac{F_n - 2}{F_n} L_0$

$x_2 = b - L_2^* = b - \dfrac{F_n - 2}{F_n} L_0$

(iii) Reject part of the interval by using the unimodality assumption. Then there remains a smaller interval of uncertainty L_2 with one experiment left in it, at a distance of L_2^* from one end and $(L_2 - L_2^*)$ from the other end.

$$L_2 = L_0 - L_2^* = L_0 \frac{F_n - 2}{F_n} L_0 = L_0 \left(1 - \frac{F_{n-2}}{F_n}\right)$$

$$= L_0 \left(\frac{F_n - F_n - 2}{F_n}\right) = \frac{F_n - 1}{F_n} L_0$$

(iv) Now place the third experiment in the interval L_2 so that the current two experiments are located at a distance $L_2^* = \frac{F_{n-3}}{F_n} L_0 = \frac{F_{n-3}}{F_{n-1}} L_2$ from each end of the interval L_2.

(v) Using unimodality property, reduce the interval L_2 to L_3 where,

$$L_3 = L_2 - L_3^* = L_2 \frac{F_n - 3}{F_n} L_2 = \frac{F_n - 2}{F_n} L_2$$

$$= \frac{F_{n-2}}{F_n} L_0$$

(vi) Continue the process of rejecting the interval and placing a new experiment in the remaining interval so that the location of the jth experiment and the interval of uncertainty end of jth experiments are:

$$L_j^* = \frac{F_{n-j}}{F_{n-(j-2)}} L_{j-1}$$

$$L_j = \frac{F_{n-(j-1)}}{F_n} L_0$$

(vii) Therefore, the ratio of the interval of uncertainty, remaining after conducting j of the 'n' predetermined experiments to the initial interval of uncertainty is,

$$\frac{L_j}{L_0} = \frac{F_{n-(j-1)}}{F_n}$$

For $J = n$

$$\frac{L_n}{L_0} = \frac{F_{n-(n-1)}}{F_n} = \frac{F_1}{F_n} = \frac{1}{F_n}$$

The ratio $\frac{L_n}{L_0}$ is useful to determine 'n' the required number of experiments.

(viii) Position of final experiment.

$$L_j^* = \frac{F_{n-j}}{F_{n-(j-2)}} L_{j-1}$$

If $j = n$ then,

$$\frac{L_n^*}{L_{n-1}} = \frac{F_{n-n}}{F_{n-(n-2)}} = \frac{F_0}{F_2} = \frac{1}{2} \text{ for all } n.$$

Thus, after conducting $(n - 1)$ experiments and discarding the appropriate interval in each step, the remaining interval will contain one experiment at its middle point. However, lie final n^{th} experiment is to be placed at the centre of present interval of uncertainty i.e. the position of the nth and $(n - 1)^{th}$ experiment is same for all values of n. Since, no new information can be gained by placing n^{th} experiment at the same location of $(n - 1)^{th}$ experiment, place n^{th} experiment close to remaining valid experiment to obtain the final interval of uncertainty to within $\frac{1}{2} L_{n-1}$.

2.4 GOLDEN SECTION METHOD

This method is same as the Fibonacci method except for the fact that in the Fibonacci method, the total number N of the experiments to be conducted has to be specified before beginning the calculation whereas this is not required in the golden section method. In this method, we start with the assumption that we are going to conduct a large number of experiments. The intervals of uncertainty after different number of experiments can be computed as follows:

$$L_2 = \lim_{N \to \infty} \left(\frac{F_{n-1}}{F_n} \right) L_0$$

$$L_3 = \lim_{N \to \infty} \left(\frac{F_{n-2}}{F_n} \right) L_0$$

$$= \lim_{N \to \infty} \left(\frac{F_{n-2}}{F_{n-1}} \frac{F_{n-1}}{F_n} \right) L_0$$

$$= \lim_{N \to \infty} \left(\frac{F_{n-1}}{F_n} \right)^2 L_0$$

In general,

$$= \lim_{N \to \infty} \left(\frac{F_{n-1}}{F_n} \right)^{k-1} L_0$$

Using the relation $F_n = F_{n-1} + F_{n-2}$ dividing by F_{n-1},

$$\frac{F_n}{F_{n-1}} = 1 + \frac{F_{n-2}}{F_{n-1}}$$

Define a ratio r as

$$r = \lim_{N \to \infty} \frac{F_n}{F_{n-1}}$$

as

$$\frac{F_n}{F_{n-1}} = 1 + \frac{F_{n-2}}{F_{n-1}}$$

Therefore,

$$r = 1 + \frac{1}{r}$$

$$r^2 - r + 1 = 0$$

This gives

$$r = 1.618$$

$\therefore$

$$L_k = \lim_{N \to \infty} \left(\frac{F_{n-1}}{F_n}\right)^{k-1} L_0 = \left(\frac{1}{r}\right)^{k-1} L_0$$

$$= \left(\frac{1}{1.618}\right)^{k-1} L_0$$

$$= (0.618)^{k-1} L_0$$

The ratio $\frac{F_{n-2}}{F_{n-1}}$ and $\frac{F_{n-1}}{F_n}$ are taken to be same for large value of N as follows:

N	2	3	4	 9	10	.... ∞
$\frac{F_{n-1}}{F_n}$	0.5	0.667	0.6	0.6181	0.618	0.618

The concept is based on golden mean. Ancient Greek architects believed that a building having the side l and b satisfying the equation will be having the most pleasing properties.

$$\frac{l+b}{l} = \frac{l}{b} = r$$

In geometry also the division of a line segment into two unequal parts so that the ratio of the whole to the larger part is same is the ratio of larger to the smaller part, being known as golden mean or golden section. Hence, the nomenclature of the method is Golden Section Method.

Procedure:

The procedure is, same as the Fibonacci method except that the location of the first two experiments is given as:

$$L_2^* = \frac{F_{n-2}}{F_n} L_o = \frac{F_{n-2}}{F_{n-1}} \cdot \frac{F_{n-1}}{F_n} L_o = \frac{L_o}{\gamma^2}$$

$$= 0.382 L_o$$

The desired can be specified to stop the procedure.

SOLVED EXAMPLES

Example 2.1: *Find maximum of f = x (1.5 – x) in the interval of (0, 1) within 10% accuracy using Dichotomous search techniques.*

Solution:

$$\frac{1}{2}\frac{L_n}{L_o} \leq \alpha \qquad \alpha = \frac{10}{100}$$

$$\therefore \quad \frac{1}{2}\frac{L_n}{L_o} \leq \frac{1}{10} \qquad L_o = 1 - 0 = 1$$

But,
$$\frac{L_n}{L_o} = \frac{1}{2^{n/2}} + \frac{\delta}{L_o}\left(1 - \frac{1}{2^{n/2}}\right)$$

Take $\delta = 0.001$ (assumed)

$$\therefore \quad \frac{1}{5} = \frac{1}{2^{n/2}} + \frac{0.001}{1}\left(1 - \frac{1}{2^{n/2}}\right)$$

$$\therefore \quad n = 6$$

Step 1:

$$x_1 = \frac{L_o}{2} - \frac{\delta}{2} = \frac{1 - 0.001}{2} = 0.4995$$

$$x_2 = \frac{L_o}{2} + \frac{\delta}{2} = \frac{1 + 0.001}{2} = 0.5005$$

$$fx_1 = x_1 (1.5 - x_1) = 0.49975$$

$$fx_2 = x_2 (1.5 - x_2) = 0.5003$$

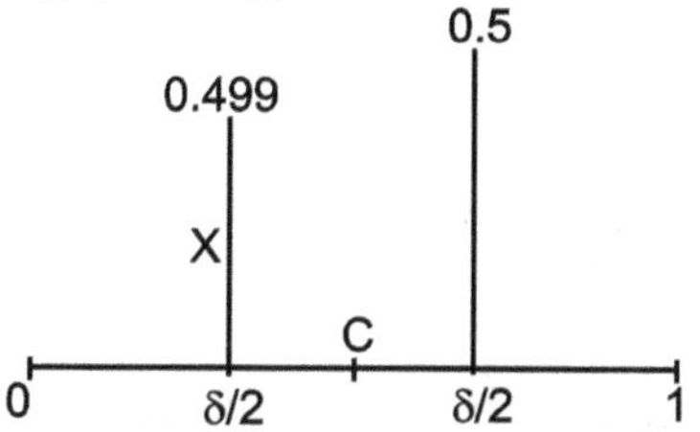

Fig. 2.3

Rejects the interval $(0, x_1) = (0, 0.5005)$

Step 2:

$$L_1 = 1 - 0.4995 = 0.5005$$

$$x_3 = \left(\frac{L_1}{2} + 0.4995\right) - \frac{\delta}{2}$$

$$= \left(\frac{0.5005}{2} + 0.4995\right) - \frac{0.001}{2}$$

$$= 0.74925$$

$$x_4 = \left(\frac{0.5005}{2} + 0.4995\right) - \frac{0.001}{2}$$

$$= 075025$$

$$f_{x_3} = 0.56249944$$

$$f_{x_4} = 0.56249994$$

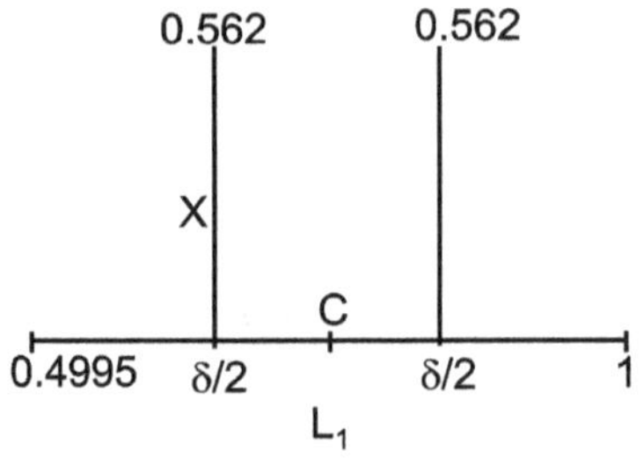

Fig. 2.4

As the values of f_x are almost same.

Consider the midpoint of $(x_3, x_4) = 0.74975$

$x^* = 0.74975 \quad f(x)^* = 0.5624999$

Example 2.2: Using Dichotomous Search Method: Find maximum of function $f(x)$ given as, $f(x) = x(5 - x)$ in the interval of $(0,1)$ to an accuracy of 10%.

Solution:

$$\frac{1}{2}\frac{L_n}{L_o} \leq \alpha \qquad\qquad L_o = 1 - 0 = 1$$

$$\alpha = \frac{10}{100} = \frac{1}{10}$$

$$\therefore \quad \frac{1}{2}\frac{L_n}{L_o} \leq \alpha \qquad\qquad \delta = 0.001 \text{ (assumed}$$

But,

$$\frac{L_n}{L_o} = \frac{1}{2^{n/2}} + \frac{\delta}{L_o}\left(1 - \frac{1}{2^{n/2}}\right)$$

$$\therefore \quad \frac{1}{5} = \frac{1}{2^{n/2}} + \frac{0.001}{1}\left(1 - \frac{1-1}{2^{n/2}}\right)$$

$$\therefore \quad n = 6 \text{ iterations}$$

Step 1:

$$x_1 = \frac{L_o - \delta}{2} = \frac{1 - 0.001}{2}$$
$$= 0.4995$$

$$x_2 = \frac{L_o}{2} + \frac{\delta}{2} = 0.5005$$

$$fx_1 = x_1(5 - x_1)$$
$$= 2.24799$$

$$fx_2 = x_2(1.5 - x_2)$$
$$= 2.25199$$

$$fx_1 < fx_2$$

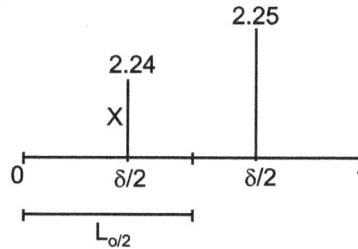

Fig. 2.5

As we want to maximize the function, reject the interval $(0, x_1)$

Step 2: New interval $(x_1, 1)$
$$= (0.4995, 1)$$
$$L_1 = 1 - 0.4995$$
$$= 0.5005$$

Centre position
$$= \frac{1 - 0.4995}{2} + 0.4995$$

$$x_3 = \left(\frac{0.5005}{2} + 0.4995\right) - \frac{0.001}{2}$$

$$x_4 = \left(\frac{0.5005}{2} + 0.4995\right) + \frac{0.001}{2}$$

$$x_3 = 0.74925$$
$$fx_3 = 3.185$$
$$x_4 = 0.75025$$
$$fx_4 = 3.1883749$$

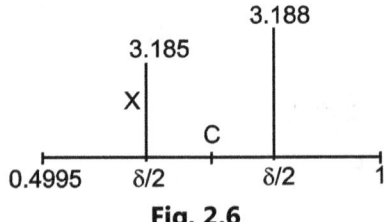

Fig. 2.6

Rejects the interval (0.4995, x₃)

Step 3: New interval (0.74925, 1)

$$\text{Centre} = \frac{1 - 0.74925}{2} + 0.74925$$

$$x_5 = \left(\frac{1 - 0.74925}{2} + 0.74925\right) - \frac{0.001}{2}$$

$$= 0.874125$$

$$x_6 = \left(\frac{1 - 0.74925}{2} + 0.74925\right) + \frac{0.001}{2}$$

$$= 0.875125$$

$$fx_5 = 3.606$$

$$fx_6 = 3.609$$

$\therefore$ fx_6 is max $\therefore$ $f^* = 3.609$ and $x^* = 0.875$

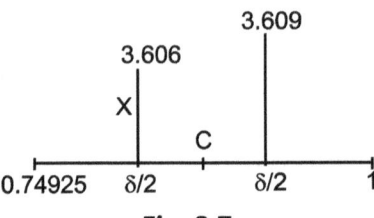

Fig. 2.7

Example 2.3: Use Fibonacci Method: To maximize $f = 16x - 0.2x^2$ in the interval (0.100) to an accuracy of 0.1%. carry out five stage **(May 2013)**

Solution:

$$\frac{1}{F_n} \leq \alpha \qquad L_0 = 100 - 0 = 100$$

$$a = 0, b = 100$$

$\therefore$ $$\frac{1}{F_n} \leq \frac{0.1}{100}$$

$$\frac{1}{F_n} \geq 1000$$

Fibonacci Numbers are,

1, 1, 2, 3, 5, 8, 13, 21, 34, 55, 89, 144, 233, 377, 610, 987, 1597

$F_n = 1597$, $F_{n-1} = 987$, $F_{n-2} = 610$ .... $F_{n-16} = 1$

∴ 16 iterations to be performed.

Stage 1:

$$L_2^* = \frac{F_{n-2}}{F_n} L_0 = \frac{610}{1597} \times 100$$

$$= 38.2 =$$

$$x_1 = a + L_2^* = 38.2$$

$$x_2 = b - L_2^* = 61.8$$

$$fx_1 = 16x_1 - 0.2 x_1^2$$

$$= 319.352$$

$$fx_2 = 224.952$$

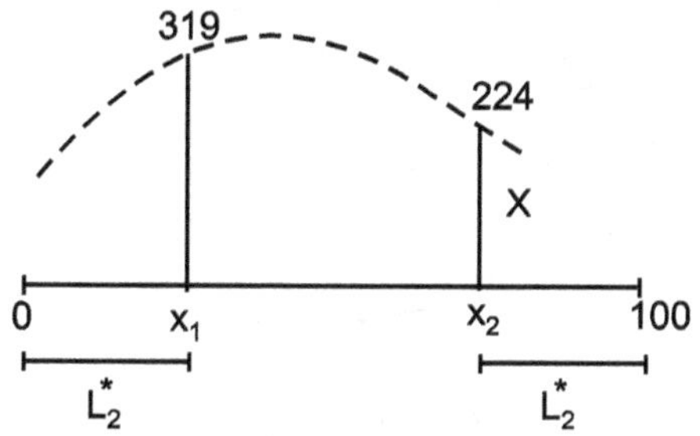

Fig. 2.8

Reject the interval $(x_2, 100) = (61.8, 100)$

Stage 2: New interval is $(0, 61.8)$

$L_2 = 61.8$ with one experiment remaining at x_1 (38.2)

$$L_3^* = \frac{F_{n-3}}{F_{n-1}} L_2 = \frac{377}{987} \times 61.8$$

$$= 23.61$$

$$x_3 = 0 + L_3^*$$

$$= 23.61$$

$$f(x_3) = 266.274$$

$$f(x_3) < f(x_1)$$

Reject the interval $(0, x_3)$

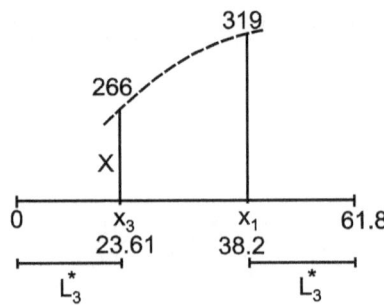

Fig. 2.9

Stage 3: New interval is (23, 61, 61.8)

$$L_3 = 61.8 - 23.61 = 38.2$$

$$L_4^* = \frac{F_{n-4}}{F_{n-2}} L_3 = \frac{233}{610} \times 38.2$$

$$= 14.59$$

$$x_4 = 61.8 - 14.59 = 47.21$$

$$fx_4 = 309.60$$

$$f(x_4) < f(x_1)$$

Reject interval $(x_4, 61.8)$ i.e. $(47.21, 61.8)$

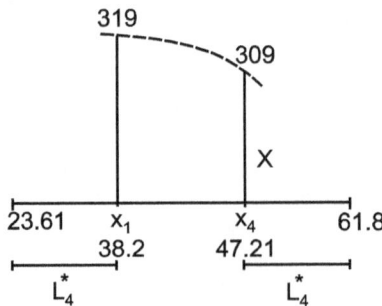

Fig. 2.10

Stage 4: New interval is (23.61, 47.26)

$$L_4 = 47.21 - 23.61 = 23.6$$

$$L_5^* = \frac{F_{n-5}}{F_{n-3}} L_4 = \frac{144}{377} \times 23.6 = 9.01$$

$$x_5 = 23.61 + 9.01 = 32.62$$

$$fx_5 = 309.1$$

$$fx_5 < fx_1$$

∴ Reject the interval (23.61, 32.62)

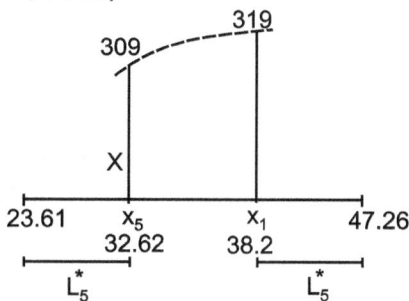

Fig. 2.11

Stage 5: New interval is (32.62, 47.26) with one experiment $x_1(38.2)$

$$L_5 = 47.26 - 32.62$$
$$= 14.59$$

$$L_6^* = \frac{F_{n-6}}{F_{n-4}} L_5$$

$$= \frac{89}{233} \times 14.59$$

$$= 5.57$$

$$x_6 = 47.26 - 5.57$$
$$= 41.61$$

$$fx_6 = 319.962$$

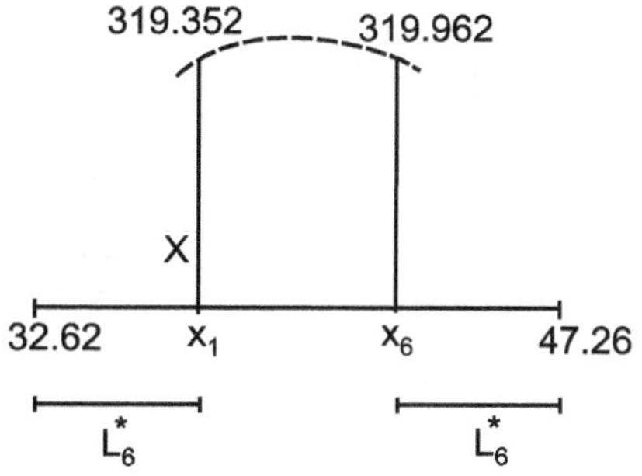

Fig. 2.12

As the value of fx_1 and fx_6 are almost same, optimal value is reached.

$$x^* = \frac{38.2 + 41.61}{2}$$
$$= 39.905$$
$$fx^* = 319.9982$$

Example 2.4: *Use Fibonacci Method:* to maximize $f = x^3(12-x)$ in the range of $(0, 12)$ within accuracy. Carry out five stages. **(Nov.2012)**

Solution:

$$\frac{1}{F_n} \leq \alpha$$

$$L_o = 12 - 0 = 12$$

$\therefore \quad \dfrac{1}{F_n} \leq \dfrac{10}{100}$

$a = 0, b = 12$

$F_n \geq 10$

$f(a) = 0, f(b) = 0$

$\therefore$ Fibonacci numbers are 1, 1, 2, 3, 5, 8, 13.

$\quad F_{n-6}, F_{n-5}, \ldots\ldots F_{n-1}, F_n$

$\therefore$ Number of iterations to be performed = 6.

Stages 1:

$$L_2^* = \frac{F_{n-2}}{F_n} L_o$$

$$= \frac{5}{13} \cdot 12 = 4.6154$$

$$x_1 = a + L_2^* = 4.6154$$

$$x_2 = b - L_2^* = 7.385$$

$$fx_1 = x_1^3 (12 - x_1)$$

$$= 726.03$$

$$fx_2 = 1858.76$$

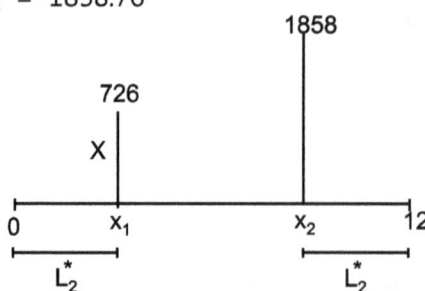

Fig. 2.13

Reject the interval $(0, x_1) = (0, 4.6154)$

Stage 2: New interval is $(x_1, 12)$

$$L_2 = (4.6154, 12)$$
$$= 12 - 4.6154 = 7.3846$$

$$L_3^* = \frac{F_{n-3}}{F_{n-1}} L_2$$

$$= \frac{3}{8} \times 7.3846 = 2.769$$

$$x_3 = 12 - 2.769 = 9.231$$
$$fx_3 = x_3^3 (12 - x_3)$$
$$= 2178.06$$
$$f(x_2) < f(x_3)$$

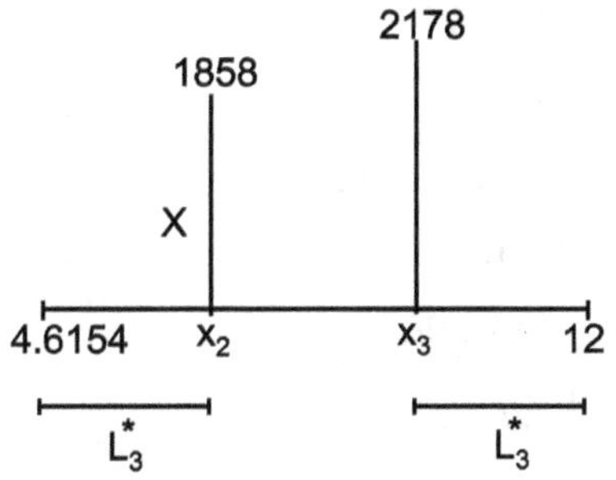

Fig. 2.14

Reject $(4.6154, x_2)$ i.e. $(4.6154, 7.385)$

Stage 3: New interval is $(x_2, 12)$

$$= (7.395, 12)$$
$$L_3 = 12 - 7.385 = 4.6154$$
$$L_4^* = \frac{F_{n-4}}{F_{n-2}} L_3$$
$$= \frac{2}{5} \times 4.6154$$
$$= 1.8462$$
$$x_4 = 12 - 1.8462 = 10.153$$
$$fx_4 = x^3 (12 - x)$$
$$= 1933.08$$
$$f(x_4) < f(x_3) \therefore \text{Reject } (x_4, 12) \text{ interval}$$

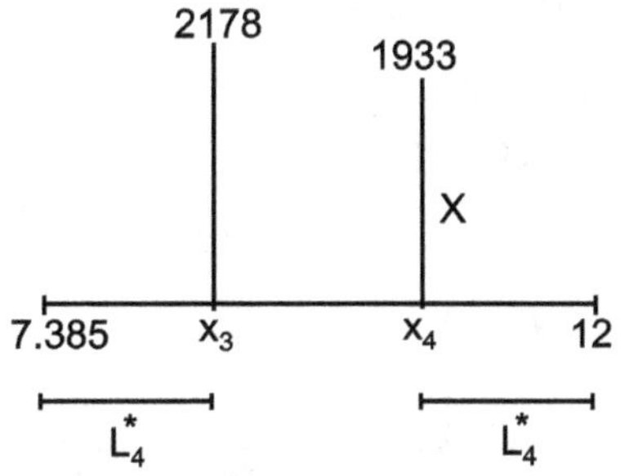

Fig. 2.15

Stage 4: New interval is (7.385, 10.153)

$$L_4 = 10.153 - 7.385 = 2.769$$

$$L_5^* = \frac{F_{n-5}}{F_{n-3}} L_4 = \frac{1}{3} \times 2.769$$

$$= 0.9226$$

$$= 1.8462$$

$$x_5 = 7.385 + 0.9226$$

$$= 8.3076$$

$$f(x_5) = 2117.296$$

$$f(x_5) < f(x_3)$$

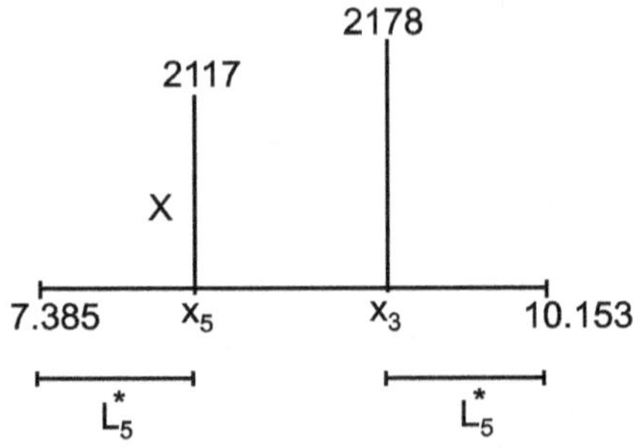

Fig. 2.16

∴ Reject the interval (7.385, x_5)

Stage 5: New interval is (8.3076, 10.153)

$$L_5 = 10.153 - 8.3076 = 1.8454$$

$$L_6^* = \frac{F_{n-6}}{F_{n-4}} L_5 = \frac{1}{2} \times 1.8454$$

$$= 0.9227$$

$$x_6 = 10.153 - 0.9227$$

$$= 9.2303$$

$$f(x_6) = 2178.1119$$

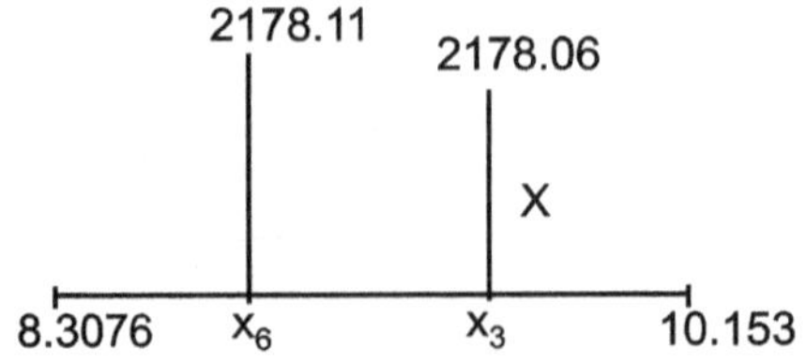

Fig. 2.17

Assuming that optimal point will lie in the region (9.2303, 9.231)

$$x^* = \frac{9.2303 + 9.231}{2} = 9.23065$$

$$f(x)^* = 2178.08$$

2.5 UNCONSTRAINED MULTIDIMENSIONAL METHODS

2.5.1 Steepest Ascent/Descent Method (Wchy's Method)

The gradient of a function is an n–component vector given as:

$$\underset{n \times 1}{\Delta f} = \begin{Bmatrix} \partial f/\partial x_1 \\ \partial f/\partial x_2 \\ \vdots \\ \vdots \\ \partial f/\partial x_n \end{Bmatrix}$$

The gradient has an important property. If we move along the gradient direction from any point in n–dimensional space, the function value increases at the faster rate. Therefore, the gradient direction is called as the direction of **steepest ascent**. It is a local property. That means the direction of steepest ascent generally varies from point to point. This concept can be used in finding out the maximum value of a function. Since the gradient vector represents the direction of steepest ascent, the negative of the gradient vector gives the direction of the steepest descent. This method based on the concept of steepest descent gives the minimum value of a function at a faster rate than any other method.

In the steepest direction method, the gradient of the function at any point gives the direction in which improvement in value of the function takes place as it happens to be with steepest gradient.

In general it can be written as

$$d = \nabla f(x^0)^T$$

where,

$$\nabla f(x) = \left(\frac{\partial f}{\partial x_1}, \frac{\partial f}{\partial x_2}, \ldots \frac{\partial f}{\partial x_n} \right)$$

Steepest Ascent/Descent Method
Algorithm:
1. Select x^0
2. Calculate $\nabla f(x)x^0$ i.e. [$\nabla f(x)$ at x^0]
3. Let $d = \nabla f(x^0)^T$ where d–direction
4. Find 't' (step length) such that t maximizes $f(x_0 + t_d)$ giving the value of t^*.
5. Then, $x^1 = x^0 + t^*d$
6. Go to Step 2.

Example 2.5: Max $z = 6x_1 - 2x_1^2 + 4x_2 - 2x_2^2 - 2x_1x_2$ with initial value (1,1) using gradient method. **(Nov. 2012)**

Solution: Iteration I :

(1) $x^0 = \begin{bmatrix} 1 \\ 1 \end{bmatrix}$ $\qquad z = 6x_1 - 2x_1^2 + 4x_2 - 2x_2^2 - 2x_1x_2 = 4$

(2) $\nabla f(x) = \left(\dfrac{\partial z}{\partial x_1}, \dfrac{\partial z}{\partial x_2} \right)$ $\qquad = (6 - 4x_1 - 2x_2 + 4 - 4x_2 - 2x_1)$

$\nabla f(x)$ at $x^0 = (0, -2)$

(3) $d = \nabla f(x^0)^T = \begin{bmatrix} 0 \\ -2 \end{bmatrix}$

(4) $(x^0 + td) = \begin{bmatrix} 1 \\ 1 \end{bmatrix} + t\begin{bmatrix} 0 \\ -2 \end{bmatrix} = \begin{bmatrix} 1 \\ 1 - 2t \end{bmatrix}$

$f(x^0 + td) = -8t^2 + 4t + 4$

To maximize $f(x^0 + td)$, $\dfrac{\partial f}{\partial t} = 0$

$\dfrac{\partial f}{\partial t} = -16t + 4 = 0$ $\qquad \therefore t^* = \dfrac{4}{16} = \dfrac{1}{4} = 0.25$

(5) $x^1 = x^0 + td = \begin{bmatrix} 1 \\ 1 \end{bmatrix} + \dfrac{1}{4}\begin{bmatrix} 0 \\ -2 \end{bmatrix} = \begin{bmatrix} 1 \\ 0.5 \end{bmatrix}$

z at $x^1 = 6x_1 - 2x_1^2 + 4x_2 - 2x_2^2 - 2x_1x_2$

$= 6 - 2 + 2 - 0.5 - 1$

$= 4.5$

Iteration II:

(1) $x^1 = \begin{bmatrix} 1 \\ 0.5 \end{bmatrix}$ z at $x^1 = 4.5$

(2) $\nabla f(x)$ at $x^1 = 6 - 4x_1 - 2x_2, 4 - 4x_2 - 2x_1$ at $(1, 0.5)$

$= (6 - 4 - 1, 4 - 4 - 1)$

$= (1, -1)$

(3) $d = \nabla f(x^1)^T = \begin{bmatrix} 1 \\ -1 \end{bmatrix}$

(4) $(x^1 + td) = \begin{bmatrix} 1 \\ 0.5 \end{bmatrix} + t\begin{bmatrix} 1 \\ -1 \end{bmatrix}$

$= \begin{bmatrix} 1 + t \\ 0.5 - t \end{bmatrix}$

(5) $f(x^1 + td) = 6(1 + t) - 2(1 + t)^2 + 4(0.5 - t) - 2(0.5 - t)^2 - 2(1 + t)(0.5 - t)$

$= 4.5 + t - 2t^2$

$\dfrac{\partial f}{\partial t} = 1 - 4t = 0 \qquad \therefore t^* = \dfrac{1}{4}$

(5) $x^2 = x^1 + t^* d = \begin{bmatrix} 1 \\ 0.5 \end{bmatrix} + \dfrac{1}{4}\begin{bmatrix} 1 \\ -1 \end{bmatrix}$

$= \begin{bmatrix} 1.25 \\ 0.25 \end{bmatrix}$

(6)   z at $x^2 = 4.625$

x	z
(1, −1)	0.4
(1, 0.5)	4.5
(1.25, 0.25)	4.625

Example 2.6: *Maximize* $f(x) = z = 2x_1x_2 - 2x_1^2 - 2x_2^2 + 6x_2$ *with* $x^o = \begin{bmatrix} 1 \\ 1 \end{bmatrix}$. *Use steepest gradient method.* **(May 2013)**

Solution: Iteration I:

(1) $x^o = \begin{bmatrix} 1 \\ 1 \end{bmatrix}$ $f(x^o) = 2x_1x_2 - 2x_1^2 - 2x_2^2 + 6x_2$

$= 4$

(2) $\nabla f(x^o) = \left(\dfrac{\partial f}{\partial x_1}, \dfrac{\partial f}{\partial x_2}\right)$

$= (2x_2 - 4x_1,\ 2x_1 - 4x_2 + 6)$ at x^o

$= (-2, 4)$

(3) $d = \nabla f(x^o)^T = \begin{bmatrix} -2 \\ 4 \end{bmatrix}$

(4) $x^1 = x^o + td = \begin{bmatrix} 1 \\ 1 \end{bmatrix} + t\begin{bmatrix} -2 \\ 4 \end{bmatrix} = \begin{bmatrix} 1 - 2t \\ 1 + 4t \end{bmatrix}$

$f(x^1) = 2x_1x_2 - 2x_1^2 - 2x_2^2 + 6x_2$

$= 4 + 20t - 56t^2$

(5) $\dfrac{\partial f}{\partial t} = 20 - (56 \times 2)t = 0 \qquad \therefore t^* = 0.18$

Iteration II:

(1) $$x^1 = x^0 + t^*d = \begin{bmatrix} 1 \\ 1 \end{bmatrix} + 0.18 \begin{bmatrix} -2 \\ 4 \end{bmatrix}$$

$$= \begin{bmatrix} 0.64 \\ 1.72 \end{bmatrix}$$

$$f(x^1) = 2x_1x_2 - 2x_1^2 - 2x_2^2 + 6x_2$$

$$= 5.784$$

(2) $\nabla f(x^1) = (2x_2 - 4x_1, 2x_1 - 4x_2 + 6)$ at x^1

$$= (0.88, 0.4)$$

(3) $$d = \nabla f(x^1)^T = \begin{bmatrix} 0.88 \\ 0.4 \end{bmatrix}$$

(4) $$x^2 = x^1 + td = \begin{bmatrix} 0.64 \\ 1.72 \end{bmatrix} + t \begin{bmatrix} 0.88 \\ 0.4 \end{bmatrix}$$

$$= \begin{bmatrix} 0.64 + 0.88\,t \\ 1.72 + 0.4\,t \end{bmatrix}$$

$$f(x^2) = 5.784 + 3.4368 - 0.8768\,t^2$$

(5) $$\frac{\partial f}{\partial t} = 3.4368 - 2 \times 0.8768\,t = 0$$

∴ $t^* = 1.96$

(6) $x^2 = \begin{pmatrix} 2.3648 \\ 2.504 \end{pmatrix}$ $f(x^2) = 9.15$

x	x f(x)
(1, 1)	4
(0.64, 1.72)	5.784
(2.36, 2.5)	9.15

Example 2.7: Minimize $f(x) = 2(x_1 - 1)^2 (x_2 - x_1)^2$ with initial value $(-1, 2)$ using gradient method. **[May 2013]**

Solution: Iterations:

(1) Select $x^0 = \begin{bmatrix} -1 \\ 2 \end{bmatrix}$

$$z = 2[x_1^2 - 2x_1 + 1] + (x_2^2 - 2x_1x_2 + x_1^2)$$

$$= 2x_1^2 - 4x_1 + 2 + x_2^2 - 2x_1x_2 + x_1^2$$

$$= 3x^2 - 4x_1 - 2x_1x_2 + x_2^2 + 2$$

z at x^0 = $3(-1)^2 - 4(-1) - 2(-1) + (2) + (2)^2 + 2$
= 3 + 4 + 4 + 4 + 2
= 17

(2) Calculate $\nabla f(x)$ at x^0

$$\nabla f(x) = \left(\frac{\partial f}{\partial x_1}, \frac{\partial f}{\partial x_2}\right)$$

= $(6x_1 - 4 - 2x_2, 2x_1 + 2x_2)$

$\nabla f(x)$ at x^0 = $(6x_1 - 4 - 2x_2, 2x_2 - 2x_1)$ at $(x^0 = -1, 2)$

= $\{[6(-1) - 4 - 2(2)], [2(2) - 2(-1)]\}$
= $\{(-6 - 4 - 4), (4 + 2)\}$
= $(-14, 6)$

(3) $(x^0 + td) = \begin{bmatrix} -1 \\ 2 \end{bmatrix} + t \begin{bmatrix} -14 \\ 6 \end{bmatrix}$

= $\begin{bmatrix} -1 - 14t \\ 2 + 6t \end{bmatrix} \to x_1, x_2$

= $3x_1^2 - 4x_1 - 2x_1x_2 + x_2^2 + 2$ at $(x^0 + td)$

= $[3(-1-14t)^2] - [4(-1-14t)] - [2(-1-14t)(2+6t)] + [(2+6t)^2] + 2$

= $3[(-1-14t)^2] - 4[-1-14t] - 2[(-1-14t)(2+6t)] +$

= $[(2+6t)^2] + 2$

= $3[+1 + 28t + 196t^2] + [4 + 56t] - 2[2 + 6t + 28t + 84t^2]$
   $+ [4 + 24t + 36t^2] + 2$

= $3 + 84t + 588t^2 + 4 + 56t + 4 + 12t + 56t + 168t^2 + 4 + 24t + 36t^2 + 2$

= $17 + 232t + 792 t^2$

(4) To maximize $f(x^0 + td)$, $\frac{\partial f}{\partial t} = 0 \Rightarrow t^*$

$\frac{\partial f}{\partial t} = 792 \times 2t^* + 232 = 0$

∴ $\boxed{t^* = -0.1465}$

(5) $x^1 = x^0 + t^*d = \begin{bmatrix} -1 \\ 2 \end{bmatrix} - 0.1465 \begin{bmatrix} -14 \\ 6 \end{bmatrix}$

$x^1 = \begin{bmatrix} 1.051 \\ 1.121 \end{bmatrix}$

Iteration II:

(1) $\quad x^1 = \begin{bmatrix} 1.051 \\ 1.121 \end{bmatrix}$

z at $x^1 = 3x_1^2 - 4x_1 - 2x_1x_2 + x_2^2 + 2$

$= 3(1.051)^2 - 4(1.051) - 2(1.051)(1.121) + (1.121)^2 + 2$

$= 3.3138 - 4.204 - 2(1.178) + 1.256 + 2$

$= 0.0101$

$= 10.1 \times 10^{-3}$

(2) $\quad \nabla f(x)$ at $x^1 = (6x_1 - 4 - 2x_2,\; 2x_2 - 2x_1)$ at x^1

$= \{6(1.051) - 4 - 2(1.121)\},\; \{2(1.121) - 21.051)\}$

$= [0.0636,\; 0.1404]$

(3) $\quad$ Let $d = \nabla f(x1)T = \begin{bmatrix} 0.064 \\ 0.14 \end{bmatrix}$

(4) $\quad x^1 + td = \begin{bmatrix} 1.051 \\ 1.121 \end{bmatrix} + t\begin{bmatrix} 0.064 \\ 0.14 \end{bmatrix} \rightarrow x_1, x_2$

$= \begin{bmatrix} 1.051 + 0.064 \\ 1.121 + 0.14 \end{bmatrix} \rightarrow x_1, x_2$

(5) $\quad f(x^1 + td) = 3x_1^2 - 4x_1 - 2x_1x_2 + x_2^2 + 2$

$= 3[(1.051 + 0.064t)^2] - 4[(1.051 + 0.064t)]$

$= 2[(1.051 + 0.064t)(1.121 + 0.14t)] + [(1.121 + 0.14t)^2] + 2$

$= 3[1.104 + 0.134561t + 0.0040] - [4.204 + 0.256t)]$

$= -2[1.1781 + 0.1471t + 0.0717t + 0.00896t^2)]$

$= + [1.256 + 0.3138t + 0.0196t^2] + 2$

$= 3.3212 + 0.4035 + 0.012t^2 - 4.204 - 0.256\,t$

$= -2.3562 - 0.242t - 0.143t - 0.0192\,t^2$

$= +1.256 + 0.3138t + 0.0196t^2 + 2$

$= 0.0078 + 0.0241t + 0.0125\,t^2$

$f(x^1 + td) = 0.0125t^2 + 0.0241t + 0.0078$

(6) $\therefore \quad \dfrac{\partial f}{\partial t} = 0.01252t + 0.024 = 0$

$\therefore \quad \boxed{t = -0.96}$

(7)
$$x^2 = x^1 + td$$
$$= \begin{bmatrix} 1.051 \\ 1.121 \end{bmatrix} - 0.96 \begin{bmatrix} 0.064 \\ 0.14 \end{bmatrix}$$

z at $x^2 = \begin{bmatrix} 0.989 \\ 0.9866 \end{bmatrix}$

z at $x^2 = 3x_1^2 - 4x_1 - 2x_1x_2 + x_2^2 + 2$

$$= 3[0.989]^2 - 4[0.989] - 2(0.989)(0.9866) + (0.9866)^2 + 2$$
$$= 2.934 - 3.956 - 1.951 + 0.9733 + 2$$
$$= 3.795 \times 10^{-4}$$

x	z
(−1, 2)	17
(1.051, 1.121)	0.0101
(0.989, 0.9866)	3.795×10^{-4}

2.5.2 Newton's Modified Method

Algorithm
(1) Select x^o
(2) Calculate $\nabla f(x^o)$ and $H^{-1}(x^o)$
(3) $\nabla x = H^{-1}(x^o) \nabla f(x^o)^T$
(4) $x^1 = x^o + \nabla x$
(5) Go to step 2.

SOLVED EXAMPLES

Example 2.8: Minimize $f(x) = 2x_1^2 + 2x_1x_2 + 2x_2^2 - 4x_1 - 6x_2$

Taking $x^o = \begin{bmatrix} 0 \\ 0 \end{bmatrix}$. Use Newton's Method.

Solution:

(1) $\quad x^o = \begin{bmatrix} 0 \\ 0 \end{bmatrix} \quad f(x^o) = 0$

(2) $\quad \nabla f(x^o) = \left(\dfrac{\partial f}{\partial x_1}, \dfrac{\partial f}{\partial x_2} \right)$

$\quad\quad\quad\quad\quad = (4x_1 + 2x_2 - 4,\ 2x_1 + 4x_2 - 6)$ at x^o
$\quad\quad\quad\quad\quad = (-4, -6)$

$$H(x^o) = \begin{bmatrix} \dfrac{\partial^2 f}{\partial x_1^2} & \dfrac{\partial^2 f}{\partial x_1 \partial x_2} \\ \dfrac{\partial^2 f}{\partial x_2 \partial x_1} & \dfrac{\partial^2 f}{\partial x_2^2} \end{bmatrix} = \begin{bmatrix} 4 & 2 \\ 2 & 4 \end{bmatrix}$$

$$H^{-1}(x^o) = \begin{bmatrix} \dfrac{1}{3} & \dfrac{-1}{6} \\ \dfrac{-1}{6} & \dfrac{1}{3} \end{bmatrix}$$

(3) $\quad \nabla x = H^{-1}(x^o)\, \nabla f(x^o)^T$

$$= -\begin{bmatrix} \dfrac{1}{3} & \dfrac{-1}{6} \\ \dfrac{-1}{6} & \dfrac{1}{3} \end{bmatrix} \begin{bmatrix} -4 \\ -6 \end{bmatrix} = \begin{bmatrix} 0.33 \\ 1.33 \end{bmatrix}$$

(4) $\quad x^1 = x^o + \nabla x$

$$= \begin{bmatrix} 0 \\ 0 \end{bmatrix} + \begin{bmatrix} 0.33 \\ 1.33 \end{bmatrix} = \begin{bmatrix} 0.33 \\ 1.33 \end{bmatrix}$$

(5) $\quad f(x^1) = 2x_1^2 + 2x_1 x_2 + 2x_2^2 - 4x_1 - 6x_2 = -4.6666$

Example 2.9: Maximize $f(x) = 6x_1 - x_1^2 + 6x_2 - 2x_2^2$ with $x^o = \begin{bmatrix} 2 \\ 2 \end{bmatrix}$.

Solution:

(1) $\quad x^o = \begin{bmatrix} 2 \\ 2 \end{bmatrix} \qquad f(x^o) = 6x_1 - x_1^2 + 6x_2 - 2x_2^2$

$$= 12$$

(2) $\quad \nabla f(x^o) = \left(\dfrac{\partial f}{\partial x_1},\ \dfrac{\partial f}{\partial x_2} \right)$

$$= (6 - 2x_1,\ 6 - 12x_2)\ \text{at}\ (2,2)$$

$$= (2, -2)$$

$$H = \begin{bmatrix} \dfrac{\partial^2 f}{\partial x_1^2} & \dfrac{\partial^2 f}{\partial x_1 \partial x_2} \\ \dfrac{\partial^2 f}{\partial x_2 \partial x_1} & \dfrac{\partial^2 f}{\partial x_2^2} \end{bmatrix} = \begin{bmatrix} -2 & 0 \\ 0 & -4 \end{bmatrix}$$

$$H^{-1}(x^o) = \begin{bmatrix} -\dfrac{1}{2} & 0 \\ 0 & -\dfrac{1}{4} \end{bmatrix}$$

(3) $$\nabla x = H^{-1}(x^o)\, \nabla f(x^o)^T$$

$$= -\begin{bmatrix} -\frac{1}{2} & 0 \\ 0 & -\frac{1}{4} \end{bmatrix} \begin{bmatrix} 2 \\ 2 \end{bmatrix}$$

$$= \begin{bmatrix} 1 \\ \frac{1}{2} \end{bmatrix}$$

(4) $$x^1 = x^o + \nabla x$$

$$= \begin{bmatrix} 2 \\ 2 \end{bmatrix} + \begin{bmatrix} 1 \\ \frac{1}{2} \end{bmatrix}$$

$$= \begin{bmatrix} 3 \\ 2.5 \end{bmatrix}$$

(5) $$f(x^1) = 6x_1 - x_1^2 + 6x_2 - 2x^2$$

$$= 11.5$$

Example 2.10: Maximize $z = 6x_1 - x_1^2 + 6x_2 - 3x_2^2$ with initial value as $x^o = (2,2)$.

Solution:

(1) $x^o = \begin{bmatrix} 2 \\ 2 \end{bmatrix}$ $\qquad z = 8$

(2) $$\nabla f(x^o) = \left[\frac{\partial f}{\partial x_1},\ \frac{\partial f}{\partial x_2} \right] \text{At } x^o$$

$$= [6 - 2x_1,\ 6 - 6x_2]\, (2,2)$$

$$= [2, -6]$$

$$H(x^o) = \begin{bmatrix} \dfrac{\partial^2 f}{\partial x_1^2} & \dfrac{\partial^2 f}{\partial x_1 \partial x_2} \\ \dfrac{\partial^2 f}{\partial x_2 \partial x_1} & \dfrac{\partial^2 f}{\partial x_2^2} \end{bmatrix}$$

$$= \begin{bmatrix} -2 & 0 \\ 0 & -6 \end{bmatrix}$$

$$H^{-1}(x^o) = \begin{bmatrix} -\dfrac{1}{2} & 0 \\ 0 & -\dfrac{1}{6} \end{bmatrix}$$

(3) $$\nabla x = -H^{-1}(x^0) \nabla f(x^0)^T$$

$$= -\begin{bmatrix} -\frac{1}{2} & 0 \\ 0 & -\frac{1}{4} \end{bmatrix} \begin{bmatrix} 2 \\ -6 \end{bmatrix}$$

$$= \begin{bmatrix} 1 \\ -1 \end{bmatrix}$$

(4) $$x^1 = x^0 + \nabla x$$

$$= \begin{bmatrix} 2 \\ 2 \end{bmatrix} + \begin{bmatrix} 1 \\ -1 \end{bmatrix}$$

$$= \begin{bmatrix} 3 \\ 1 \end{bmatrix}$$

(5) $$z(x^1) = 6x_1 - x_1^2 + 6x_2 - 3x_2^2$$

$$= 12$$

2.6 CONSTRAINED EXTERNAL PROBLEMS

The optimization problems having continuous objective function and equality or inequality type constraints are discussed in this section. The solution of such problems, having differentiable objective function and equality type constraints can be obtained by a methods, but the most common is the *Lagrange multipliers method*.

2.6.1 Problem with all Equality Constraints

The use of Lagrange function can best be understood with the help of an example. Let us consider a simple two–variable problem having a single equality type constraint.

Maximize or minimize $z = f(x_1, x_2)$,

Subject to $g(x_1, x_2) = b$,

$x_1, x_2 \geq 0$

The objective function as well as constraint should be differentiable w.r.t x_1 and x_2. The constraint function can be replaced by another differentiable function $h(x_1, x_2)$ such that

$h(x_1, x_2) = g(x_1, x_2) - b = 0.$

The problem, then, reduces to

Maximize or minimize $z = f(x_1, x_2)$,

Subject to $h(x_1, x_2) = 0$,

$x_1, x_2 \geq 0$

The Lagrangian function can now be formulated as

$L(x_1, x_2, \lambda) = f(x_1, x_2) - \lambda h(x_1, x_2)$,

Where λ is the Lagrange for the maximum or minimum of $f(x_1, x_2)$, subject to the constraint $h(x_1, x_2) = 0$, can be obtained as

$$\frac{\partial L}{\partial x_1} = 0,$$

$$\frac{\partial L}{\partial x_2} = 0,$$

and

$$\frac{\partial L}{\partial \lambda} = 0,$$

where $\quad L = L(x_1, x_2, \lambda)$

If $f = f(x_1, x_2)$ and $h = h(x_1, x_2)$, the above three conditions are given by

$$\frac{\partial L}{\partial x_1} = \frac{\partial f}{\partial x_1} - \lambda \frac{\partial h}{\partial x_1} = 0 \quad \text{or} \quad \frac{\partial f}{\partial x_1} = \lambda \frac{\partial h}{\partial x_1},$$

$$\frac{\partial L}{\partial x_2} = \frac{\partial f}{\partial x_2} - \lambda \frac{\partial h}{\partial x_2} = 0 \quad \text{or} \quad \frac{\partial f}{\partial x_2} = \lambda \frac{\partial h}{\partial x_2},$$

and $\quad \frac{\partial L}{\partial \lambda} = 0 - h = 0 \quad \text{or} \quad -h = 0$

The necessary conditions for external of $f(x_1, x_2)$, subject to $h(x_1, x_2) = 0$, are thus given by

$$f_1 = \lambda h_1,$$
$$f_2 = \lambda h_2,$$

and $\quad -h = 0,$

These necessary conditions are also the sufficient conditions, when for a maximization problem, the objective function is concave and for a minimization problem, it is convex.

2.6.2 Necessary and Sufficient Conditions for a General NLPP

A general NLPP having n variables and m constraints (n > m), can be expressed as maximize or minimize

$$z = f(x), \, x = (x_1, x_2, \dots, x_n),$$

Subject to $\quad g^i(x) = b_i, \quad i = 1, 2, \dots, m,$

$$x \geq 0.$$

The constraint can also be written as

$$h^i(x) = g^i(x) - b_i = 0, \, i = 1, 2, \dots, m.$$

By introducing that all function L, f and hi are differentiable partially w.r.t. $x_1, x_2, \dots, x_n$ and $\lambda_1, \lambda_2, \dots, \lambda_m$, the necessary conditions for the objective function to be a maximum or a minimum are

$$\frac{\partial L}{\partial x_j} = \frac{\partial f}{\partial x_j} - \sum_{i=1}^{m} \lambda_1 \frac{\partial h^i}{\partial x_j} = 0, \quad j = 1, 2, \dots, n,$$

And $\quad \dfrac{\partial L}{\partial \lambda} = -h(x) = 0$

Form the first condition, $\lambda = \dfrac{\partial f}{\partial x_j} / \dfrac{\partial h}{\partial x_j}$, for j = 1, 2, ...,n.

These necessary conditions provide and optimal solution to the problem. The sufficient conditions for determine whether the solution results in maximization or minimization of the objective function, the (n–1) principal minors of the following determinant are solved:

$$\Delta_{n+1} = \begin{vmatrix} 0 & \dfrac{\partial h}{\partial x_1} & \dfrac{\partial h}{\partial x_2} & \cdots & \dfrac{\partial h}{\partial x_n} \\ \dfrac{\partial h}{\partial x_1} & \dfrac{\partial^2 f}{\partial x_1^2} - \lambda \dfrac{\partial^2 h}{\partial x_1^2} & \dfrac{\partial^2 f}{\partial x_1 \partial x_2} - \lambda \dfrac{\partial^2 h}{\partial x_1 \partial x_2} & \cdots & \dfrac{\partial^2 f}{\partial x_1 \partial x_n} - \lambda \dfrac{\partial^2 h}{\partial x_1 \partial x_n} \\ \dfrac{\partial h}{\partial x_2} & \dfrac{\partial^2 f}{\partial x_2 \partial x_1} - \lambda \dfrac{\partial^2 h}{\partial x_2 \partial x_1} & \dfrac{\partial^2 f}{\partial x_1^2} - \lambda \dfrac{\partial^2 h}{\partial x_1^2} & \cdots & \dfrac{\partial^2 f}{\partial x_2 \partial x_n} - \lambda \dfrac{\partial^2 h}{\partial x_2 \partial x_n} \\ \vdots & & & & \\ \dfrac{\partial h}{\partial x_n} & \dfrac{\partial^2 f}{\partial x_n \partial x_1} - \lambda \dfrac{\partial^2 h}{\partial x_n \partial x_1} & \dfrac{\partial^2 f}{\partial x_n \partial x_2} - \lambda \dfrac{\partial^2 h}{\partial x_n \partial x_2} & \cdots & \dfrac{\partial^2 f}{\partial x_n^2} - \lambda \dfrac{\partial^2 h}{\partial x_n^2} \end{vmatrix}$$

It the signs of minors Δ_3, Δ_4, Δ_5 etc are alternatively +ve and –ve , the stationary points is a local maxima and if all the minors are negative. The local stationary points is a minima.

SOLVED EXAMPLES

Example 2.11 : *Use method of Lagrangian multiplier to solve the following.*

Minimize $\quad z = 3x_1^2 + 2x_2 + 3x_3^2 + 10x_1 + 9x_2 + 16x_3 - 50$

Subject to $\quad 2x_1 + x_2 + 2x_3 = 40$
$\quad\quad\quad\quad\;\; x_1, x_2\, x_3 \geq 0$

Solution: The objective function and the constraint are differentiable w.r.t x_1, x_2 and x_3 and the lagrangian function can be written as,

$$L(x, \lambda) = 3x_1^2 + 2x_2 + 3x_3^2 + 10x_1 + 9x_2 + 16x_3 - 50 - \lambda(2x_1 + x_2 + x_2 + 2x_3 - 40)$$

The necessary conditions for the maximum or minimize are,

$\dfrac{dL}{dx_1} = 6x_1 + 10 - 2\lambda = 0$

$\dfrac{\partial L}{\partial x_2} = 2 + 9 - \lambda = 0 \;\boxed{\lambda = 11}$

$\dfrac{\partial L}{\partial x_3} = 6x_1 + 10 - 2\lambda = 0$

$\dfrac{\partial L}{\partial \lambda} = (2x_1 + x_2 + 2x_3 - 40) = 0$

By solving above equation

$$x_1 = 2$$
$$x_2 = 34$$
$$x_3 = 1$$

These the stationary point is (x_1, x_2, x_3)

$$= (2, 34, 1)$$
$$z_{min} = 3(4) + 2 \times 34 + 3(1) + 10 x^2 + 9 \times 34 + 16 \times 1 - 50$$
$$= 12 + 68 + 3 + 20 + 306 + 16 - 50$$

$$\boxed{z_{min.} = 375}$$

Example 2.12: *Use Lagrange multiples Technique to,*

Minimize $\quad z = 5x_1 + x_2 - (x_1 - x_2)^2$

Subject to $\quad x_1 + x_2 = 4$,

and $\quad x_1, x_2 \geq 0$, [Nov. 2012]

Solution: The lagrangian function for above problem can be formed as,

$$L(x, \lambda) = 5x_1 + x_2 - (x_1 - x_2)^2 - \lambda(x_1 + x_2 - 4)$$

The necessary conditions for the objective function to be maximum areas are as

$$\frac{\partial L}{\partial x_1} = 5 - 2(x_1 - x_2) - \lambda = 0 \quad \ldots(1)$$

$$\frac{dL}{dx_2} = 1 + 2(x_2 - x_2) - \lambda = 0 \quad \ldots(2)$$

and $\quad \dfrac{dL}{d\lambda} = -(x_1 + x_2 - 4) = 0 \quad \ldots(3)$

Solving eqs. (1) (2) and (3) we get,

$$x_1 = \frac{5}{2} = 1.666$$

$$x_2 = \frac{3}{2} \text{ and } \lambda = 3$$

$$= 1.5$$

With z max $\quad = 13$

Example 2.13: *Use langrange multiplier technique to*

Minimize $\quad z = x_1^2 + 2x_2^2 + 3x_1 + 7x_2$

Subject to $\quad x_1 + x_2 = 5$

Solution: The objective function are differentiable w.r.t. x_1 and x_2. The constraint can be replanted by another differentiable function as,

$$x_1 + x_2 - 5 = 0$$

The Langrangian function can be written as,

$$L(x_1, x_2, \lambda) = x_1^2 + 2x_2^2 + 3x_1 + 7x_2 - \lambda(x_1 + x_2 - 5)$$

The necessary condition for a maxima or minima are,

$$\frac{\partial L}{\partial x_1} = 2x_1 + 3 - \lambda = 0 \qquad \ldots(1)$$

$$\frac{\partial L}{\partial x_2} = 4x_2 + 7 - \lambda = 0 \qquad \ldots(2)$$

$$\frac{\partial L}{\partial \lambda} = -(x_1 + x_2 - 5) = 0 \qquad \ldots(3)$$

From (1) and (3)

$$2x_1 + 3 = 4x_2 + 7$$

Or $\quad 2x_2 + x_1 = 2$

And from (3) $\quad x_2 + x_1 = 5$

Which gives $x_1 = 4$, $x_2 = 1$ and $\lambda = 11$

Since the problem is of maximization and the objective function is concise. The necessary conditions are also sufficient condition for maximization of the objects function.

$$z_{max.} = 8 + 2 + 12 + 7 = 29$$

Example 2.14: *Determine the optimal solution for the following NLPP and check whether it maximizes or minimizes the objective function.*

Optimize $\quad z = x_1^2 - 10x_1 + x_2^2 - 6x_2 + x_3^2 - 4x_3$

Subject $\quad x_1 + x_2 + x_3 = 7$

$\quad x_1 + x_2 + x_3 \geq 0$

Solution: The lagrangian function can be formed as,

$$L(x, \lambda) = x_1^2 - 10x_1 + x_2^2 - 6x_2 + x_3^2 - 4x_3 - \lambda(x_1 + x_2) + x_3 - \lambda)$$

The necessary conditions for z to be maximum or minimum are,

$$\frac{\partial L}{dx_1} = 2x_1 - 10 - \lambda = 0 \quad , \quad \frac{\partial L}{\partial x_2} = 2x_2 - 6 - \lambda = 0$$

$$\frac{\partial L}{\partial x_3} = 2x_3 - 4 - \lambda = 0 \quad , \quad \frac{\partial L}{\partial \lambda} = (x_1 + x_2 + x_3 - 7) = 0$$

The resulting solution is $x_1 = 4$, $x_2 = 2$, $x_3 = 1$ and $\lambda = -2$

The determine whether this solution is a maximum or minimum stationary point two principal minors Δ_3 and Δ_4 need to be solved.

$$\Delta_3 = \begin{bmatrix} 0 & \dfrac{\partial h}{\partial x_1} & \dfrac{\partial h}{\partial x_2} \\ \dfrac{\partial h}{\partial x_1} & \dfrac{\partial^2 f}{\partial x_1^2} - \lambda \dfrac{\partial^2 h}{\partial x_1^2} & \dfrac{\partial^2 f}{\partial x_1 \partial x_2} - \lambda \dfrac{\partial^2 h}{\partial x_1 \partial x_2} \\ \dfrac{\partial h}{\partial x_2} & \dfrac{\partial^2 f}{\partial x_2 \partial x_1} - \lambda \dfrac{\partial^2 h}{\partial x_2 \partial x_1} & \dfrac{\partial^2 f}{\partial x_2^2} - \lambda \dfrac{\partial^2 h}{\partial x_2^2} \end{bmatrix}$$

$$= \begin{bmatrix} 0 & 1 & 1 \\ 1 & 2 & 0 \\ 2 & 0 & 2 \end{bmatrix} = -4$$

$$\Delta_4 = \begin{bmatrix} 0 & \dfrac{\partial h}{\partial x_1} & \dfrac{\partial h}{\partial x_2} & \dfrac{\partial h}{\partial x_3} \\ \dfrac{\partial h}{\partial x_1} & \dfrac{\partial^2 f}{\partial x_1^2} - \lambda \dfrac{\partial^2 h}{\partial x_1^2} & \dfrac{\partial^2 f}{\partial x_1 \partial x_2} - \lambda \dfrac{\partial^2 h}{\partial x_1 \partial x_2} & \dfrac{\partial^2 f}{\partial x_1 \partial x_3} - \lambda \dfrac{\partial^2 h}{\partial x_1 \partial x_3} \\ \dfrac{\partial h}{\partial x_2} & \dfrac{\partial^2 f}{\partial x_2 \partial x_1} - \lambda \dfrac{\partial^2 h}{\partial x_2 \partial x_1} & \dfrac{\partial^2 f}{\partial x_2^2} - \lambda \dfrac{\partial^2 h}{\partial x_2^2} & \dfrac{\partial f^2}{\partial x_2 \partial x_3} - \lambda \dfrac{\partial^2 h}{\partial x_2 \partial x_3} \\ \dfrac{\partial h}{\partial x_3} & \dfrac{\partial^2 f}{\partial x_3 \partial x_1} - \lambda \dfrac{\partial^2 h}{\partial x_3 \partial x_1} & \dfrac{\partial^2 f}{\partial x_n \partial x_2} - \lambda \dfrac{\partial^2 h}{\partial x_n \partial x_2} & \dfrac{\partial^2 f}{\partial x_3^2} - \lambda \dfrac{\partial^2 h}{\partial x_3^2} \end{bmatrix}$$

$$= \begin{bmatrix} 0 & 1 & 1 & 1 \\ 1 & 2 & 0 & 0 \\ 1 & 0 & 2 & 0 \\ 1 & 0 & 0 & 2 \end{bmatrix} = -12$$

Since the principal minors D3 and D4 are the solution $x_1 = 4$, $x_2 = 2$ and $x_3 = 1$ minimizes the objective function and

$$z_{min.} = 16 - 40 + 4 - 12 + 7 - 4 = -35$$
$$z_{min.} = x_1^2 - 10x_1 + x^2 - 6x_2 + x_3^2 + 4x_3^2$$

Where
$x_1 = 4$
$x_2 = 2$
$x_3 = -1$

$\boxed{z_{min.} = -35}$

2.6.3 Constrained External Problem with more than One Equality Constraint

The non-linear programming problem having n variables and m constraints (m < n), can be expressed in the general form as.

Maximize (or minimize)   Z = f (x)

Subject to $h^i(x) = 0, i = 1, 2, ..., m,$

The Lagrangian function can be formed as,

$$L(x, \lambda) = f(x) - \sum_{i=1}^{m} \lambda_i h^i(x)$$

Where $\lambda_i, (I = 1, 2 ..., m)$ are the Lagrangian multipliers. As in the previous cases, here again it is assumed that the functions L (x, λ), f (x) and $h^i(x)$ are partially differentiable w.r.t. x and λ.

The necessary conditions for the optimum solution are,

$$\frac{\partial L}{\partial x_j} = 0, j = 1, 2, ..., n,$$

And $$\frac{\partial L}{\partial \lambda_j} = 0, i = 1, 2, ..., m,$$

The sufficiency condition for the stationary point to be a maxima or minima are obtained by solving the principal minors of the bordered Hessian matrix,

$$H^B = \begin{pmatrix} O & | & P \\ \hline P^T & | & Q \end{pmatrix}_{(m+n) \times (m+n)}$$

$$P = \begin{pmatrix} h_1^1(x) & h_2^1(x) & \cdots & h_n^1(x) \\ h_1^2(x) & h_2^2(x) & & h_n^2(x) \\ \vdots & & \cdots & \\ h_1^m(x) & h_2^m(x) & \cdots & h_n^m(x) \end{pmatrix}_{m \times n}$$

P^T = Transpose of P,

And
$$Q = \begin{bmatrix} \dfrac{\partial^2 L}{\partial x_1^2} & \dfrac{\partial^2 L}{\partial x_1 \partial x_2} & \cdots & \dfrac{\partial^2}{\partial x_1 \partial x_n} \\ \dfrac{\partial^2 L}{\partial x_2 \partial x_1} & \dfrac{\partial^2 L}{\partial x_2^2} & \cdots & \dfrac{\partial^2 L}{\partial x_2 \partial x_n} \\ \vdots & & & \vdots \\ \dfrac{\partial^2 L}{\partial x_n \partial x_1} & \dfrac{\partial^2 L}{\partial x_n \partial x_2} & \cdots & \dfrac{\partial^2 L}{\partial x_n^2} \end{bmatrix}$$

Where O is an m × m null matrix,

If (x^*, λ^*) is the stationary point for the function $L(x, \lambda)$ and H^B is the corresponding bordered Hessian matrix, the sufficient but not necessary condition for the maxima and minima is determined by the signs of the last $(n - m)$ principal minors of H^B, starting with the principal minor of the order $(2m + 1)$

x^* maximizes the function if the signs alternate, starting with $(-1)^{m+1}$ and x^* minimizes the function if all the sings are same and of the (-1) type.

Example 2.15: *Solve the following non–linear programming problem. Using the lagrangian multipliers.*

Optimize $Z = 4x_1^2 + 2x_2^2 + x_3^2 - 4x_1 x_2$

$x_1 + x_2 + x_3 = 15$

$2x_1 - x_2 + 2x_3 = 20$

$x_1, x_2, x_3 \geq 0$

Solution: The lagrangian function can be constructed as,

$L(x, \lambda) = 4x_1^2 + 2x_2^2 + x_3^2 - 4x_1 x_2 - \lambda(x_1 + x_2 + x_3 - 15)$
$\qquad - \lambda(2x_1 - x_2 + 2x_3 - 20)$

The necessary condition a stationary point,

$\dfrac{\partial L}{\partial x_1} = 8x_1 - 4x_2 - \lambda_1\, 2\lambda_2 = 0$

$\dfrac{\partial L}{\partial x_2} = 4x_1 - 4x - \lambda_1 - \lambda_2 = 0$

$\dfrac{\partial L}{\partial x_3} = 2x_3 - \lambda_1 - 2\lambda_2 = 0$

$\dfrac{\partial L}{\partial \lambda_1} = -(x_1 + x_2 + x_3 - 15) = 0$

And $\dfrac{\partial L}{\partial \lambda_2} = -(2x_1 - x_2 + 2x_3 - 20) = 0$

The solution of these simultaneous and gives,

$$x_1 = 3.667$$
$$x_2 = 3.334$$
$$x_3 = 08$$
$$\lambda_1 = 4.445$$
$$\lambda_2 = 5.778$$

Next step was to determine whether stationary point is a maximum or a minimum the bordered blessing matrix is as,

$$H^B = \begin{bmatrix} O & P \\ P^T & O \end{bmatrix} = \begin{bmatrix} 0 & 0 & 1 & 1 & 1 \\ 0 & 0 & 2 & -1 & 2 \\ 1 & 2 & 8 & -4 & 0 \\ 1 & -1 & -4 & 4 & 0 \\ 1 & 2 & 0 & 0 & 2 \end{bmatrix} = 72 > 0$$

$H^B = 72$ is = +ve hence x_0 is a minimum point.

Thus the solution,

$$\lambda_0 = (x_1, x_2, x_3) = (3.667, 3.334, 8)$$

Minimizes the objective function and $Z_{min.} = 4x_1^2 + 2x_2^2 + x_3^2 - 4x_1 x_2$

$$Z_{min.} = 4(3.667)^2 + 2(3.333)^2 + 8^2 + 4 \times 3.667 \times 3.333$$
$$= 91.12$$
$$= \boxed{Z_{min.} = 91.12}$$

Example 2.16: *Use the method of lagrangian multiplier* [May 2012]

Maximize $\quad Z = 6x_1 + 8x_2 - x_1^2 - x_2^2$

Subject to $\quad 4x_1 + 3x_2 = 16$

$\quad 3x_1 + 5x_2 = 15$

Where $x_1 + x_2 \geq 0$

Solution: Construed the lagrangian function

$$L(x, \lambda) = 6x_1 + 8x_2 - x_1^2 - x_2^2 - \lambda_1(4x_1 + 3x_2 - 15) - \lambda(3x_1 + 5x_2 - 14)$$

The necessary condition for a stationary point are,

$$\frac{\partial L}{\partial x_1} = 6 - 2x_2 - 4\lambda_1 \, 3\lambda_2 = 0$$

$$\frac{\partial L}{\partial x_2} = 8 - 2x_2 - 3\lambda_1 - 5\lambda_2 = 0$$

$$\frac{\partial L}{\partial \lambda_1} = -(4x_1 + 3x_2 - 15) = 0$$

And
$$\frac{\partial L}{\partial \lambda_2} = -(3x_1 - 5x_2 - 14) = 0$$

The solution of there simultaneous equation gets $x_1 = 3$ and $x_2 = 1$

The bordered Hessian matrix at this solution is,

$$H^B = \begin{bmatrix} 0 & 0 & 4 & 3 \\ 0 & 0 & 3 & 5 \\ \hline 4 & 3 & -2 & 0 \\ 3 & 5 & 0 & -2 \end{bmatrix} = 121 > 0$$

The stationary point $x_o = (x_1, x_3) = (3, 1)$ is a minima and hence minimizes the objective function.

$$Z_{min.} = 6 \times 3 + 8 \times 1 - (3)^2 - 1$$
$$= 13 + 8 - 9 - 1$$
$$= 16$$

Example 2.17: Minimize $f(x) = 3x_1^2 + 4x_2^2 + 5x_1x_2 - 8x_2$

Subject to $x_1 + x_2 = 4$

Solution: The lagrangian function for the given problem can be written as,

$$L(x_1, x_2, \lambda) = 3x_1^2 + 4x_2^2 + 5x_1 x_2 - 8x_2$$
$$- \lambda (x_1 + x_2 - 4)$$

The necessary conditions for the function to be minimum are,

$$\frac{\partial L}{\partial x_1} = 6x_1 - 5x_2 - \lambda = 0$$

$$\frac{\partial L}{\partial x_2} = 8x_1 - 5x_2 - 8 - \lambda = 0$$

$$\frac{\partial L}{\partial \lambda} = x_1 + x_2 - 4 = 0$$

Solution above equation are get,

$$x_1 = 1.83$$
$$x_2 = 2.17$$
$$Z = -8.33$$

2.6.4 Non–Linear Programming Problem with Inequality Constraints

One Inequality Constraint

Consider a general non–linear programming problem having one inequality constraint of the type.

Maximize $\quad Z = f(x_1, x_2, ..., x_n)$

Subject to $\quad g(x_1, x_2, ..., x_n) \leq b,$

$\quad x_1, x_2, ..., x_n \geq 0.$

Introducing a slack variable S in the form of S^2 so as to ensure that it is always non–negative, the constraint equation can be modified to

$$h(X) + S^2 = 0,$$

where, $\quad h(X) = g(X) - b \leq 0$

The problem can now be expressed as

Maximize $\quad Z = f(X),$

Subject to $\quad h(X) + S^2 = 0$

$\quad x \geq 0,$

Which is an (n + 1) variable, single equality constraint problem of constrained optimization. The lagrangian can be constructed as,

$$L(X, S, \lambda) = f(X) - \lambda [h(X) + S^2]$$

The necessary conditions for the stationary point are,

$$\frac{\partial L}{\partial x_j} = \frac{\partial f}{\partial x_j} - \lambda \frac{\partial h}{\partial x_j} = 0, \, j = 1, 2, ..., n.$$

$$\frac{\partial L}{\partial \lambda} = [h(X) + S^2] = 0,$$

And $\quad \dfrac{\partial L}{\partial S} = -2S\lambda = 0$

The condition $\dfrac{\partial L}{\partial S} = 0$ implies that either S = 0 or λ = 0. If S = 0, then condition $\dfrac{\partial L}{\partial \lambda} = 0$ given h(X) = 0. Thus either λ or h(X) = 0.

i.e., $\lambda.h.(X) = 0.$

Since S^2 has been taken to be a non–negative slack variable, h(X) ≤ 0.

This implies that when h(X) ≤ 0 λ = 0;

And when λ > 0, h(X) = 0,

The necessary conditions for maximization problem can thus be summarized as.

Example 1: Maximize f(X), Subject to h(X) ≤ 0.

Necessary conditions: $\dfrac{\partial f}{\partial x_j} - \lambda \dfrac{\partial h}{\partial x_j} = 0$

$$\lambda\, h(X) = 0$$
$$h(X) \leq 0$$
$$\lambda \geq 0$$

These necessary conditions are also called Kuhn–Tucker conditions. In case of minimization problem, the constraint would be of the type.

$$g(X) \geq b,$$
$$h(X) = g(X) - b \geq 0,$$

which modifies to the quality constraint,

$$h(X) - s^2 = 0$$

Following an analysis similar to the one for maximization problem, the Kuhn–Tucker conditions for the minimization non–linear programming problem can be obtained.

Example 2: Minimize f(X), subject to h(X) ≥ 0

Kuhn–Tucker conditions: $\dfrac{\partial f}{\partial x_j} - \lambda \dfrac{\partial h}{\partial x_j} = 0$

$$\lambda\, h(X) = 0$$
$$h(X) \geq 0$$
$$\lambda \geq 0$$

For single constraint non–linear programming problem, the Kuhn–Tucker conditions are also the sufficient conditions for

- The maximization problem, when f(X) is concave and h(X) is convex.
- The minimization problem, when both f(X) and h(X) are concave.

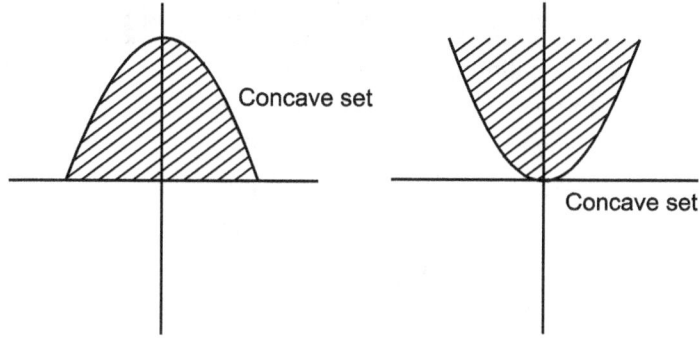

Fig. 2.18

Example 2.18:

Solve the NLPP:

Maximize $\quad Z = 4x_1 - x_1^3 + 2x_2^2$,

Subject to $\quad x_1 + x_2 \leq 1$,

$\quad x_1, x_2 \geq 0$

Solution: The problem can be put as:

$$f(X) = 4x_1 - x_1^3 + 2x_2$$
$$h(X) = x_1 + x_2 - 1$$

The problem is of maximization and Kuhn–Tucker conditions are

$$\frac{\partial f(X)}{\partial x_j} - \lambda \frac{\partial h(X)}{\partial x_j} = 0$$

$$\lambda\, h(X) = 0$$
$$h(X) \leq 0$$
$$\lambda \geq 0$$

Applying these conditions, we get

$$4 - 3x_1^2 - \lambda = 0 \qquad \ldots \text{(i)}$$
$$2 - \lambda = 0, \qquad \ldots \text{(ii)}$$
$$\lambda(x_1 + x_2 - 1) = 0, \qquad \ldots \text{(iii)}$$
$$x_1 + x_2 - 1 \leq 0, \qquad \ldots \text{(iv)}$$

Form (ii) $\lambda = 2$, therefore from (iii) $x_1 + x_2 - 1 = 0$. These results satisfy the conditions ... (v) And (v), Solution of (i), (ii) and (iii) yields.

$$x_1 = 0.8165,$$

And $\quad x_2 = 1 - 0.1835$

It can be easily observed that f(X) is concave in X, while h(X) is a convex function. Hence the solution $X^* = (0.8165, 0.1835)$ maximizes the objective function which comes to $Z_{max} = 0.0887$.

THEORETICAL QUESTIONS

1. Write short notes on non–linear programming [Nov. 11, May 12]
2. Define Fibonacci number [Nov. 11]
3. Explain Hessian matrix with its significance [Nov. 11]
4. Explain following terms:
   (i) Local and Global optima [Nov. 11, May 12]
   (ii) Concave and convex function [Nov. 11]
   (iii) Local and Global maxima
   (iv) Unimodal function

5. What is the different between Dichotomous search and Global section method?
6. Distinguish between exterior and interior penalty function method.
7. What is a Hessian matrix explain clearly what is meant by positive definite and semi definite matrix and negative definite and negative semi definite matrix.
8. Explain (1) Local and Global minima (2) Algoritrum of Newton's method.
9. Explain the necessary conditions for optimality in a constrained multi variable NLP optimizations problem using the method or Lagrange multiplies.
10. Explain the algorithm of Newton's method what are its advantages over steepest gradient technique.
11. Explain the algorithm of Lagrange multiplier technique.
12. Explain the algorithm of steepest gradient method.
13. Compare the various one dimensional search techniques in NLP.
14. Compare Newton's method with steepest gradient method.

NUMERICAL PROBLEMS

1. Find the minimum of $f = x^2(x - 2)$ in the internal (0.0, 2.0) with three interactions using Dichotomous search method **[Nov. 11]**
2. Use Fibonacci method to maximize $z = 10x^2 - 4x^3$ in the interval (0,2) with n = 5 upto 3 iteration. **[Nov. 11]**
3. Use Fibonacci method to maximize $z = x^3(12 - x)$ in the range of (0,12) with 10% accuracy carry out five stages. **(Nov. 12)**
4. Use Fibonacci method to find the minimum value of the function $z = x^2 + \frac{128}{x}$ in the range 0 to 10 to an accuracy of 0.5% carry out computations for the first war stages only.
5. Use Fibonacci method to minimize $f = 3x^2 - 36x$ in the range 0 to 10, to an accuracy of 1% carry out first 4 iterations only.
6. Use the golden section method to minimize $z = 2x^2 - 16x$ in the range of 0 to 10 carry out tone the first four iterations only.
7. Use gold section method to minimize $F = 3x^2 - 36x$ in the range 0 to 10 to an accuracy of 1% carry out first 4 iterations only.
8. Maximize $f(x) = 6x_1 - 2x_1^2 + 4x_2 - 2x_2^2 - 2x_2$ with initial value (1,1) using gradient method.
9. Use the steepest gradient method to maximize $f(x) = 4x_1 + 6x_2 - 2x_1^2 - 2x_2^2$ take the starting point as (0,0) and carry out the first two iterations only.

10. Use steepest gradient method to maximize $f(x) = 8x_2 + 2x_1x_2 - 3(x_1^2 + x_2^2)$ take the starting point as (1,1) and carry out only two iterations.

11. Use steepest gradient method to maximize $Z = 6x_1 + 8x_2 - x_1^2 - x_2^2 - 35$ take starting point as (0,0)

12. Use Newton's method to minimize $f(x) = 8x_1^2 + 5x_2^2 - 10 x_1x_2 - 18 x_1$. Take the starting point as (0, 0).

13. Use Newton's method to maximize $f(x) = 9x_1 - x_2 + 8x_2 - 2x_2^2$. Take the starting point as (0,0).

14. Use Lagrange multiplier technique to

   minimize $Z = 2x_1^2 - 24x_1 + 2x_2^2 - 8x_2 + 2x_3^2 - 12x_3 + 20$

   Subject to the constraints: $x_1 + x_2 + x_3 = 1$, $x, x_2, x_3 \geq 0$

15. Use Lagrange multiplier technique

   to minimize $Z = 2x_1^2 - 3x_1^2 + 18 x_2$

   subject to $2x_1 + x_2 = 8$

16. Use the method of Lagrangian multiplier to solve the following NLPP. Does the solution maximize or minimize the objective function?   **[Dec. 2014]**

   Optimize $Z = 2x_1^2 + x_2^2 + 3x_3^2 + 8 x_2 + 6x_3 - 100$

   Subject to $x_1 + x_2 + x_3 = 20$

   $x_1, x_2, x_3 \geq 0$

17. Use Lagrange multiplier technique to minimize $f = \frac{1}{2}\left(x_1^2 + x_2^2 + x_3^2\right)$

   Subject to $x_1 + 2x_2 + 3x_1 = 1$

   $3x_1 + 2x_2 + x_3 \geq 2$

■■■

Unit 3

STOCHASTIC PROGRAMMING

3.1 SEQUENCING MODEL

3.1.1 Introduction

Sequencing model deals with the situation in which the effectiveness measure (time, cost, distance etc) is a function of the order or sequence of performing a series of jobs (tasks). The selection of the appropriate order in which waiting customers may be served is called sequencing.

The schedules show an optimal order i.e. sequence and time in which jobs are processed as well as show timetables for jobs, equipment, people, materials, facilities and all other resources that are needed to support the production plan. The schedule should use resources efficiently to give low cost and high utilizations.

The purpose of sequencing are as follows:
- Minimizing total elapsed time.
- Minimizing idle time of machine.
- Minimizing in-process inventory cost.
- Minimizing the cost of being late.
- Minimizing customers waiting time.
- Meeting promised delivery dates.
- Keeping stock level low.
- Giving preferred working patterns, etc.

3.1.2 Notations and Terminology

t_{ij} = Processing time for job i on machine j.
T = Total elapsed time for processing all jobs. This also include idle time, if any.
I_{ij} = Idle time on machine j, from the end of job (i-1) to the short of job i.

Terminology:
- **Number of Machines:** The no. of machines refer to no. of service facilities through which a job must pass before it is assumed to be completed.
- **Processing Time:** It is the time required by a job on each machine.
- **Processing Order:** If refers to the order in which machines are required for completing the job.
- **Idle Time of a Machine:** If is the time for which a machine does not have a job to process.
- **Total Elapsed Time:** It is the time interval between starting of the first job and completing the last job including the idle time in a particular order by the given set of machines.

- **No Passing Rule:** It refers to the rule of maintaining the order in which jobs are to be processed on the given machine. For example, if n number of jobs has to pass through two machines m_1 and m_2 in order m_1 and m_2; then each job should go to machine m_1, first and then m_2.

3.1.3 Analytical Methods have been Developed for Solving only Five Simple Cases

- n jobs and one machine (A)
- n jobs and two machine (A and B)
- n Jobs and three machine (A, B and C)
- 2 jobs and m machines
- n jobs and m machines.

According to our syllabus we have to see only n jobs through 2, 3 and m machines.

3.1.4 Assumptions in Sequencing Problem

- Only one operation is carried out on a machine at a particular time.
- Each operation once started, must be completed.
- An operation must be completed before starting the next operation.
- Only one machine of each type is available.
- Processing time on different machines are exactly known and are independent of the order of jobs in which they are to be processed.
- Time taken by the job in moving from one machine to another is negligible.
- Order of completion of jobs are independent of the sequence of job.
- All the jobs are ready for processing before the time period begins.
- Time taken by the job in moving from one machine to another is negligible.

3.1.5 Processing 'n' Jobs Through Two Machines

Step to be followed: We have n jobs to be processed on 2 machines, for those n jobs we have the processing time on each machine.

Step 1: Sequencing of the job select the smallest processing time from the given list of processing time i.e. $A_1, A_2, \ldots\ldots A_n$ and $B_1, B_2 \ldots B_n$ resp.

(a) If the minimum processing time is A_R then do the Rth job first in the sequence.

(b) It the minimum processing time is B_s then do the sth job last in the sequence.

(c) Remove the assigned jobs from the table. If the table is empty, stop and go to next step, if not follow the above steps.

Step 2: Idle time of the machine.

(a) Calculate the start time and finish time for each machine.

(b) Calculate the idle time for machine 1 and 2.

   (i) Idle time for machine M_1

      = (Total elapsed time) − (Time when the last job in the sequence finished on machine M_1)

(ii) Idle time for machine M_2

= Time at which the first job in the sequence finished on machine M_1 + $\sum_{j=2}^{n}$ {(Time when the jth job in a sequence starts on machine M_2) − (Time when the $(j-1)^{th}$ job in a sequence finishes on machine M_2]}

Job Sequence	Machine A (Time)			Machine B (Time)			Idle
	Processing	In	Out	Processing	In	Out	

SOLVED EXAMPLES

Example 3.1: *Five jobs are to be processed on 2 machine M_1 and M_2 in order M_1, M_2, processing time is in hours. Find the sequence of the total elapsed and idle time.*

Jobs	Machine A	Machine B
1	5	2
2	1	6
3	9	7
4	3	8
5	10	4

Solution:

Step 1: Sequencing

(a)

Jobs	Machine A	Machine B
1	5	2
~~2~~	~~1~~	~~6~~
3	9	7
4	3	8
5	10	4

Smallest processing time for machine A and machine B is 1 i.e. for job 2. So place the job2 first in sequence and cancel if from the table.

2				

(b)

Jobs	Machine A	Machine B
~~1~~	~~5~~	~~2~~
3	9	7
4	3	8
5	10	4

Smallest processing time for machine B is 2 i.e. for job 1, so place it last in the sequence. And then remove it from the list.

| 2 | | | 1 |

(c)

Jobs	Machine A	Machine B
3	9	7
~~4~~	~~3~~	~~8~~
5	10	4

Smallest processing time for machine A is 3 i.e. for job 4, so place it second in the sequence and then remove it from the table.

| 2 | 4 | | 1 |

(d)

Jobs	Machine A	Machine B
3	9	7
~~5~~	~~10~~	~~4~~

Smallest processing time for machine B is 4 i.e. for job 5, so place it second last in the sequence and remove it from the table.

| 2 | 4 | | 5 | 1 |

(e) At last place the remaining job in the blank box of the sequence.

| 2 | 4 | 3 | 5 | 1 |

Step 2: Elapsed time and idle time.

Optimal Sequence	Machine A			Machine B			Idle	
	Processing Time	In Time	Out Time	Processing Time	In Time	Out Time	Machine A	B
2	1	0	1	6	1	7	-	1
4	3	1	4	8	7	15	-	-
3	9	4	13	7	15	22	-	-
5	10	13	23	4	23	27	-	1
1	5	23	28	2	28	30	30 - 28 = 2	1
								3

Total elapsed time = 30 hrs.
Idle time for machine A = 2 hrs.
Idle time for machine B = 3 hrs.

Note:

- It there are equal smallest times, one for each machine, then place the job on machine 1 first in the sequence and other in machine 2 at last in the sequence.
- It the equal smallest processing time are both for machine A, select the job with lower processing time in machine B for placing 1st in the sequence.
- It the equal smallest time are both for machine B, select the one with lower processing time in machine A, for placing last in the sequence.

Example 3.2: *There are seven jobs, each of which has to go through the machine A and machine B in the order AB, processing time in hours are given as,*

Job	1	2	3	4	5	6	7
Machine A	3	12	15	6	10	11	9
Machine B	8	10	10	6	12	1	3

Determine a sequence of these jobs they will minimize the total elapsed time.

Solution: Step 1: Sequencing the jobs

Jobs	Machine A	Machine B
1	3	8
2	12	10
3	15	10
4	6	6
5	10	12
6	11	1
7	9	3

(a)

						6

(b)

1						6

(c)

1					7	6

(d)

1	4				7	6

(e)

1	4			2	7	6

(f)

1	4	5		2	7	6

(g)

1	4	5	3	2	7	6

Step 2: Elapsed time and idle time

Job Sequence	Machine A				Machine B			
	Processing	Start	Finish	Idle	Processing	Start	finish	Idle
1	3	0	3		8	3	11	3
4	6	3	9		6	11	17	-
5	10	9	19		12	19	31	2
3	15	19	34		10	34	44	3
2	12	34	46		10	46	56	2
7	9	46	55		3	56	59	-
6	11	55	66	67-66 =1	1	66	67	7 / 17

Total elapsed time = 67 hrs.

Idle time for machine A = 1 hrs.

Idle time for machine B = 17 hrs.

3.1.6 Processing n Jobs through Three Machines

In this sequencing problem the description is as follows:

1. Only three machines are involved i.e. Machine A, Machine B and Machine C.
2. We have n jobs to be processed in the prescribed order.
3. No passing of job is permitted.

The problem again is to find the optimum sequence of jobs which minimizes the elapsed time (T).

When,

1. The minimizes time on machine A is ≥ maximum time on machine B and /or
2. The minimizes time on machine C is ≥ maximum time on machine B then,

The problem can be converted to equivalent problem involving n jobs and two machines. These two machine are denoted by G and H and their corresponding processing time are given by,

$$G_1 = A_1 + B_1 \text{ and } H_1 = B_1 + C_1$$

Example 3.3: *Five jobs are to be processed in three departments A, B and C in the sequence A-B-C. The time required for each job in each department is given below. Determine the sequence in which the jobs are to be processed if the total elapsed time is to be minimized.*

Job	Time in hours		
	A	B	C
1	13	9	14
2	12	8	9
3	11	7	12
4	15	10	13
5	16	11	15

Tabulate the processing sequence and determine the total elapsed.

Solution: Step 1 - Check for the condition

Minimize time of machine A = 11
Maximum time of machine B = 11
Minimize time of machine C = 9

∴ Min. Time of machine A ≥ Maximum time of machine B
11 = 11

∴ We can solve the above problem by converting 3 departments to 2 fictitious operations.

Step 2: Sequencing:

Job	G = A + B	H = B + C
1	22	23
2	20	17
3	18	19
4	25	23
5	27	26

(a)

				2

(b)

3				2

(c)

3			1	2

(d)

3	4		1	2

(e)

3	4	5	1	2

Step 3: Elapsed Time:

Optimal Sequence	Machine A			Machine B				Machine C			
	Processing	Start	Finish	Processing	Start	Finish	Idle	P	S	F	I
3	11	0	11	7	11	18	11	12	18	30	18
4	15	11	26	10	26	36	8	13	36	49	6
5	16	26	42	11	42	53	6	15	53	68	4
1	13	42	55	9	55	64	2	14	68	82	0
2	12	55	67	8	67	75	3	9	82	91	0
							30				28

Minimum elapsed time is 91 hrs.

Idle time for department A = 91-67 = 24 hrs.

Idle time for department B = 30 + (91 − 75) = 46 hrs.

Idle time for department C = 28 hrs.

Example 3.4: *Solve the following sequencing problem involving 3 machines, n-jobs and no passing, to obtain the sequence of jobs to be processed so as to minimize the total time elapsed. Determine the total elapsed time and idle hours of the machines, if any, Tabulate the results indicating the schedule of processing of all jobs.*

Jobs	Time in hours		
	Machine A	Machine B	Machine C
1	6	5	9
2	7	7	11
3	3	8	8
4	4	5	9
5	5	6	12
6	10	4	9
7	16	7	10
8	12	3	14

Solution: Step 1 - Check for the condition

Minimum time of machine A = 3

Maximum time of machine B = 8

Minimum time of machine = 8

The condition,

$$\text{Minimum time of machine C} \geq \text{maximum time of machine B}$$
$$\text{i.e } 8 = 8$$

∴ It is satisfied.

Step 2: Sequencing

Job	G = A + B	H = B + C
~~1~~	~~11~~	~~14~~
2	14	18
3	11	16
~~4~~	~~9~~	~~14~~
5	11	18
6	14	13
~~7~~	~~23~~	~~17~~
8	15	17

(a)

4							

(b)

4							6

(c)

4	1						6

(d)

4	1					8	6

(e)

4	1	3				8	6

(f)

4	1	3			7	8	6

(g)

4	1	3	5	2	7	8	6

(h)

4	1	3	5	2	7	8	6

Step 3: Elapsed Time:

Optimal Sequence	Machine A			Machine B				Machine C			
	Processing	Start	Finish	Processing	Start	Finish	Idle	P	S	F	I
4	4	0	4	5	4	9	4	9	9	18	9
1	6	4	10	5	10	15	1	9	18	27	-
3	3	10	13	8	15	23	-	8	27	35	-
5	5	13	18	6	23	29	-	12	35	47	-
2	7	18	25	7	29	36	-	11	47	58	-
7	16	25	41	7	41	48	5	10	58	68	-
8	12	41	53	3	53	56	5	14	68	82	-
6	10	53	63	4	63	67	7	9	82	91	-
							22				9

Minimum elapsed time is 91 hours.

Idle time for machine A = 91 – 63 = 28 hours.
Idle time for machine B = (91 ÷ 67) + 22
= 46 hours
Idle time for machine C = 9 hours

3.1.7 Processing n Jobs through m Machines

In this sequencing problem use we have:
1. n jobs to be performed, which are denoted by 1, 2, 3, ……, i, …….. n.
2. There are m machines, denoted by A, B, C, ……, K.
3. Each job is to be processed in the prescribed order ABC ……. k.
4. No passing of jobs is permitted. (i.e. same order over each machine is maintained)
5. The actual processing time for the n jobs on each machine is known.

The problem is to find optimum sequence of jobs which minimizes the elapsed time T. Here the conditions which are to be satisfied are:

(i) The minimum time on machine A ≥ maximum time on machine B,C…… K-1
(ii) The minimum time on machine K ≥ maximum time on machine B,C……K-1

In this problem, we have to replace m machines by an equivalent two machine problem. These two fictitious machines are denoted by 'a and b' and their corresponding processing times are given by,

$$a_i = A_i + B_i + \ldots\ldots +(K-1)_i$$
$$b_i = B_i + C_i + \ldots\ldots + K_i$$

SYSTEMS APPROACH IN CIVIL ENGG. (B.E. Civil Sem. - I)   STOCHASTIC PROGRAMMING

Example 3.5 : *Four jobs 1, 2, 3 and 4 are to be processed on each of the five machines A, B, C, D and E in the order ABCDE. Find the total minimum elapsed time if no passing of job is permitted.*

Machine job	A	B	C	D	E
1	7	5	2	3	9
2	6	6	4	5	10
3	5	4	5	6	8
4	8	3	3	2	6

Solution: Step 1 Check for the condition:

$$\text{Minimum A} = 5$$
$$\text{Maximum B} = 6$$
$$\text{Maximum C} = 5$$
$$\text{Maximum D} = 6$$
$$\text{Minimum E} = 6$$

Minimum of machine E $\geq$ maximum B, C and D

i.e. $6 \geq 6, 5$ and 6

∴ The condition is satisfied, so we can convert m machines to two machines.

Step 2: Replacing m machines by 2 machines.

Job	a = A + B + C + D	b = B + C + D + E
1	17	19
2	21	25
3	20	23
4	16	14

Step 3: Sequencing

Job	a	b
1	17	19
2	21	25
3	20	23
4	16	14

(a)

		4

(b)

1			4

(c)

1		3	4

(d)

1	2	3	4

Step 4: Elapsed time and Idle time

Job Sequence	Machine A			Machine B				Machine C				Machine D				Machine F			
	P	S	F	P	S	F	I	P	S	F	I	P	S	F	I	P	S	F	I
1	7	0	7	5	7	12	7	2	12	14	12	3	14	17	14	9	17	26	17
2	6	7	13	6	13	19	1	4	19	23	5	5	23	28	6	10	28	38	2
3	5	13	18	4	19	23	-	5	23	28	-	6	28	34	-	8	38	46	-
4	8	18	26	3	26	29	3	3	29	32	1	2	34	36	-	6	46	52	-
							11				18				20				19

Total elapsed time = 52 hours

Idle time for m/c A = 52 – 26 = 26 hrs

Idle time for m/c B = (52-29) + 11 = 34 hrs

Idle time for m/c C = (52-32) + 18 = 38 hrs

Idle time for m/c D = (52- 36) + 20 = 36 hrs

Idle time for m/c E = 19 hrs

Example 3.6 : *Four jobs 1, 2, 3 and 4 are to be processed on each of the four machines A, B, C and D in the order ABCD. The processing time in minimum are given in the table. Find for no passing the minimum elapsed time.*

Machine Jobs	A	B	C	D
1	58	14	14	48
2	30	10	18	32
3	28	12	16	44
4	64	16	12	42

Solution: **Step 1:** check for condition

  Minimum processing time of Machine A = 28
  Miximum processing time of Machine B = 16
  Minimum processing time of Machine C = 18
  Miximum processing time of Machine D = 32

So, the condition minimum A and minimum D ≥ maximum B and C is satisfied.

So we can convert m machine to two m/cs.

Step 2: Replacing m machines by 2 machines.

Jobs	a = A + B + C	b = B + C + D
1	86	76
2	58	60
3	56	72
4	92	70

Step 3: Sequencing

Jobs	a	b
~~1~~	~~86~~	~~76~~
~~2~~	~~58~~	~~60~~
~~3~~	~~56~~	~~72~~
4	92	70

(a)

3			

(b)

3			2

(c)

3	1		2

(d)

3	1	4	2

Step 4: Elapsed Time and Idle time.

job Sequence	Machine A			Machine C				Machine B				Machine D			
	P	S	F	P	S	F	I	P	S	F	I	P	S	F	I
1	28	8	28	16	28	44	28	12	44	56	44	44	56	100	56
2	58	28	86	14	86	100	42	14	100	114	44	48	114	162	14
3	64	86	150	12	150	162	50	16	162	178	48	42	178	220	16
4	30	150	180	18	180	198	18	10	198	208	20	32	220	252	-
							138				156				86

Total elapsed time = 252 minimum
Idle time for m/c A = 72 minimum
Idle time for m/c B = 156 + (252 − 208) = 200 minimum
Idle time for m/c C = 138 + (252 − 198) = 192 minimum
Idle time for m/c D = 86 minimum.

3.2 QUEUING THEORY

3.2.1 Introduction

'Queuing' is the common situation which everyone have faced in their day to day life, i.e. waiting in line. Queues are generally observed at bus stands, taxi stop, restaurants, ticket booths, doctor's clinic, bank counter etc. Queue is formed at a queuing system when either the customers who need service are waiting due to increased no. of customers then the service facilities, or the services is inefficient and take more time in serving the customers.

Queuing theory is applied to various situations where it is not possible to evaluate the exact no. of customers and their time of arrival and service rate of service facility or time required to serve. This theory is used to determine the level of service that can balance the two following cost:
1. Cost of providing the service
2. Increase in cost due to delay in offering service.

The first cost is related with the service facilities and their operations, while the second represents the cost of customer's waiting time.

If we increase the existing service facilities it would reduce the customer's waiting time and it will result in long queues. This shows that an increase in the level of service increases the cost of operation service but decrease the cost of waiting and vice-a-versa.

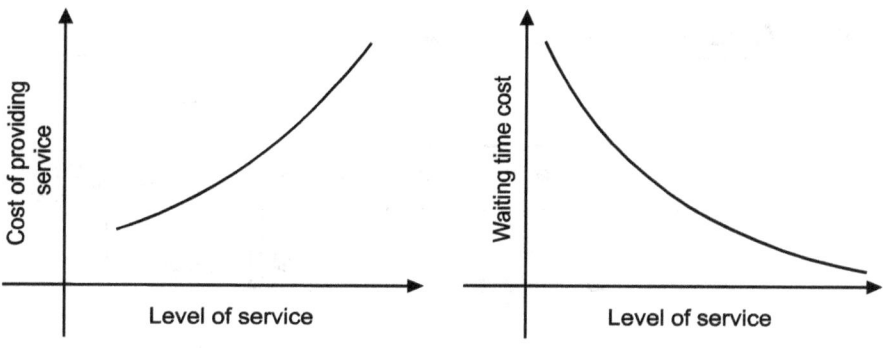

Fig. 3.1

Cost of operating = Cost of providing service + Waiting time Cost

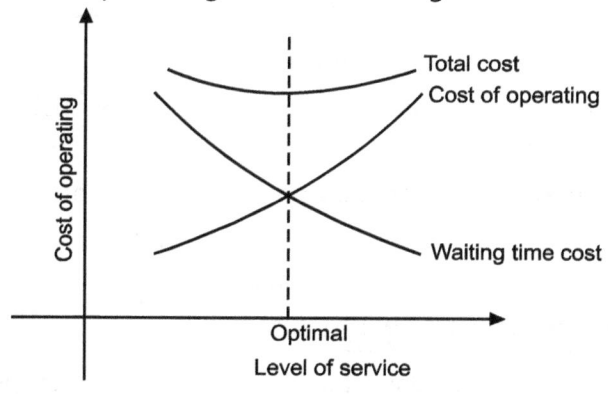

Fig. 3.2

The optimum service level is one that minimizes the sum of the two costs.

3.2.2 Applications of Queuing Models

- Queuing theory can be applied to the various business situations where customers are involved such as restaurants, cinema halls, banks, petrol pumps, doctor's clinic etc.
- It is also used for manufacturing units.
- It is successfully used in determining the no. of docks to be constructed for the trucks and ships, such that the sum of the two cost is minimized.
- It can be applied for machines repair and maintenance so that the sum of the cost of repair and cost of production loss from downtime is minimum.
- Scheduling the distribution of scarce war material.
- Planning the jobs in production control.
- Reducing the congestion due to traffic delay at toll booth.
- Solution of inventory control problem.

3.2.3 The basic Queuing Model Consist of

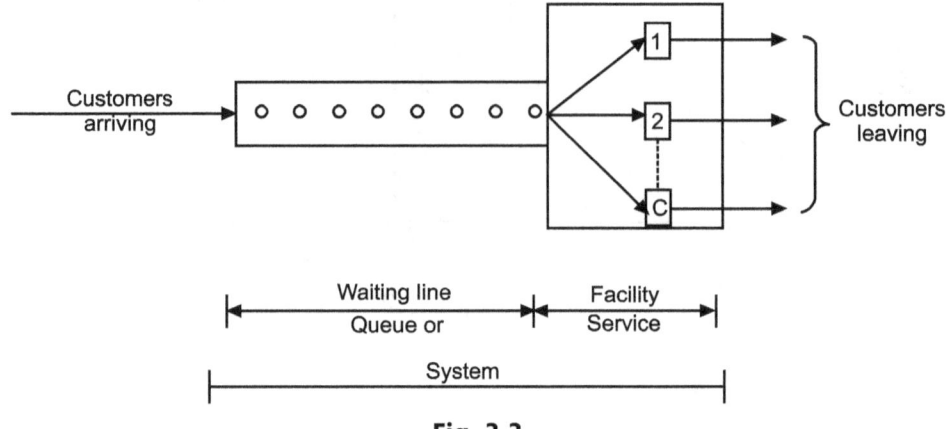

Fig. 3.3

1. **Customer:** The arriving unit who requires services. The customers may be persons, machines, vehicles, parts, etc.
2. **Queue (Waiting Line):** The customers who are waiting to be serviced.
3. **Service System:** The process or facility which is performing the services of the customer. It can be single or multi-channelled.

3.2.4 Characteristic of Queuing Theory

1. Units arrive at regular or irregular intervals of time at a given point called the service centre. All these units are called entries or arrivals of customers.
2. There is one or more of service channel or service stations or service facilities which are assembled at the service centre. If the service station is empty (free), the arriving customers will be served immediately and if they are not free the customers will wait until they are served. As soon as the customers are served they leave the system.

3.2.5 Operating Characteristics of a Queuing System

1. **Queue Length (L_q):** The number of customers in the queue waiting to get service.
2. **System Length (L_s):** The number of customers entering the system i.e. customers waiting for service as well as customers already been served.
3. **Waiting Time in the Queue (W_q):** The time for which a customer has to wait in the queue to get service.
4. **Total Time in the System (W_s):** The time elapsed between the arrival of the customer till the time he leaves the system is the total time in the system.
5. **Utilization Factor (P):** It is the proportion of time a server actually spends with the customer. It is also called traffic intensity.

3.2.6 Kendall's Notation for Representing Queuing Models

The queuing model notations are introduced by D.G.Kendall and A.M.Lee. The complete notation can be expressed as:

$$(a/b/c) : (d/e/f)$$

Where,

- a = Arrival distribution
- b = Departure distribution
- c = Number of parallel service channels in the system
- d = Service discipline
- e = Maximum number of customers allowed in the system,
- f = Calling source or population.

As shown earlier, different models in queuing theory are classified by using the special notation described by D. G. Kendall's and A. M. Lee, in the form of (a/b/c). Later A.M. Lee in 1966 added the symbols d and c to the notation.

Now the standard format used to describe main characteristic of parallel queues is as follows:

$$\{ (a / b / c) : (d / e) \}$$

where,

- a = Arrivals distribution
- b = Service time (or departures) distribution
- c = Number of service channels (servers)
- d = Maximum number of customers allowed in the system (in queue plus in service)
- e = Queue (or service discipline)

Other descriptive notations are used for the arrival and service times distribution (i.e. to replace notation a and b) as follows:

- M = Markovian/Exponential interarrival time or service time distribution
- D = Deterministic / Constant interarrival time or service time.
- G = General distribution of service time (departures).
- GI = General probability distribution - normal, uniform or any empirical distribution for interarrival time.
- E_k = Erlang - k distribution for interarrival or service time with parameter k (i.e. if k = 1, Erlang is equivalent exponential and if k = ∞. Erlang is equivalent to deterministic).

For example, a queuing system in which the number of arrivals is described by a Poisson probability distribution, the service time is described by an exponential distribution and there is a single server, would be represented by M/M/1.

The Kendell notation now will be used to define the class to which a queuing model belongs. The usefulness of a model for a particular situation is limited by its assumptions.

Symbols for d,

FCFS = First Come, First Served
LCFS = Last Come, First Served
SIRO = Service in Random Order
GD = General Service Discipline

The symbols e and f represent a finite (N) on infinite (∞) number of customers in the system and calling source respectively.

For example, $(M/E_k/1)$: (FCFS/N/∞) represents Poisson arrival, Erlangian departure, single server, 'first come first served' discipline, maximum allowable customers N in the system and infinite population model.

3.2.7 Classification of Queuing Models

The various types of queuing models can be classified as follows:

(a) Probabilistic Queuing Models:

1. **Model I:** It is also knowon as Erlang Model. This model is represented symbolically as (M/M/1) : (FCFS/∞/∞). This represents Poisson arrival, Poisson departure, single server, first come, first served service discipline, infinite number of customer allowed in the system and infinite population. As the Poisson and exponential distributions are related to each other, both of them are denoted by the symbol. 'M' due to Markovian property of exponential distribution.

2. **Model II:** It is called as General Erlang Model. This model is also represented by (M/M/I): (FCFS/∞/∞), it is general queuing model in which the arrival and service rates depends upon the length of the queue. Some persons desiring service may not join the queue since it is too long, thus affecting the arrival rate. Similarly, service rate is also affected by the length of the queue.

3. **Model III:** It is represented by (M/M/1) : (SIRO/∞/∞). It is essentially the same as Model I, except the service discipline is SIRO instead of FCFS.

4. **Model IV:** This model is represented by (M/M/1) : (FCFS/N/∞). In this model the capacity of the system is finite, say N. So the number of arrivals cannot exceed N.

5. **Model V:** This is represented by (M/M/1) : (FCFS/n/M). It is again a finite system. Here, the probability of an arrival depends upon the number of potential customer available.
6. **Model VI:** It is represented by (M/M/c): (FCFS/∞/∞). This is the same as model I, except that there are c service channels working in parallel.
7. **Model VII:** We can represent this model by (M/E_k/1) : (FCFS/∞/∞). Here we have Erlang service time with k phases instead of exponential service time.
8. **Model VIII:** It is represented by (M/M/1) : (GD/m/n), where m ≤ n. This model represents machine repair problem with a single repairman. Here n is total number of machines out of which m is number of machines which are brokendown or forming a queue and GD represents a general service discipline.
9. **Model IX:** It is represented by (M/M/c): (GD/m/n), m ≤ n. This is same as model VIII, except that there are c repairmen, c < n.
10. **Model X:** This is called power supply model.

(b) Deterministic Model:

11. **Model XI:** This model is represented by (D/D/1): (FCFS/∞/∞). Here interarrival time as well as service time are fixed and known with certainty. Therefore, this model is called as deterministic model.

(c) Mixed Queuing Model:

12. **Model XII:** This model is represented by (M/D/I) : (FCFS/∞/∞). Here, arrival rate is Poisson distributed while the service rate is deterministic or constant.

3.2.8 Model 1, Single Channel Poisson Arrivals with Exponential Service, Infinite Population Model [(M/M/1) : (FCFS/∞/∞)]

Let us consider a single-channel system with Poisson arrivals and exponential service time distribution. Both the arrivals and service rates are independent of the number of customers in the waiting line. Arrivals are handled on 'First Come, First Served' basis. And the arrival rate l is less than the service rate μ.

The following mathematical notation (symbols) will be used in connection with queuing models.

η = No. of customers, in the system at the time t

λ = Mean arrival rate, i.e. number of arrivals per unit of item

μ = Mean service rate per busy server, i.e. number of customers served per unit of time

λdt = Probability that an arrival enters the system between t and $t + dt$ time interval i.e. within time interval dt.

$1 - \lambda dt$ = Probability that no arrival enters the system within interval dt plus higher order terms in dt

μ = Mean service rate per channel

μdt = Probability of one service completion between t and $t + dt$ time interval i.e. within time interval dt.

$1 - \mu dt$ = Probability of no service rendered during the interval dt plus higher order terms in dt.

p_n = Steady state probability of exactly n customers in the system.

$p_n(t)$ = Transient state probability of exactly n customers in the system at time t, assuming the system started its operation at time zero.

$p_{n+1}(t)$ = Transient state probability of having $n + 1$ customers in the system at time t.

$p_{n-1}(t)$ = Transient state probability of having $n - 1$ customers in the system at time t.

$p_n(t+dt)$ = Probability of having n customers in the system at time $t + dt$.

L_q = Expected number of customers in the queue

W_q = Expected waiting time per customers in the queue

W_s = Expected time a customer spends in the system

L_n = Expected number of customers waiting in line excluding those times when the line is empty i.e. expected number in non-empty queue

W_n = Expected time a customer waits in line if e has to wait at all

To determine the properties of the single-channel system, it is necessary to find an expression for the probability of n customers in the system at time t, i.e., $P_n(t)$, for, if $P_n(t)$ is know, the expected number of customer in the system and hence the other characteristics can be calculated. In place of finding an expression for $P_n(t)$, we shall first find the expression for $p_n(t+dt)$.

The probability of n units in the system at time $t + dt$ can be determined by summing up probabilities of all the ways this event could occur. The event can occur in four mutually exclusive and exhaustive ways:

Table 3.1

Event	No. of Units at Time t	No. of Arrivals in Time dt	No. of Services in Time dt	No. of Units at Time t + dt
1	n	0	0	n
2	n + 1	0	1	n
3	n − 1	1	0	n
4	n	1	1	n

Now we compute the probability of occurrence of each of the events, remembering that the probability of a service or arrival is $\mu\,dt$ or $\lambda\,dt$ and $(dt)^2 \to 0$.

∴ Probability of event 1 = Probability of having n units at time t × Probability of no. arrivals × Probability of no. services

$$= p_n(t) \cdot (1 - \lambda dt)(1 - \mu dt)$$
$$= p_n(t) \cdot [1 - \lambda dt - \mu dt + \lambda u(dt)^2]$$
$$= p_n(t)\,[1 - \lambda dt - \mu dt]$$

Similarly, Probability of event 2 $= p_{(n+1)}(t) \cdot (1 - \lambda dt)(\mu dt)$
$$= p_{(n+1)} \cdot \mu dt$$

Probability of event 3 $= p_{(n-1)}(t) \cdot [\lambda dt \cdot (1 - \mu dt)]$
$$= p_{n-1}(t) \cdot [\lambda dt]$$

Probability of event 4 $= p_n(t) \cdot (\lambda dt)(\mu \cdot dt)$
$$= p_n(t) \cdot [\lambda \mu\,(dt)^2]$$

Note that other events are not possible because of the small value of dt that causes $(dt)^2$ to approach zero.

Since one and only one of the above events can happen, we can obtain $P_n(t + dt)$, where $n > 0$, by adding the probabilities of above four events.

∴ $$p_n(t + dt) = p_n(t)\,[1 - \lambda dt - \mu dt] + p_{(n+1)}(t)\,[\mu dt] + p_{n-1}(t)\,[\lambda dt] + 0$$

OR

$$p_n(t + dt) = p_n(t) - p_n(t)\,[\lambda dt + \mu dt] + p_{(n+1)}(t)\,[\mu dt] + p_{n-1}(t)\,[\lambda dt]$$

OR

$$\frac{p_n(t + dt) - p_n(dt)}{dt} = -(\lambda + \mu) \cdot p_n(t) + \mu \cdot p_{n+1}(t) + \lambda p_{n-1}(t)$$

Taking the limit when $dt \to 0$, we get the following differential equation which given the relationship between p_n, p_{n-1}, p_{n+1} at any time t, mean arrival rate λ and mean service rate μ:

$$\frac{d}{dt}[p_n(t)] = \lambda p_{n-1}(t) + \mu\,p_{n+1}(t) - (\lambda + \mu)\,p_n(t), \quad \text{where } n > 0 \qquad \ldots \text{(a)}$$

After solving for $p_n(t + dt)$ where $n > 0$, it is necessary to solve for $p_n(t + dt)$ where $n = 0$, i.e. to solve for $p_0(t + dt)$. If $n = 0$, only two mutually exclusive events can occur as shown below in the table.

Table 3.2

Event	No. of Units at Time t	No. of Arrivals in Time dt	No. of Services in Time dt	No. of Units at Time t + dt
1	0	0	–	0
2	1	0	1	0

$\therefore$ Probability of event 1 = Probability of having no. unit at time t × Probability of no. arrivals × Probability of no.services

$= p_0(t) \times (1 - \lambda dt) \times 1$

and Probability of event 2 = Probability of having no. unit at time t × Probability of no. arrivals × Probability of no.services

$= p_1(t) \times (1 - \lambda dt) \times (\mu dt)$

Note that is no units were in the system, the probability of no service would be 1. Probability of having no unit in the system at time $t + dt$ is given by summing of the probabilities of above two events.

$\therefore \quad p_0(t + dt) = p_0(t) \cdot (1 - \lambda dt) + p_1(t) \cdot (\mu dt)(1 - \lambda dt)$

$\qquad \qquad = p_0(t) - p_0(t)(\lambda dt) + p_1(t)(\mu dt)$

OR

$p_0(t + dt) - p_0(t) = -p_0(t) \cdot (\lambda dt) + p_1(t)(\mu dt)$

OR

$\dfrac{p_0(t + dt) - p_0(t)}{dt} = \mu p_1(t) - \lambda p_0(t)$

When $dt \to 0$, the differential equation which indicates the relationship between probabilities p_0 and p_1 at any time t, mean arrival rate λ at mean service rate μ, is

$$\dfrac{d}{dt}[p_0(t)] = \mu p_1(t) - \lambda p_0(t), \text{ where } n = 0 \qquad \ldots \text{(b)}$$

Equation (a) and (b) provide relationships involving the probability density function $p_n(t)$ for all values of n but still we do not know the value of $p_n(t)$.

Assuming the steady state condition for the system, when the probability of having n units in the system becomes independent of time, we get

$$p_n(t) = p_n$$

$$\frac{d}{dt}[p_n(t)] = 0$$

Therefore, for a steady state system the differential equation (a) and (b) reduce the difference equations (c) and (d).

$$0 = \lambda p_{n-1} + \mu p_{n+1} - (\lambda + \mu) p_n, \quad \text{where } n > 0 \qquad \ldots (c)$$

$$0 = \mu p_1 + \lambda p_0, \quad \text{where } n = 0 \qquad \ldots (d)$$

From equation (d), we have $p_1 = \dfrac{\lambda}{\mu} \cdot p_0$

Putting $n = 1$ in equation (c), we have

$$0 = \lambda p_0 + \mu p_2 - (\lambda + \mu) p_1$$

$$\therefore \quad p_2 = \frac{\lambda + \mu}{\mu} \cdot \left(\frac{\lambda}{\mu} \cdot p_0\right) - \frac{\lambda}{\mu} \cdot p_0$$

$$= \frac{\lambda}{\mu} \cdot p_0 \left(\frac{\lambda + \mu}{\mu} - 1\right)$$

$$= \left(\frac{\lambda}{\mu}\right)^2 \cdot p_0$$

Similarly, for $n = 2$, equation (c) gives

$$p_3 = \left(\frac{\lambda}{\mu}\right)^3 \cdot p_0$$

$$\vdots$$

$$p_n = \left(\frac{\lambda}{\mu}\right)^n \cdot p_0, \quad \text{when } n > 0 \qquad \ldots (e)$$

Equation (e) gives p_n in terms of p_0, λ and μ. Finally, an expression for p_0 in terms of λ and μ must be obtained. The easiest way to do this is to recognize that the probability that the channel in busy in the ratio of the arrival rate of service rate $\left(\dfrac{\lambda}{\mu}\right)$. Thus, p_0 and 1 minus this ratio.

i.e.

$$p_0 = 1 - \frac{\lambda}{\mu} \qquad \ldots (f)$$

Hence,

$$p_n = \left(\frac{\lambda}{\mu}\right)^n \cdot \left(1 - \frac{\lambda}{\mu}\right) \qquad \ldots (g)$$

Having know the value of p_n, we can find the various operating characteristics of the system.

1. Expected number of units in the system (waiting + serving) L_s is obtained by using the definition of an expected value:

$$E(x) = \sum_{i=0}^{i=\infty} x_i p_i$$

$$\therefore \quad L_s = \sum_{n=0}^{n=\infty} n p_n$$

or,
$$L_s = \sum_{n=0}^{\infty} n \left(\frac{\lambda}{\mu}\right)^n \left(1 - \frac{\lambda}{\mu}\right)$$

$$= \left(1 - \frac{\lambda}{\mu}\right) \cdot \sum_{n=0}^{\infty} n \left(\frac{\lambda}{\mu}\right)^n$$

$$= \left(1 - \frac{\lambda}{\mu}\right) \left[0 \left(\frac{\lambda}{\mu}\right)^0 + 1\left(\frac{\lambda}{\mu}\right)^1 + 2\left(\frac{\lambda}{\mu}\right)^2 + 3\left(\frac{\lambda}{\mu}\right)^3 + \ldots \right]$$

$$= \left(1 - \frac{\lambda}{\mu}\right) \left[0 + \frac{\lambda}{\mu} + 2\left(\frac{\lambda}{\mu}\right)^2 + 3\left(\frac{\lambda}{\mu}\right)^3 + \ldots \right]$$

The series within brackets is an infinite series of the form $0, a, 2a^2, 3a^3, \ldots xa^x, \ldots$ for such an infinite series, if a is a constant of less than one, the sum of given by the formula,

$$S_\infty = \frac{a}{(1-a)^2}$$

$$\therefore \quad L_s = \left(1 - \frac{\lambda}{\mu}\right) \left[\frac{\lambda/\mu}{(1 - \lambda) \cdot \mu_2}\right]$$

$$= \frac{\lambda/\mu}{1 - \lambda/\mu} = \frac{\lambda}{\mu - \lambda} \qquad \ldots \text{(h)}$$

2. Expected number of units in the queue,

L_q = Expected number of units in the system – Expected number in service (Single server),

$$\therefore \quad L_q = L_s - \frac{\lambda}{\mu} = \frac{\lambda}{\mu - \lambda} - \frac{\lambda}{\mu}$$

$$= \lambda \left[\frac{\mu - \mu + \lambda}{\mu(\mu - \lambda)}\right]$$

$$= \frac{\lambda}{\mu} \cdot \frac{\lambda}{\mu - \lambda} \qquad \ldots \text{(i)}$$

Note that the expected number in service is 1 times the probability that the service channel is busy i.e., $1 - \dfrac{\lambda}{\mu}$.

3. Expected time per unit in the system (expected time a unit spends in the system),

$$W_s = \dfrac{\text{Expected number of units in the system}}{\text{Arrival rate}}$$

$$= \dfrac{L_s}{\lambda} = \dfrac{\lambda}{(\mu - \lambda) \cdot \lambda} = \dfrac{1}{\mu - \lambda} \qquad \ldots \text{(j)}$$

4. Expected waiting time per unit in the queue,

$$W_q = W_s - \dfrac{1}{\mu} = \dfrac{1}{\mu - \lambda} - \dfrac{1}{\mu} = \dfrac{\lambda}{\mu} \cdot \dfrac{1}{\mu - \lambda} \qquad \ldots \text{(k)}$$

5. Variance of queue length

By definition we have

$$\text{Var}(n) = E(n)^2 - [E(n)]^2$$

$$= \sum_{n=1}^{\infty} n^2 p_n - \left[\sum_{n=0}^{\infty} n\, p_n\right]^2$$

[∵ for n = 0, both terms are zero only]

$$= \sum_{n=0}^{\infty} n^2 \cdot \left(1 - \dfrac{\lambda}{\mu}\right)\left(\dfrac{\lambda}{\mu}\right)^n - [L_s]^2$$

$$= \left(1 - \dfrac{\lambda}{\mu}\right) \sum_{n=1}^{\infty} n^2 \left(\dfrac{\lambda}{\mu}\right)^n - \left(\dfrac{\lambda}{\mu - \lambda}\right)^2$$

$$= \left(1 - \dfrac{\lambda}{\mu}\right)\left[1 \cdot \dfrac{\lambda}{\mu} + 2^2 \left(\dfrac{\lambda}{\mu}\right)^2 + 3^2 \cdot \left(\dfrac{\lambda}{\mu}\right)^3 + \ldots\right] - \left(\dfrac{\lambda}{\mu - \lambda}\right)^2$$

$$= \dfrac{\lambda}{\mu} \cdot \left(1 - \dfrac{\lambda}{\mu}\right)\left[1 - 2^2 \cdot \dfrac{\lambda}{\mu} + 3^2 \left(\dfrac{\lambda}{\mu}\right)^2 + \ldots\right] - \left(\dfrac{\lambda}{\mu - \lambda}\right)^2$$

Let, $\quad S = 1 + 2^2 \dfrac{\lambda}{\mu} + 3^2 + \left(\dfrac{\lambda}{\mu}\right)^2 + \ldots$

$$= 1 + 2^2 p + 3^2 p^2 + \ldots \qquad \left[\because p = \dfrac{\lambda}{\mu}\right]$$

Integrating, both sides w.r.t. p from 0 to p, we have,

$$\int_0^p S \cdot dp = \int_0^p (1 + 2^2 p + 3^2 p^2 + \ldots) \, dp$$

$$= [p + 2p^2 + 3p^3 + \ldots]_0^p$$

$$= p + 2p^2 + 3p^3 + \ldots = p(1 + 2p + 3p^2 + \ldots)$$

$$= p \cdot \frac{1}{1-p^2} = \frac{p}{1-p^2}$$

Now differentiating both sides w.r.t. p, we have

$$S = \frac{1}{(1-p)^2} + p \cdot (-2) \cdot (1-p)^{-3} (-1)$$

$$= \frac{1}{(1-p)^2} + \frac{2p}{(1-p)^3}$$

$$= \frac{1+p}{(1-p)^3} = \frac{1+\frac{\lambda}{\mu}}{\left(1-\frac{\lambda}{\mu}\right)^3}$$

$$\therefore \quad \text{var}_{(n)} = \frac{\lambda}{\mu}\left(1-\frac{\lambda}{\mu}\right) \cdot \frac{\left(1+\frac{\lambda}{\mu}\right)}{\left(1-\frac{\lambda}{\mu}\right)^3} - \left(\frac{\lambda}{\mu-\lambda}\right)^2$$

$$\therefore \quad \text{Variance of queue length} = \frac{\frac{\lambda}{\mu}\left(1+\frac{\lambda}{\mu}\right)}{\left(1-\frac{\lambda}{\mu}\right)^2} - \frac{\frac{\lambda^2}{\mu^2}}{\left(1-\frac{\lambda}{\mu}\right)^2} = \frac{\frac{\lambda}{\mu}}{\left(1-\frac{\lambda}{\mu}\right)^2} \quad \ldots (l)$$

6. **Average length of non-empty queue (length of queue that is formed from time to time). L_n**: for a non-empty queue, the number of units in the system should be at least 2 (one in service and other in the queue). Probability of a non-empty queue,

$$= \sum_{n=0}^{\infty} p_n - (p_0 + p_1)$$

$$= 1 - \left(p_0 + \frac{\lambda}{\mu} p_0\right) = 1 - p_0\left(1 + \frac{\lambda}{\mu}\right)$$

$$= 1 - \left(1 - \frac{\lambda}{\mu}\right)\left(1 + \frac{\lambda}{\mu}\right) = \left(\frac{\lambda}{\mu}\right)^2$$

Now average length of non-empty queue,

$$L_n = \frac{\text{Average length of queue}}{\text{Probability of non-empty queue}}$$

$$= \frac{\frac{\lambda}{\mu} \cdot \frac{\lambda}{\mu - \lambda}}{\left(\frac{\lambda}{\mu}\right)^2} = \frac{\mu}{\mu - A} \qquad \ldots \text{(m)}$$

7. Average waiting time is non-empty queue

$$\omega_n = \frac{1}{\mu - \lambda} \qquad \ldots \text{(n)}$$

8. Probability of queue being greater than or equal to k,

$$p(\geq k) = \sum_{n=0}^{\infty} p_n - \sum_{n=0}^{n=k-1} p_n$$

$$= 1 - [p_0 + p_1 + p_2 + \ldots, p_{k-1}]$$

$$= 1 - \left[p_0 + \frac{\lambda}{\mu} + p_0 + \left(\frac{\lambda}{\mu}\right)^2 p_0 + \ldots + \left(\frac{\lambda}{\mu}\right)^{k-1} p_0\right]$$

$$= 1 - p_0 \left[1 + \frac{\lambda}{\mu} + \left(\frac{\lambda}{\mu}\right)^2 + \ldots + \left(\frac{\lambda}{\mu}\right)^{k-1}\right]$$

$$= 1 - p_0 \frac{1 - \left(\frac{\lambda}{\mu}\right)^k}{1 - \frac{\lambda}{\mu}} = 1 - \left(1 - \frac{\lambda}{\mu}\right) \cdot \frac{1 - \left(\frac{\lambda}{\mu}\right)^k}{1 - \frac{\lambda}{\mu}} = \left(\frac{\lambda}{\mu}\right)^k \qquad \ldots \text{(O a)}$$

9. Probability of queue being greater than k,

$$p(> k) = \left(\frac{\lambda}{\mu}\right)^{k+1} \qquad \ldots \text{(O b)}$$

10. Probability that the queue is non-empty,

$$p(n > k) = 1 - p_0 - p_1$$

$$= 1 - \left(1 - \frac{\lambda}{\mu}\right) - \frac{\lambda}{\mu}\left(1 - \frac{\lambda}{\mu}\right)$$

$$= \left(\frac{\lambda}{\mu}\right)^2 \qquad \ldots \text{(O c)}$$

11. Probability density function of waiting time distribution

$$= \begin{bmatrix} \dfrac{\lambda}{\mu}(\mu-\lambda)\cdot e^{-(\mu-\lambda)t}, & t > 0 \\ \dfrac{\lambda}{\mu}(\mu-\lambda) & , t = 0 \end{bmatrix} \qquad \ldots (p)$$

12. Probability density function of (waiting + service) time distribution

$$= (\mu-\lambda)\cdot e^{-(\mu-\lambda)t} \qquad \ldots (q)$$

3.2.9 Service Mechanism

It is the process which shows. The way in which service is provided to customers and the manner in which they leave the service centre.

This process/Mechanism is characterized by,

(a) The arrangement of service facilities

(b) Queue disciplining

(c) Service distribution.

(a) Arrangement of Service Facilities:

The capacity of the service facility is measured in terms of customers that can be served simultaneously and effectively. The service channels may be in series or in parallel or mixed.

(i) **Single or in Series Arrangement:** In series arrangement it consist of the sequence of the service facility such that the customers goes through one facility after another in a sequence, so that the complete service is received. The facilities work independently of each other.

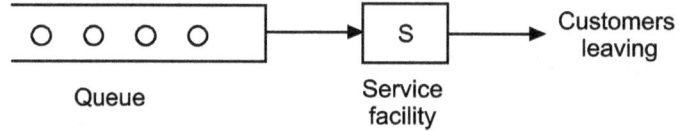

Single Queue, Single Server

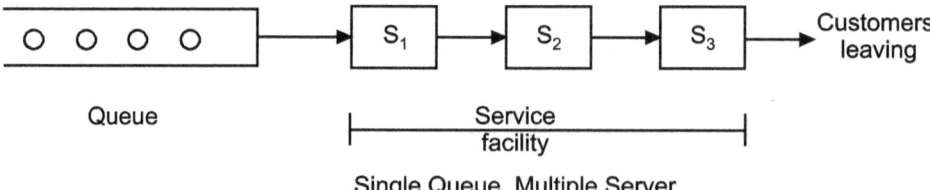

Single Queue, Multiple Server

Fig. 3.4

(ii) Parallel Arrangement: In this arrangement there are number of service facilities in parallel and the customers may join the queue of his choice or may be served by any service facility.

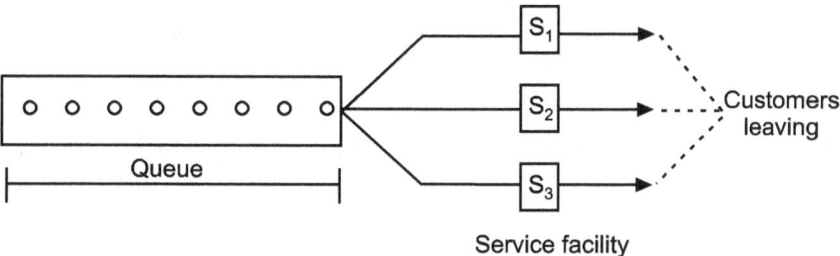

Fig. 3.5

(iii) Mixed Arrangement: In this arrangement service facilities are provided in series as well as parallel.

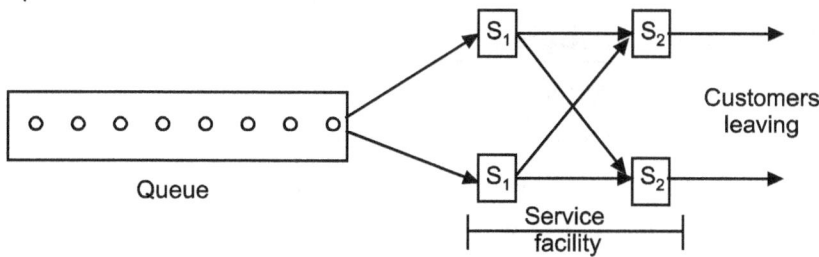

Fig. 3.6

(b) Queue Discipline:

It is the rule by which customers are selected from the queue for service. The most common is "first come, first served", in this the customers are served as they come. Then the other is 'last come, first served', and the according to the importance or urgency the customers.

(c) Service Distribution:

It represent the pattern in which the number of customers leave the system.

3.2.10 Assumptions of Queuing Model

- The customer arrives for service at the service centre randomly.
- The service discipline followed is first come first served.
- Customer who needs the service joins the queue and wait for their turn and leaves only after getting the service.
- Service centres serve the customers continuously.
- Service centres serve one customer at a time.
- The waiting space for the customers in the queue is infinite.
- The customers coming are also infinite.
- The rate of arrival is less than the rate of service.

3.2.11 Limitations of Queuing Model

- The waiting space for the customer is limited.
- The arrival rate depends on the service facility. It means that customer has the choice to join the queue, on seeing a long queue or may leave the service centre without being served.
- The arrival rate will have peak and slack period during which the arrival rate can be more or less than the average.
- The customers are finite and the finite and the service discipline may not be first come, first served.
- The service facility may break down and also the services may be provided in groups not individually.

3.2.12 Mathematical Symbols of Queuing Model

L_s = Mean length of the system.
 = No. of customers in the queue + No. being queue serve
L_q = Mean length of the queue (no. of customers in the queue)
W_s = Mean time a customer's spends waiting in the system (Queue time + service time)
W_q = Mean time spent waiting in the queue.
A = Mean arrival rate (no. of arrivals per unit of time)
S = Mean service time rate (no. of customers served per unit of time)
P_i = Probability that service facility is idle.
P_b = Probability that service facility is busy.
P_n = Probability that there are 'n' no. of customers in the queue.

Formula:

$$L_s = A / (S - A)$$
$$L_q = A^2 / S(S - A)$$
$$W_s = 1 / (S - A)$$
$$W_q = A / S(S - A)$$
$$P_b = A / S$$
$$P_i = 1 - \frac{A}{S}$$
$$P_n = \left(1 - \frac{A}{S}\right)\left(\frac{A}{S}\right)^n$$

SOLVED EXAMPLES

Example 3.7: Aeroplane arrives at airport at am average rate of 8 planes per week and their arrival pattern follows poison distribution. On an average 12 planes are loaded and unloaded with exponential distribution per week. So determine.
(i) The chance that a plane will be directly taken for loading and unloading and the proportion of time required for this process.
(ii) The average queue length and no. of planes in the system.
(iii) Average time spent by the plane waiting in the queue and in the system.
(iv) The probability that there are two planes in the queue.

Given:
$$A = 8 \text{ planes per week}$$
$$S = 12 \text{ planes per week.}$$

Solution:

(i) $P_b = \dfrac{A}{S} = \dfrac{8}{12} = 0.66$

$P_i = 1 - \dfrac{A}{S} = 0.34$

(ii) $L = \dfrac{A}{S-A} = \dfrac{8}{12-8} = \dfrac{8}{4} = 2$

$L_q = \dfrac{A^2}{S(S-A)} = \dfrac{8^2}{12(4)} = 1.33$

(iii) $W_s = \dfrac{1}{S-A} = \dfrac{1}{12-8} = \dfrac{1}{4} = 0.25$

$W_q = \dfrac{A}{S(S-A)} = \dfrac{8}{12(4)} = \dfrac{8}{48} = \dfrac{1}{6} = 0.167$

(iv) $n = 2 = \left(1 - \dfrac{A}{S}\right)\left(\dfrac{A}{S}\right)^n$

$= \left(1 - \dfrac{8}{12}\right)\left(\dfrac{8}{12}\right)^2$

$= 0.148$

Example 3.8: Cars came to the workshop to receive service to increase its efficiency. The average time between two arrivals is 60 second and arrivals are assumed to be in Poisson distribution. The average service time is 40 second.

Determine:
1. Average queue length
2. Average length of workers in system.

3. Average no. of cars being attended including the cars being attended.
4. Mean waiting time of an arrival
5. Type of policy to be established.

Determine whether to go in for an additional service centre which minimizes the combined cost of attendants idle time and cost of car's waiting time. Assume the charges of a car ₹ 40/ hr and that of service centre ₹ 15 /hr.

Solution:

(i) $A = \dfrac{1}{60}$ per second = 1 per min.

$S = \dfrac{1}{40}$ per second = 1.5 per min

(ii) $L_q = \dfrac{A^2}{S(S-A)} = \dfrac{1}{1.5(105)} = 1.33$

(iii) $L_n = \dfrac{S}{S-A} = \dfrac{1.5}{0.5} = 3$ cars

(iv) $L_s = \dfrac{A}{S-A} = \dfrac{1}{0.5} = 2$ cars

(v) $W_q = \dfrac{A}{S(S-A)} = \dfrac{1}{1.5(0.5)} = 1.33$ min

(vi) $P_i = 1 - \dfrac{A}{S} = 1 - \dfrac{1}{1.5} = \dfrac{1}{3}$

Idle time cost of one allotment $= \dfrac{1}{3} \times 8 \times 15 =$ ₹ 39.97 / day

Waiting time cost of cars $= w_q \times$ No. of cars / day $\times$ cost

$= \left(\dfrac{4}{3} \times \dfrac{1}{60}\right) \times (8 \times 60) \times 40$

$=$ ₹ 425.60 / days.

Idle time cost is much more than idle time cost, therefore additional service centre can be started.

Example 3.9: *Truck arrive at a loading site in a pattern which can be characterized by the poisson distribution at an average of 20 trucks per hr. The loading by shovel is done at a rate of 22 per hr. per shovel. The cost of truck is ₹ 800 per hr. whereas the cost of shovel is ₹ 500 per hr. Find the optimum no. of shovels to be used.*

Solution:

A = 20 trucks per hr.

B = 22 trucks per hr.

1. $L_q = \dfrac{A^2}{A(S-A)}$

   $= \dfrac{20^2}{20(22-20)} = \dfrac{40}{4} = 10$ trucks

   Cost of lost time of trucks $= 10 \times 8 \times 800$

   $= ₹ 64000/-$

   Cost of one shovel $= 1 \times 8 \times 500$

   $= ₹ 4000$

   ∴ Total cost $= 64000 + 4000$

   $= 68000/-$

2. It we have two shovels working $A = 20$

   $S = 44$

   then, $L_q = \dfrac{A^2}{S(S-A)} = \dfrac{20^2}{44(44-20)} = \dfrac{400}{1056}$

   $= 0.3787$ trucks

   Cost of lost time of trucks $= 0.38 \times 8 \times 800$

   $= ₹ 2432/-$

   Cost of two shovel $= 2 \times 8 \times 500 = 8000$

   It there are 3 shovels then,

   The cost of three shovels $= 3 \times 8 \times 500$

   $= ₹ 12000/-$

   As such employing three shovels is out of questions.

   ∴ Optimum no. of shovels $= 2$

3.3 SIMULATION

3.3.1 Introduction

Simulation is representation of reality through the use of a model or other devices which will react in the same manner as reality under a given set of conditions. Simulation is also defined as "The use of system model that has the designed characteristics of reality in order to produce the essence of actual operation".

A simulated model may be defined as one which depicts the working of a large scale system of men, material, machines and information over a period of time in a simulated environment of the actual real world condition.

Simulation is an imitation of reality. For e.g. The testing of an aircraft model in a wind tunnel from which we can determine the performance of the actual aircraft, planetarium represents a beautiful simulation of the planet system, labours are trained on simulated equipments, New/Learning drivers are trained on simulated vehicles etc.

When a complex system is formulated into a mathematical model for which a computer programme is developed and the problem is solved by using high speed computer and hence it is named as computer simulation or system simulation.

In system approach we have discussed a no. of operations research tools and techniques for solving various types of managerial decision making problems. Linear programming, dynamic programming, queuing theory, network models etc are the few techniques which cannot tackle the managerial problems. Each technique has its own limitations.

The technique of simulation is successfully used by the designers and analysts in physical science and it has become an important tool for dealing with complicated problems of managerial decision-making.

3.3.2 Advantages of the Simulation Technique

- Simulation gives solution to a problem by allowing experimentation model of the system without disturbing the real system.
- Simulation helps the management to know the difficulties which can be arrived due to introduction of new machine, equipment or process.
- As simulation is free from difficult mathematics, so it can be easily understood by everyone (i.e. technical and non-technical)
- Simulation models are flexible and can be modified according the real situation.
- Computer simulation can compress the performance of a system over several years and involving large calculation into a few minutes of computer running.
- Simulation technique is simpler than mathematical model and is considered quite superior to the mathematical analysis.
- Simulation is advantageous to train people on simulated model before putting them into real system. Because of this trainees gain self confidence, increase efficiency and moreover they become well known / familiar with the real system.

3.3.3 Limitations of the Simulation Technique

- Simulation model is subjected to uncertainties so it doesn't produce optimum results.
- In many situations it is not possible to identity all the variables that affects the system of simulation.
- Simulation is costlier and time consuming technique.
- In a very large and complex problem, large no. of variables and their interrelationship makes the problem more complicated.

3.3.4 Applications of Simulation

- It is used in design field to design specific structures like dams, spillways, power plants, aircrafts, spaceships, satellites etc.

- It is used to evaluate, the area under a curve, to estimate the value of TT, study of particle diffusion.
- It is also used to design weapon system, war strategies and tactics.
- It is used to determine. Population growth, environmental effect on human health.
- It also include customer behaviours, price determination, economic fore casting, port folio selection and capital budgeting.
- It also help in designing queuing system, inventory control, scheduling of production process.

3.3.5 Monte Carlo Simulation

This method of simulation was developed by two mathematicians, during World War II. This technique provided an approximate but a workable solution to the problem. Due to the success of the technique, it become most popular technique and found many applications in business and industry, it has now become a very important tool of operation researcher's in their research.

The Monte Carlo simulation technique involves conducting of repetitive experiments on the model of the system under study with known probability distribution to draw random samples with the help of random number. It a system is not described by a standard distribution, than an empirical probability distribution is constructed.

The Monte Carlo simulation technique consist of following steps:

1. Setting up a probability distribution for variables to be analysed.
2. Then random numbers and then assign an appropriate set of random numbers to represented value or range of values for each random variable.
3. Conduct the simulation experiment using random sampling.
4. Repeat the above step until all the required numbers of simulation runs has been generated.
5. Design and implement a course of action and maintain control.

Example 3.10 : *A sample of 100 arrivals of automobiles at a toll booth is found to be according the following distribution.*

Time of Arrivals in Min.	0.5	1.0	1.5	2	2.5	3	3.5	4	4.5	5
Frequency	2	6	10	24	20	15	10	7	4	2

A study of service time reveal the following distribution.

Service Time in Min.	0.5	1	1.5	2	2.5
Frequency	13	22	37	20	8

Estimate the average waiting time, the percentage waiting time of the vehicle, average idle time and percentage idle time of the server for 10 arrivals. Use the following random no.

Arrival	16	77	23	02	77	28	06	24	25	93
Service Time	56	65	05	61	86	90	92	10	79	80

Solution: Step 1: Assignment of random no. to arrivals.

Time between arrivals	Frequency (f)	Cumulative Frequency (CF)	CF %	Random No.
0.5	2	2	0.02	0 to 1
1	6	8	0.08	2 to 7
1.5	10	18	0.18	8 to 17
2	24	42	0.42	18 to 41
2.5	20	62	0.62	42 to 61
3	15	77	0.77	62 to 76
3.5	10	87	0.87	77 to 86
4	7	94	0.94	87 to 93
4.5	4	98	0.98	98 to 99
5	2	100	1.00	98 to 99

Step 2: Assignment of random no. for service facility.

Service Time	Frequency (f)	Cumulative Frequency (CF)	CF %	Random No.
0.5	13	13	0.13	0 to 12
1	22	35	0.35	12 to 34
1.5	37	72	0.72	35 to 71
2	28	92	0.92	72 to 91
2.5	8	100	1.00	92 to 98

Step 3: Idle time and Waiting time.

R_1	Random No.	16	77	23	02	77	28	06	24	25	93
R_2	Time between Arrivals (Tab. 1)	1.5	3.5	2	1	3.5	2	1	2	2	4.5
R_3	Time of Arrival in Min. on Simulation Clock.	1.5	5	7	8	11.5	13.5	14.5	16.5	18.5	22.5
R_4	Random No.	56	65	05	61	86	90	92	10	79	80
R_5	Length of Service Time in Min. (Tab.2)	1.5	1.5	0.5	1.5	2	2	2.5	0.5	2	2
R_6	Time of Start	1.5	5	7	8	11.5	13.5	15.5	18	18.5	22.5
R_7	Time of Finish	3	6.5	7.5	9.5	13.5	15.5	18	18.5	20.5	24.5
R_8	Waiting Time (Min.) of Customers	–	–	–	–	–	–	1	1.5	–	–
R_9	Idle Time of Server (Min.)	1.5	2	0.5	0.5	2	–	–	–	–	2

Note: R_3 is Cumulative of R_2, R_4 is service time given for random no.,

$R_7 = R_6 + R_5$, $R_8 = R_6 - R_3$

Sum of waiting time of customer = 2.5 min

Sum of idle time of servers = 8.5 min.

(i) Total elapsed time = 24.5 min

(ii) % Customer waiting time = $\frac{2.5}{24.5} \times 100 = 10.20$

(iii) % Idle time of server = $\frac{8.5}{24.5} \times 100 = 34.69$

(iv) Average waiting time of customer = $\frac{2.5}{10} = 0.25$ min

(v) Average idle time of server = $\frac{8.5}{10} = 0.85$ min.

Example 3.11: The inter arrival time and the service time in a waiting line model have the following frequency distribution based on 100 such arrivals.

Inter-arrival Time in Min.	1	2	3	4	5	6	7
Frequency	4	10	13	22	30	14	7
Service Time in Min.	1	2	3	4	5	6	
Frequency	3	8	25	39	16	9	

Estimate the average customer waiting time and the percentage waiting time, average idle time and percentage idle time of the service facility and the average queue length by simulating 10 arrivals. Use the following random numbers.

Arrivals	23	58	56	44	80	36	97	26	71	62
Service	60	21	68	76	52	08	25	84	38	05

Solution: Step 1: Assignment of random numbers to arrivals.

Inter-arrival Time in Mins.	Frequency (f)	(CF)	CF %	Random No.
1	4	4	0.04	0-3
2	10	14	0.14	4-13
3	13	27	0.27	14-26
4	22	49	0.49	27-48
5	30	79	0.79	49-78
6	14	93	0.93	78-92
7	7	100	1.00	93-99

Step 2: Assignment of random no. for service facility.

Inter-arrival Time in Mins.	Frequency (f)	(CF)	%CF	Random No.
1	3	3	0.03	0-2
2	8	11	0.11	3-10
3	25	36	0.36	11-35
4	39	75	0.75	36-74
5	16	91	0.91	75-90
6	9	100	1	91-99

Step 3: Waiting time and idle time.

Random No.	23	58	56	44	80	36	97	26	71	62
Time between Arrivals (Tab.1)	3	5	5	4	6	4	7	3	5	5
Time of Arrival in Min. on Simulation Clock	3	8	13	17	23	27	34	37	42	47
Random No.	60	21	68	76	52	08	25	84	38	05
Length of Service Time in Min. (Tab. 2)	4	3	4	5	4	2	3	5	4	2
Time of Start	3	8	13	17	23	27	34	37	42	47
Time of Finish	7	11	17	22	27	29	37	42	46	49
Waiting Time (Min.) of Customers	-	-	-	-	-	-	-	-	-	-
Idle Time of Server (Min.)	3	1	2	-	1	-	5	-	-	1

Sum of waiting time of customers = 0 mins.

Sum of idle time of server = 12 mins.

(i) Total elapsed time = 49 mins

(ii) % customer waiting time = $\frac{0}{49} \times 100 = 0$

(iii) % idle time of server = $\frac{12}{49} \times 100 = 24.49$

(iv) Average waiting time of customer = $\frac{0}{10} = 0$

(v) Average idle time of server = $\frac{12}{10} = 1.2$ min.

THEORETICAL QUESTIONS

1. Five jobs are to be processed in 3 departments A, B and C in the sequence A-B-C. The time required for each job in each department is given below. Determine the sequence in which the jobs are to be processed if the total elapsed time is to be minimized.

   Tabulate the processing sequence and determine the total elapsed.

Job	Time in hrs.		
	A	B	C
1	13	9	14
2	12	8	9
3	11	7	12
4	15	10	13
5	16	11	15

2. A company has 6 jobs which are to be processed on 3 machines A, B and C in order ABC. The processing time in minutes for each job on each machine is as given below. Find the optimal sequence of the jobs so as to minimize the total time elapsed. Also find the idle time on each machine.

Machine \ Job	1	2	3	4	5	6
A	36	24	58	72	86	74
B	14	24	22	4	12	24
C	38	24	46	94	56	72

3. Find the sequence that minimizes the total time required for performing the following jobs on three machines in the order A-B-C. find the total elapsed time & idle times of machine B and C.

Job	Processing Time in Min.		
	A	B	C
1	8	3	8
2	3	4	7
3	7	5	6
4	2	2	9
5	5	1	10
6	1	6	9

4. Solve the following sequencing problem involving 3-machines, n jobs & no passing, to obtain the sequence of jobs to be processed so as to minimize the total time elapsed. Determine the total elapsed time and idle hours of the machines, if any. Tabulate the results indicating the schedule of processing of all the jobs.

Jobs	Time in hrs.		
	Machine A	Machine B	Machine C
1	6	5	9
2	7	7	11
3	3	8	8
4	4	5	9
5	5	6	12
6	10	4	9
7	16	7	10
8	12	3	14

5. What is sequence? What are the assumptions in sequencing problem.
6. Solve: It is given that,
   (a) Arrival and service follow poisson process.
   (b) Customers arrive at a rate of 12 per hr.
   (c) Service rate is 15 customers per hr.
   So, determine,
   (i) What is the average no. of customers waiting for service.
   (ii) What is the average time, a customer must wait in queue.
   (iii) What is the average time for a customers to be in the system.
7. What are the various components of a queuing model? Discuss their characteristics.
8. Explain Kendal's notation.
9. Arrivals at a telephone booth follow poison distribution with an inter arrival time of 10 min. The length of the phone call is assumed to be distributed exponentially with a mean of 3 minutes finds,
   (i) The probability that an arrival will have to wait before the phone is free.
   (ii) The average queue length
   (iii) The average no. of customers in the system.
   (iv) Average waiting time of customers in the queue.
   (v) Average waiting time of customers in the system.
10. Explain the Monte Carlo method of simulation.
11. Give any two applications of simulation in the field of civil engineering.
12. State advantages and limitations of simulation technique.

13. The inter arrival time and the service time in a waiting line model have the following frequency distribution based on 100 such arrivals.

Inter Arrival Time in Mins.	3	6	9	12	15	18
Frequency	6	9	25	37	16	7

Service Time in Min.	4	6	8	10	12
Frequency	4	10	18	44	24

Calculate:

(a) The average waiting time and percentage waiting time of an arrival.

(b) The average idle time and percentage idle time of the server.

(c) Mean queue length:

Simulate 10 arrivals and use the following random numbers:

Arrival	15	19	61	49	54	73	85	96	31	22
Service Time	9	11	90	64	37	29	43	78	87	56

14. A sample of 100 arrivals of automobiles at both is found to be according to the following distribution:

Time between Arrivals in Min.	0.5	1.0	1.5	2.0	2.5	3.0	3.5	4.0	4.5	5.0
Frequency	2	6	10	24	20	15	10	7	3	2

The time take for service follows the distribution.

Service Time in Min.	0.5	1.0	1.5	2.0	2.5
Frequency	13	22	37	20	8

Estimate the average % waiting time and idle time of a customer by simulation for next 10 arrivals. Use the following random numbers.

Arrivals	16	77	23	02	77	28	06	24	25	93
Service	56	65	05	61	86	90	92	10	79	80

15. Solve the following sequencing problem involving 3-machines, n-jobs and no passing. To obtain the sequence of jobs to be processed so as to minimize the total time elapsed. Determine the total elapsed time and idle hours of the machines, if any, tabulate the results indicating the schedule of processing of all the jobs.

Jobs	Time in hours.		
	Machine A	Machine B	Machine C
1	6	5	9
2	7	7	11
3	3	8	8
4	4	5	9
5	5	6	12
6	10	4	9
7	16	7	10
8	12	3	14

16. A sample of 200 arrivals of customers in a super-market is according to the following distribution: **[Nov. 2012]**

Time between Arrivals in Min.	0.5	1.0	1.5	2.0	2.5	3.0	3.5	4.0	4.5	5.0	5.5
Frequency	4	12	22	48	38	28	22	12	8	4	2

The time taken for service, follows the distribution ;

Time in Min.	0.5	1.0	1.5	2.0	2.5	3.0	3.5	4.5
Frequency	12	18	38	60	32	16	14	10

Estimate the average % waiting time and idle time of a customer by simulation for next 10 arrivals. Use the following random numbers.

Arrivals : 9, 73, 25, 33, 76, 53, 01, 35, 86, 34

Service : 54, 20, 48, 05, 64, 89, 47, 42, 96, 24

17. Solve the following sequencing problem involving 3- machines, n-jobs and no passing, to obtain the sequence of jobs to be processed so as to minimize the total time elapsed. Determine the total elapsed time and idle hours of the machines, if any. Tabulate the results indicating the schedule of processing of all the jobs. **[Nov. 2013]**

Jobs	Time in hours		
	Machine A	Machine B	Machine C
1	6	5	9
2	7	7	11
3	3	8	8
4	4	5	9
5	5	6	12
6	10	4	9
7	16	7	10
8	12	3	14

18. A sample of 100 arrivals of automobiles at toll booth is found to be according to the following distribution : **[May 2013]**

Time between Arrivals Min	0.5	1.0	1.5	2.0	2.5	3.0	3.5	4.0	4.5	5.0
Frequency	2	6	10	24	20	15	10	7	4	2

The time taken for service follows the distribution;

Service Time in Min.	0.5	1.0	1.5	2.0	2.5
Frequency	13	22	37	20	8

Estimate the average % waiting time and idle time of a customer by simulation for next 10 arrivals. Use the following random numbers.

Arrivals	16	77	23	02	77	28	06	24	25	93
Service	56	65	05	61	86	90	92	10	79	80

Unit 4

DYNAMIC PROGRAMMING

4.1 INTRODUCTION

In real finance world, decisions must often be made in a sequential manner over time. Earlier decisions may affect the feasibility and performance of later decision. In such environments, myopic decisions that optimize only the immediate impact are usually suboptimal for the overall process. To find optimal strategies, one must consider current and future decisions simultaneously. These types of multi-stage decision problems are the typical settings where one employs dynamic programming. Dynamic programming is a useful mathematical technique for making a sequence of interrelated decisions. It provides a systematic procedure for determining the optimal combination of decisions. In contrast to linear programming, there does not exist a standard mathematical formulation of the dynamic programming problem. Rather, dynamic programming is a general type of approach to problem solving, and the particular equations used must be developed to fit each situation. Therefore, a certain degree of ingenuity and insight into the general', structure of dynamic programming problems is required to recognize when and how a problem can be solved by dynamic programming procedures. These abilities can best be developed by an exposure to a wide variety of dynamic programming applications and a study of the characteristics that are common to all these situations.

The two terms 'dynamic' and 'programming', convey a particular significance – programming" is used in mathematical sense of selecting an optimal allocation of resources and it is dynamic in the sense that it is particularly useful problems where decisions are taken at several distinct stages.

Dynamic programming therefore is a mathematical technique for solving certain types of problem in which a sequence of decisions have to be made at several distinct stages. Dynamic programming represents more of a approach rather than a technique with rigid rules such as simples method of linear programming. It divides the problems into series of sub-problems proceeding to it. In lieu of its general approach, dynamic programming can be used to solve many types of problems. The only restriction being that problem involved must be capable of being split up into-sub problem (or alternatively the decision process must be split into several stages)

This technique was originated in 1950 by Richard Bellman and G.B Dantzig and was Initially referred to as the stochastic linear programming.

4.2 CHARACTERISTICS OF DYNAMIC PROGRAMMING PROBLEMS

Basic characteristics of dynamic programming are as follows:
- A single n variable problem can be divided into n problems of single variable, provided the objective function of the optimization problem is separable with respect to stage.
- The problem can be divided into stages with a policy required at each stage.
- With each stage, a number of states are associated.
- The policy decision transforms the present state into a state associated with the next stage.
- At a given stage for a given state, the recursive relationship identifies the optimal decision, given the optimal decision for each state at the previous stage.
- The solution moves back ward or forward stage by stage, till optimal decision for the last stage is determined. From this solution the optimal decision for other stages are determined.

4.3 APPLICATION OF DYNAMIC PROGRAMMING IN CIVIL ENGINEERING

- Reservoir Operation,
- Water Allocation,
- Capacity Expansion,
- Irrigation Scheduling,
- Water Quality Control,
- Shortest Route Problems
- Slope Stability Analysis
- Reliability Analysis,
- Resource Allocation,
- Biological Sequence Manipulation
- Cargo Handling
- Cargo Loading
- Equipment Replacement
- Fund Allocation
- Risk Management.
- Production Scheduling

4.4 ADVANTAGES OF DYNAMIC PROGRAMMING

- In dynamic programming unlike linear programming'. the formation for linear and non linear problems is the same. Thus no extra labour is required for non linear problems.
- In dynamic programming, the incorporation of constraints is easier than linear programming and non linear programming. The constraints serve a useful purpose. In this case, the constraints limit the feasible region and reduce the computational time.
- The stochastic nature of the problem can be easily considered in dynamic programming

4.5 DISADVANTAGES OF DYNAMIC PROGRAMMING

- In dynamic programming, there are no set procedures (algorithm) to solve any decision or allocation problem
- Dynamic programming cannot provide one time period (single stage) solution to problems unlike linear programming
- Design and formulation of recursive equations can be very complex and frustrating.

4.6 TERMINOLOGY OF DYNAMIC PROGRAMMING

- **Stage:** The dynamic programming can be decomposed into a sequence of smaller sub-problems called stages of the original problem. At each stage, there are number of decision alternatives and a decision is made by selecting the most suitable, out of the given list.
- **State Variable:** State variables are the variables whose specify the conditions of the process for making decisions. Stages variables depend on the type of problems. At any stages of the decision-making process there could be a finite or infinite number of stages. For example, in production scheduling of Ready Mix Concrete Plant, state variables may relate to plant capacity and current inventory.
- **Decision Variables:** Decision variable are the unknowns in the given problem that need to be determined. For example, in a problem on minimum cost production of Ready Mix Concrete per cubic meter. decision variables will be" quality of Ready Mix Concrete.
- **Return Function:** Return function represents the contribution of each stage and it depends on the nature of the problem. At each stage, a decision is made which can be affecting the state of the system at the next stage and help in arriving at the optimal solution at the current stage. Each decision that is made has benefit and is

described in an algebraic equation called as return function. Since for every set of decisions a return on each decision is obtained. This return functions depends on the state variable as well as the decision made at particular stage.

- **Recursive Relationship:** Recursive Relationship represents a mathematical expression connecting the optimal solution of the earlier stages and the return function from the current stage; it therefore shows the total contribution till the stages. The recursive relationship is established for each stage that's general from is as under

$$f_n = r_n + f_{n-1}$$

Where f_n = optimal valve of all earlier stages up to and including its stage Rn= return function at the nth stages.

The recursive relationship may be additive or multiplicative.

- **Forward and Backward Solution:** A dynamic programming can be solved in different ways. One can either start from initial stage and go to the final solution in which case it is called forward solution. Alternatively, one can start from the final stage and go back to the initial stage which is called the backward solution.

4.7 STAGES FOR SOLUTION THROUGH DYNAMIC PROGRAMMING

Basic steps to a problem through dynamic programming requires following basic stages:

Stage 1 : Identify the decision variables and specify the objectives to be optimized.

Stage 2 : Divide the given problem into a number sub–problem. Each stage refers to a group of sub–problems.

Stage 3 : Write a general recursive relationship for determining the optimal policy. Also decide whether forward or backward method is to be followed to solve the problem.

Stage 4 : Determine the optimal valve of each of the sub–problems at the first stage.

Stage 5 : Utilized the optimal values of the first stage to determine optimal values of the sub–problems at the second stage. This requires repeating stage 4 for the second stage.

Stage 6 : Follow through stages 4 and 5 for each of the succeeding stages.

Stage 7 : Backtrack to find the overall optimal decision and its value at each stage. The problem may have more than one optimal policy.

4.8 BELLMAN'S PRINCIPAL OF OPTIMALITY

Dynamic programming reduces the computational effort involved in problem requiring sequential decision making. Dynamic programming is closely associated with the name of Richard Bellman who has stared the principal of dynamic programming as under:

"An optimal policy has the property that whatever the initial state and initial decisions are, the remaining decision must constitute an optimal policy with regard to the stage resulting from the first decision."

If an optimal state X results in a state Y, this initial state to this final state, the portion of the original must be optimum. That is every part of optimal policy is optimal.

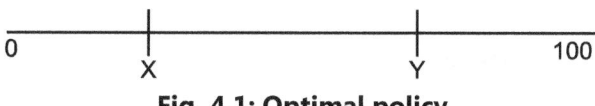

Fig. 4.1: Optimal policy

Based on this principal of optimality, the solution procedure starts by solving a one–stage problem and then sequentially adding a series of one–stage problem that are solved until the overall optimal of the initial process is obtained. The solution procedure is based on a backward induction process. In this process, the problem is solved by solving the problem in the last stages and working backward towards the first stage, making optimal decision at each stage of the problem.

The exact recursion relationship varies with the nature of the problem. In general it is written as:

$$F_n(s_n) = \underset{d_n}{\text{Optimal}} \{r_n(S_n, d_n) * f_{n-1}(S_{n-1})\}$$

Where

$$S_{n-1} = t_n(S_n, d_n)$$

i.e.

$$F_n^* = \underset{\text{oF}}{\text{Optimal value}} (r_n + f^n(n-1))$$

4.9 REPRESENTATION OF DYNAMIC PROGRAMMING

4.9.1 Single Stage Decision Process

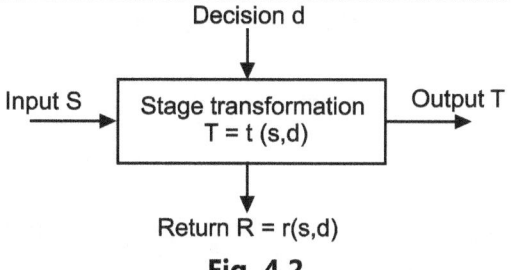

Fig. 4.2

It can be represented by a rectangular block. It is a component of the multistage problem. Any decision process is–characterised by certain input parameters S, certain decision variables d and output parameters T representing the outcome obtained as a result of making the decision. There is a return function R, which measures the effectiveness of the decisions that are made and the outputs that result from these decisions. For a single–stage decision process, the output is related to input through a stage transformation function denoted by:

$$T = t(S, d)$$

Since the input stage of the system influences the decisions we make the return function can be represented as

$$R = r(S, d)$$

4.9.2 Multistage Decision Process

The functional relationship among stage, state, decision and return function may be described as shown below.

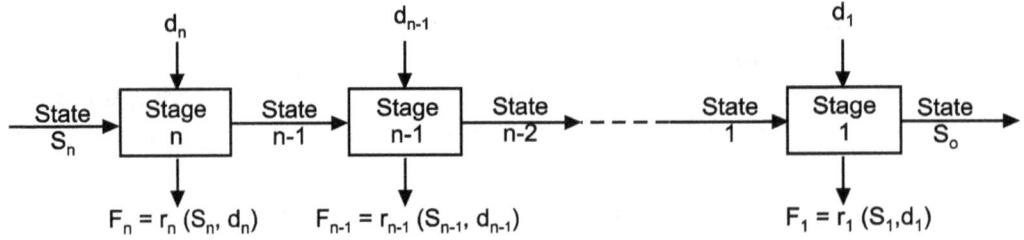

Fig. 4.3

where, n = stage number

S_n = state input to stage n from stage n + 1

Its value is the status of the system resulting from the previous (n + 1) stage decision.

d_n = decision variable at stage n

$f_n = r_n(S_n, d_n)$ = return function for stage n

Further, suppose that there are n stages at which a decision is to be made. These n stages are all interconnected by the relationship.

$$S_n - 1 = S_n * d_n$$

i.e. output at stage n = input to stage n ∗ decision at stage n where ∗ represents any mathematical operation.

At each stage of the problem, there are two inputs:

(i) State variable S_n

(ii) Decision variable d_n

The state input relates the present stage back to the previous stage.

The decision d_n is made at stage n for optimising the total return over the remaining (n–1) stages. The decision d_n which optimise the output at stage n produces two outputs – the, return function $r_n(S_n, d_n)$ and the new state variable S_{n-1}. The return function, function of the state variable S_n and decision variable d_n indicates about the state of the process at beginning of the next stage (n – 1) and is denoted as $S_n–1 = t_n(S_n, d_n)$ where t_n represents a state transformation function.

4.10 COMPUTATIONAL PROCEDURE IN DP

1. It begins by sub–optimising the last component, numbered 1.

$$f_1^*(S_1) = d_1^{opt}[R_1, (d_1, S_1)]$$

The best value of the decision variable d_1 (denoted as d_1^*) is that which makes the return function R_1 to assume its optimal value, denoted as f_1^*. Both f_1^* and d_1^* depend on the input that component receives from the upstream that is S_i. Since the value S_i is not known at this time, we solve this last stage of sub–optimisation for a range of possible values of S_1 and the results are written in a tabular form.

2. Move up the serial system to include the last two components. In this two stage sub.–optimisation,

$$f_2^*(S_2) = d_2^{opt} d_1 [R_2(d_2, S_2) + R_1(d_1, S_1)]$$
$$= d_2^{opt}[R_2(d_2, S_2) + f_1^*(S_1)]$$

A range of possible values of S_2 must be considered and for each one, d_2^* must be found so as to optimise $\left[R_2 + f_1^*(S_1)\right]$ and write the result in a tabular form.

3. The process continues until, the next step is to optimise the i end components.

$$f_1^*(S_1) = d_i, d_i - 1 \ldots d_i^{opt}[R_i + R_{i-1} \ldots R_1]$$
$$= \underset{d_i}{opt}\left[R_1(d_i, S_i) + f_{i-1}^*(S_i - 1)\right]$$

4. The sub–optimisation procedure is continued until stage n is needed.

$$f_n^*(S_n) = \underset{d_n}{opt}\left[R_n(d_n, S_n) + f_{n-1}^*(S_n - 1)\right]$$

SOLVED EXAMPLES

Example 4.1: *Miss Vaishali the project manager of ABC construction company is planning a business tour from Pune to Kolkata. She intends to cover. One city from each of the company's different zone on route.*

The network shows clearly the three intermediate stages and three possible choices of route at all but the last cities. The travel time between the two cities inclusive of the working time is given below the arrow between the cities. Which intermediate cities should she visit to minimize the time required to get from A to K?

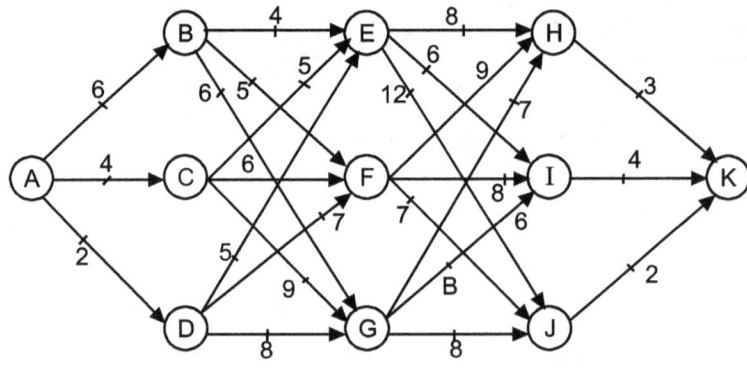

Fig. 4.4

Solution: The solution can be obtained by starting from the first city and going to the destination called forward solution.

$$f_n = \text{Optimal valve of } (r_n + f^*_{n-1})$$
$$= (r_n - f_{n-1})^*$$

Where
r_n = Distance travelled in the nth stage
F_{n-1} = Optimal distance travelled up to $(n-1)^{th}$ stage.

Stage 1: At stage I the recursive relationship takes form.

$$f_1 = [r_n + f_{o*}]^*$$

Since there is no stage prior to first stage, hence f_{o*} is zero.

Therefore, for input at stage 1st node ($S_1 = B$)

$$r_1 = 6, f_o^* = 0$$
$$f_1^* = 6 + 0 = 6$$

Similarly, for input at stage $S_1 = C$

$$r_1 = 4, f_o^* = 0 \qquad f_1^* = 4 + 0 = 4$$

And for input at stage $S_1 = D$

$$r_1 = 2, f_o^* = 0 \qquad f_1^* = 2 + 0 = 2$$

These are shown in table. Route from A to 1st stage.

Stage Rode (S_1)	Node at the Proceeding (n–1 = 0 stage) A Input to the Stage Node	Optimal Input Value of the Node at Stage 1 = f_1^*
B	6 + 0 = 6	6
C	4 + 0 = 4	4
D	2 + 0 = 2	2

Stage 2: At stage 2, the recursive equation takes the from

$$f_2 = [r_2 + f_1^*]^*$$

Where r_2 is the return function at the stage 2 (distance travelled is stage 2) and f_2^* is the optimal distance travelled to the proceeding stage (1st stage). For input $S_2 = E$ and preceeding node B, r_2 and f_1^* values would be $r_2 = 4$, $f_1^* = 6$ (value taken from f_1^* column or stage 1)

For preceding note C is considered then

$$r_2 = 5 \text{ and } f_1^* = 4$$

Similarly is preceding node D considered then

$$r_2 = 6 \text{ and } f_1^* = 2$$

Therefore, when stage mode $S_2 = E$, the optimal value $f_2 *$ (i.e. minimum distance upto the node E) from previous nodes.

$\therefore$ f_2^* minimum $[4 + 6 = 10]$
$[5 + 4 = 09]$
$[5 + 2 = 07]$

This is shown in table.

Stage Node (S_2)	Node [S] at the Preceding Stage (i.e. First Stage)			Optimal Input Value of the Node at Stage 2 = f_2^*
	B	C	D	
	Input to the Stage Node S_2			
E	4 + 6 = 10	5 + 4 = 9	5 + 2 = 7	7
F	5 + 6 = 11	6 + 4 = 10	7 + 2 = 9	9
G	6 + 6 = 12	9 + 4 = 13	8 + 2 = 10	10

Stage 3: At stage 3 the recursive equation become

$$f_3 = [r_3 + f_2^*]^*$$

Input at the nodes at stage 3 are shown in table.

Stage Node (S_3)	Node [S] at the Preceding Stage (i.e. First Stage)			Optimal Input Value of the Node at Stage 3 = f_3^*
	E	F	G	
	Input to the Stage Node (S_3)			
H	8 + 7 = 15	9 + 9 = 18	7 + 10 = 17	15
I	6 + 7 = 13	8 + 9 = 17	6 + 10 = 16	13
J	12 + 7 = 19	7 + 9 = 16	8 + 7 = 15	15

Stage 4: At the stage 4 the recursive equation becomes

$$f_4 = [r_4 + f_3^*]^* \text{ Input at stage 4 are shown in table}$$

Optimal distance from A to stage 4.

Stage Rode (S_4)	Nodes at the Proceeding (i.e. Third) Stage			OPTIMAL Input value of the Stage Node $S_4 = f_4^*$
	H	I	J	
k	3 + 15 = 18,	4 + 13 = 17,	3 + 15 = 18	17

Optimal solution:

The shortest distance between start to destination is 17. To identity optimal route, we need to connect optimal values at different stages. This is shown in table below.

Optimal route between A to K

Stage (S_n)	Optimal Input at the Stage S_n	Optimal Input of the Proceeding $(S_n - 1)^{th}$ Stage comes Point Node	Route Indentured S_o Ear
4	$f_4^* = 17$	$f_3^* = 13, I$	I – K
3	$f_3^* = 13$	$f_2^* = 7, E$	E – I – K
2	$f_2^* = 7$	$f_1^* = 2, D$	D – E – I – K
1	$f_1^* = 2$	$f_0 = 0, A$	A – D – E – I – K

∴ **Optimal route is A – D – E – I – K**

Example 4.2: A pipeline is proposed to be laid between to placed numbered as 1 to 11. The pipe lines can be laid along different routes. The costs C_{ij} of laying the pipe alone the different possible routes from places i to j are given below:

$C_{1,2} = 25$	$C_{1,3} = 29$	$C_{1,4} = 31$
$C_{2,5} = 24$	$C_{2,6} = 22$	$C_{2,7} = 25$
$C_{3,5} = 26$	$C_{3,6} = 20$	$C_{3,7} = 18$
$C_{4,5} = 23$	$C_{4,6} = 22$	$C_{4,7} = 21$
$C_{5,8} = 16$	$C_{5,9} = 28$	$C_{5,10} = 28$
$C_{6,8} = 17$	$C_{6,9} = 19$	$C_{6,10} = 24$
$C_{7,8} = 28$	$C_{7,9} = 27$	$C_{7,10} = 29$
$C_{8,11} = 32$	$C_{9,11} = 33$	$C_{8,11} = 31$

Use dynamic programming to determine the minimum cost and the carries on ding route laying pipeline. Write recursive equation at each stage.

Solution: Stage 1:

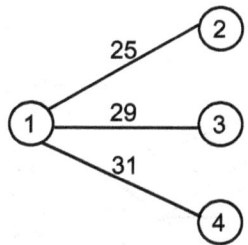

Fig. 4.5

At stage 1: The recursive equation takes the form,

$$f_1 = [r_1 + f_0^*]^*$$

since there is no stage prior to first stage hence f_0^* is zero.

Therefore. For input at stage I node (i.e. $S_1 = 1$)

$$R_1 = 25, \; f_0^* = 0$$
$$f_1^* = 25 + 0 = 25$$

Similarly, input at stage $S_1 = 2$

$$r_1 = 29, \; f_0^* = 0, \; f_1^* = 29 + 0 = 29$$

and for input at stage $S_1 = 3$

$$r_1 = 31, \; f_0^* = 0, \; f_1^* = 31 + 0 = 31$$

These are shown in below:

Table route form place 1 to first stage:

Stage node (S_1)	Nodes at the Proceeding (n–1 = 0) Stage	Optimal Input Value of the Node at Stage 1 $S_1 = f_1^*$
	1	
	Input to the Stage Node	
2	25 + 0 = 25	25
3	29 + 0 = 29	29
4	31 + 0 = 31	31

At stage 2:

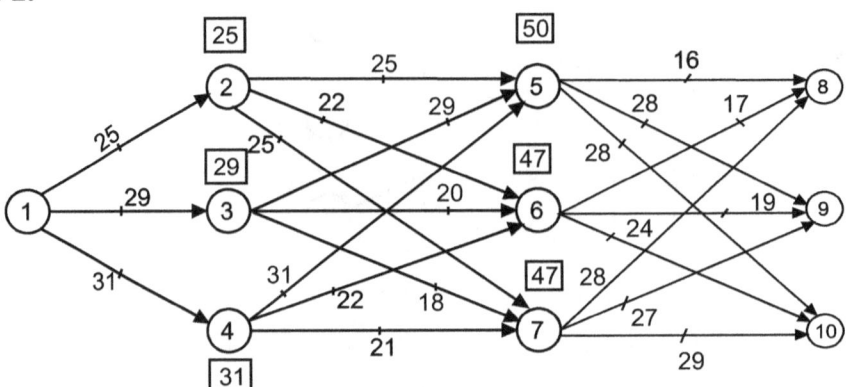

Fig. 4.6

At stage 2, the recursive equation = $f_2 = [r_2 + f_1^*]^*$, where r_2 is the return function at the stage 2 and f_1^* is the optimal distance travelled proceeding stage. For input $S_2 = 5$ and preceding rode 2, r_2 and f_1^* value would be.

$r_2 = 24$, $f_1^* = 25$ (= value taken from f_1^* column of stage 1) And if preceding node 3 is considered then $r_2 = 26$ and $f_1^* = 29$.

Similarly, if preceding node 4 considered, then $r_2 = 26$ and $f_1^* = 31$

Therefore, when stage $S_2 = 5$ the optimal value f_2^* form previous nodes

∴ f_2^* = Minimum [25 + 25 = 49, 26 + 29 = 55, 23 + 31 = 54] = 50

Table 4.1: Optimal distance form place 1 to second stage

Stage Node (S_2)	Nodes at the Proceeding (i.e. First Stage) Stage			Optimal Input Value of the Stage Node at Stage 2 f_2^*
	2	3	4	
	Input to the Stage Node (S_2)			
5	25 + 25 = 50,	29 + 29 = 58,	31 + 31 = 62	50
6	25 + 22 = 47,	29 + 20 = 49,	31 + 22 = 53	47
7	25 + 25 = 50,	29 + 18 = 47,	31 + 21 = 52	47

Similarly at stage 3

At stage 3, the recursive equation becomes

$$f_3 = [r_3 + f_2^*]^*$$

Input at the nodes at stage 3 care shown in table.

Table 4.2: Optimal Distance From Place 1 to Stage 3

Stage Node (S_3)	Node (S) at the Proceeding (i.e. Second) Stage			Optimal Input Value of the Stage Node at Stage 2 f_3^*
	5	6	7	
	Input to the stage node (S_3)			
5	50 + 16 = 66,	47 + 17 = 64,	47 + 28 = 75	64
6	50 + 28 = 78,	47 + 19 = 66,	47 + 27 = 74	66
7	50 + 28 = 78,	47 + 24 = 71,	47 + 29 = 76	71

Stage 4: At stage 4, the recursive equation becomes

$$f_4 = [r_4 + f_3^*]^*$$

Input at place / stage 4 are shown in table.

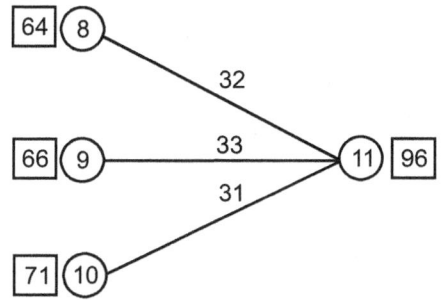

Fig. 4.7

Table 4.3: Optimal Distance Form place 1 to Stage

Stage Node (S_4)	Nodes at the Proceeding (i.e. Third Stage) Stage			Optimal Input Value of the Stage Node at Stage 2 f_2^*
	8	9	10	
	Input to the Stage Node (S_4)			
11	64 + 32 = 96,	66 + 33 = 99,	71 + 31 = 102	96

Stage 5: The pipeline can be laid along the route shown in Fig. 4.8.

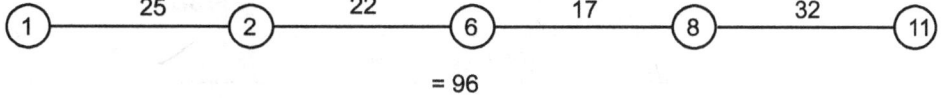

= 96

Fig. 4.8

and minimum cost = 96 units.

Example 4.3: *A pipe line is to be laid form point 1 to point 8. The unit cost of laying the pipe line considering various routes from place i to place J are given below. Use dynamic programming to find the route which will be cheapest.* **(Nov. 2012)**

From i to j	1–2	1–3	1–4	2–5	2–6	3–6	3–7	4–7	5–8	6–8	7–8
Unit Cost in Thousand of ₹	6	5	6	8	4	9	10	7	6	3	5

Solution: Stage 1

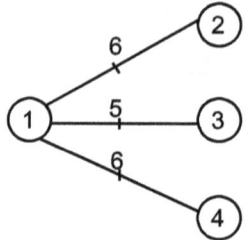

Fig. 4.9 (a)

At stage 1, the recursive equation is

$$f_1 = [r_1 + f_0^*]^*$$

∴ Since there is no stage period to first stage hence f_0^* is zero.

There for input at stage 1 node (i.e., $S_1 = 1$)

$r_1 = 6$ $\quad f_0^* = 0$ $\quad f_1^* = 6 + 0 = 06$

Similarly for input at stage $S_1 = 2$

$r_1 = 5$ $\quad f_0^* = 0$ $\quad f_1^* = 5 + 0 = 05$

And for input at stage $S_1 = 3$

$r_1 = 6$ $\quad f_0^* = 0$ $\quad f_1^* = 6 + 0 = 06$

These are shown in below.

Table 4.4: Route from Place 1 to First Stage

Stage Node (S_1)	Nodes at the Proceeding (n–1 = 0) Stage	Optimal Input Value of the Node at Stage $1 = f_1^*$
	1	
	Input to the Stage Node	
2	6 + 0 = 6	
3	5 + 0 = 5	5
4	6 + 0 = 6	

At stage 2:

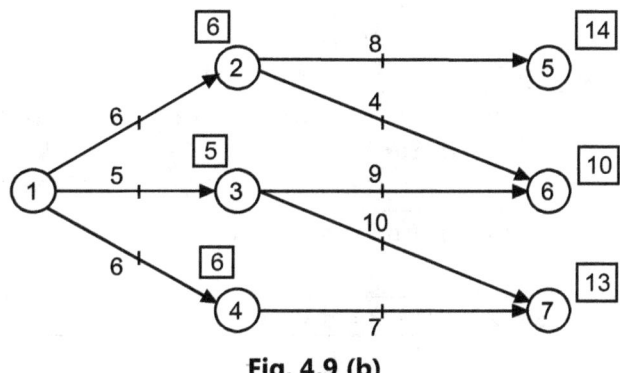

Fig. 4.9 (b)

At stage 2, the recursive equation

$$f_2 = [r_2 + f_1^*]^*$$

where r_2 is the return function at the stage 2 and f_1^* is the optimal distance travelled up to proceeding stage.

Table 4.5: Route from Place 1 to Second Stage

Stage Node (S_2)	Nodes at the Proceeding (1 – First Stage)			Optimal Input Value of the Node at Stage 2 = f_2^*
	2	3	4	
	Input to the Stage Node			
5	6 + 8 = 14	–	–	14
6	6 + 4 = 10	5 + 9 = 14	–	10
7	–	5 + 10 = 15	6 + 0 = 6	13

At stage 3:

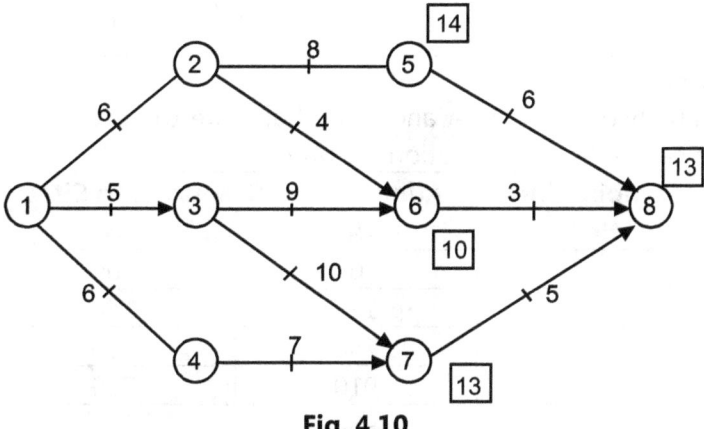

Fig. 4.10

At stage 3, the recursive equation

$$f_3 = [r_3 + f_2^*]^*$$

Table 4.6: Route from Place 1 to Third Stage

Stage node (S_3)	Node at the Proceeding Stage (i.e. Second) Stage			Optimal Input Value of the Stage Node at Stage 2 f_3^*
	5	6	7	
	Input to the Stage Node (S_3)			
8	14 + 6 = 20,	10 + 3 = 13,	13 + 5 = 18	13

Stage 4:

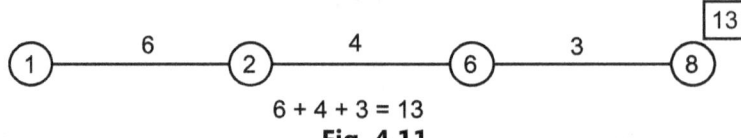

6 + 4 + 3 = 13
Fig. 4.11

The pipe line can be laid along the route shown and minimum cost = 6 + 4 + 3 = 13 thousand rupees.

Example 4.4: *It is proposed to develop hydropower project on reservoir across 3 possible river sites. The total finical resource available is 400 cores rupees. The return functions for each of the possible investment are given below. The available resources is to be allocated optimally to these developments using dynamic programming the maximum return and give the allocation to various sites.*

Resources Allocated	Return from Sites		
	A	B	C
0	0	0	0
100	120	140	300
200	750	550	500
300	910	700	700
400	980	800	750

Solution: Method – I:

We can select any two sites (say A and B) and allocate the available resources between two sites. There can be five combinations as under

Combination No.	Allocation of Resources to Sites	
	A	B
1	0	0
2	120	140
3	750	550
4	910	700
5	980	800

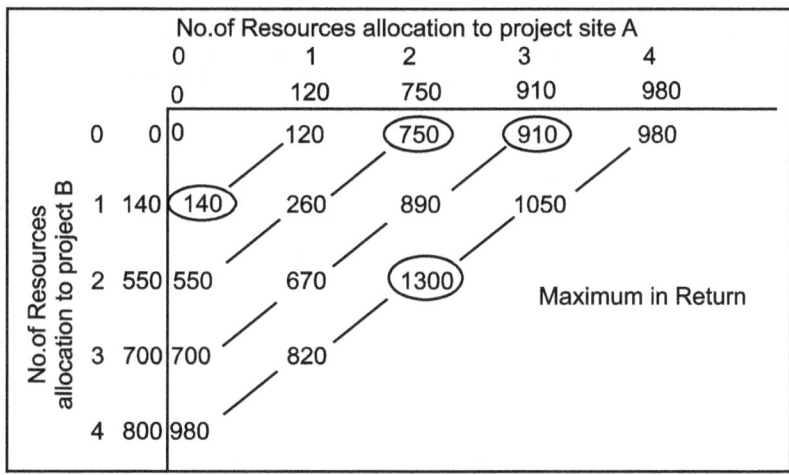

Fig. 4.12

For different allocation of resources the circled Figures 4.12 and 4.13 along the diagonal line indicate the maximum in Return. The circled Figures 4.12 and 4.13 in the above table have following significance

No of Resources Decided to be Allocated the Project (A and B) out of the no of Four	Circled Fig. 4.12 along the Diagonal of Resources Line		Best Possible Combination of Resources Allocation between the Project v	
	Diagonal of Resources	Circled Fig. 4.13	A	B
4	4 – 4	1300	2	2
3	3 – 3	910	3	0
2	2 – 2	750	2	0
1	1 – 1	140	0	1

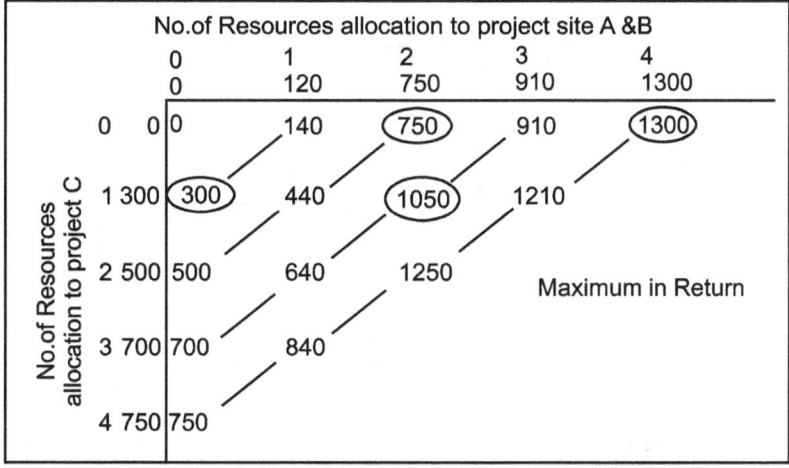

Fig. 4.13

Thus the optimal allocation among three site and maximum return is

Project	Resources Allocated	Maximum Return
A	200	750
B	200	550
C	0	0
	400	1300

Maximum Return = 1300 $\Rightarrow q_1 = 200$

$$R_1 = 750$$
$$q_2 + q_3 = q - q_1 = 400 - 200$$
$$= 200$$

$q_1 = 200$ $q_2 = 200$ $q_3 = 000$
$R_1 = 750$ $R_1 = 550$ $R_3 = 000$
     $R_{max} = 1300$

Method II:

Resources Allocated	Return from Sites		
	1	2	3
0	0	0	0
100	120	140	300
200	750	550	500
300	910	700	700
400	980	800	750

Solution:

Step 1:

Resources Allocated q	Return R_3	$R_3 = f_3^*(q_3)$	q_3^*
0	0	0	0
100	300	300	100
200	500	500	200
300	700	700	300
400	750	750	400

Step 2:

q	q₂	q₃	R₃	R₂	R₂ + R₃
0	0	0	0	0	0
100	0	100	300	000	300
	100	0	000	140	140
200	0	200	500	000	500
	100	100	300	140	440
	200	0	000	550	550
300	0	300	700	000	700
	100	200	500	140	640
	200	100	300	550	850
	300	0	000	700	700
400	0	400	750	000	750
	100	300	700	140	840
	200	200	500	550	1050
	300	100	300	700	1000
	400	0	000	800	800

q₂	f₂(q₂)					f₂*(q₂)	q₂*
	0	2	4	6	8		
0	0					00	0
100	300	140				300	0
200	500	440	550			550	200
300	700	640	850	700		850	200
400	750	840	1050	1000	800	1050	200

Step 3:

q	Q₁	q−q₁ = q₂ + q₃	R₂ +R₃	R₁	R₁ +R₂ + R₃
0	0	0	0	0	0
100	0	100	300	0	300
	100	0	0	120	120
200	0	200	550	0	550
	100	100	300	120	420
	200	0	0	750	750

...Conti.

300	0	300	850	0	850
	100	200	550	120	670
	200	100	300	750	105
	300	0	0	910	910
400	0	400	105	0	1050
	100	300	850	120	970
	200	200	550	750	1300
	200	200	300	970	1210
	0	0	00	980	980

Max. R = 1300 ⟹ q_1 = 200 units R_1 = 750

$q_2 + q_3 = q - q_1 = 400 - 200 = 200$

$$\begin{bmatrix} q_1 = 200 & q_2 = 200 & q_3 = 0 \\ R_1 = 750 & R_2 = 550 & R_3 = 0 \end{bmatrix}$$

Example 4.5: *A company has proposals to invest ₹ 600 million in three possible projects. The returns depend upon the level of investment as given below. Determine the, amount can be each project so that the total returns are maximum.*

Investment in ₹ Million	Returns from Projects		
	A	B	C
0	0	00	0
100	70	80	120
200	170	160	180
300	320	220	300
400	360	330	350
500	420	440	410
600	520	510	500

Write the recursive equation at each stage. In case the amount available in ₹ 400 million, what would be the investment policy?

Solution: $F_3(q_3) = R_3(q_{3c})$

Step 1:

q	q_3	$R_3 = f_3^*(q_3)$	q_{3c}
0	0	0	0
100	100	120	100
200	200	180	200
300	300	300	300
400	400	350	400
500	500	410	500
600	600	500	600

Where, q = Investment in Project

Step 2:

$$f_2^*(q_2) = \underset{q_2}{\text{Max.}} \left[R_2(q_2) + f_2^*(q_3) \right] = \underset{q_2}{\text{Max.}} R_2 + R_3$$

q	q_2	q_3^*	$R_2(q_2)$	q_3^*	$R_2 + R_3$
0	0	0	0	0	0
100	0	100	0	120	120
	100	0	80	0	80
200	0	200	0	180	180
	100	100	80	120	200
	200	0	160	0	160
300	0	300	0	300	300
	100	200	80	180	260
	200	100	160	120	280
	300	0	220	0	220
400	0	400	0	350	350
	100	300	80	300	380
	200	200	160	180	340
	300	100	220	120	340
	400	0	330	0	330
500	0	500	0	410	410
	100	400	80	350	430
	200	300	160	300	460
	300	200	220	180	40
	400	100	330	120	450
	500	0	440	0	440
600	0	600	0	510	510
	100	500	80	410	490
	200	400	160	350	510
	300	300	220	300	520
	400	200	330	180	510
	500	100	440	120	560
	600	0	510	0	510

q \ q_2	$F_2(q_2) = R_2 + R_3$							$f_2^*(q_2)$	q_2^*
	0	100	200	300	400	500	600		
0	0							0	0
100	120	80						120	0
200	180	200	160					200	100
300	300	260	280	220				300	00
400	350	380	340	340	330			380	100
500	410	480	460	400	450	440		460	200
600	510	490	510	520	510	560	510	560	500

q	q_1	$q_2 + q_3 =$ $q - q_1$	R_1	$R_2 + R_3$	$R_1 + R_2 + R_3$
0	0	0	0	0	0
100	0	100	0	120	120
	100	0	70	0	70
200	0	200	0	200	200
	100	100	70	120	190
	200	0	170	0	170
300	0	300	0	300	300
	100	200	70	200	270
	200	100	170	120	290
	300	0	320	0	320
400	0	400	0	380	380
	100	300	70	300	370
	200	200	170	200	370
	300	100	320	120	$\boxed{440}$
	400	0	360	0	360
500	0	500	0	460	460
	100	400	70	380	450
	200	300	170	300	470
	300	200	320	200	$\boxed{520}$
	400	100	360	120	480
	500	0	42	0	420
600	0	600	0	560	560
	100	500	70	460	530
	200	400	170	380	550
	300	300	320	300	$\boxed{620}$
	400	200	360	200	560
	500	100	420	120	540
	600	0	52	0	520

When,

q = ₹ 600 million

Max. return = 620 unit

q_1 = ₹ 300 million R_1 = 320

q_2 = 0 R_2 = 0

q_3 = ₹ 300 million R_3 = 300

It q = ₹ 400 million

q_1 = ₹ 300 million R_1 = 320
q_2 = ₹ 100 million R_2 = 120
q = ₹ 400 million   R = 440

Method 2:

Solution: We can select project A and B and Invest the available amount between two skis. There can be seven combinations as under.

Combination No.	Allocation of Investment	
	A	B
1	0	0
2	70	80
3	170	160
4	320	220
5	360	330
6	420	440
7	520	510

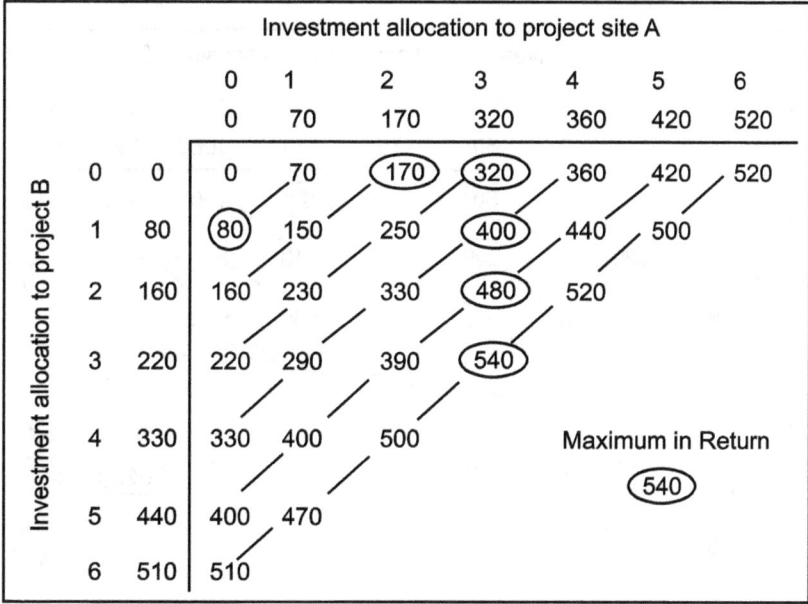

Fig. 4.14

For different investment of money the circle Figs. 4.14 and 4.15 alone the diagrams line indicate the maximum in return. The circle Figs. 4.14 and 4.15 in the above as following significant

Amount of Investment Decided to be Allocated the Project (A and B) out of 600 Million	Circle Fig. along the Diagonal of Invest Recovery		Best Possible Combination of Investment Allocated between the Projects	
	Diagonal of Investment	Circle Fig. 4.15	A	B
600	6–6	540	300	300
500	5–5	480	300	200
400	4–4	480	300	100
300	3–3	320	300	0
200	2–2	170	200	0
100	1–1	80	0	100

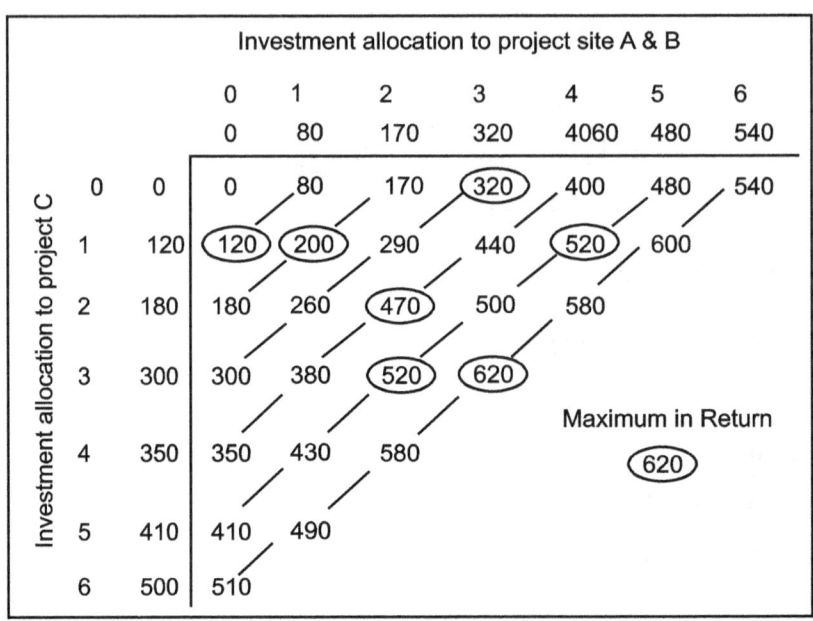

Fig. 4.15

Thus, the optimal allocation of investment many there site maximum return is:

Project	Investment Allocated	Maximum Return
A	300	320
B	000	000
C	300	300
		620

$$q = ₹\,600 \text{ million}$$

Then maximum return = 620

$q_1 = ₹\,300$ million $R_1 = 320$
$q_2 = ₹\,0$ million $R_2 = 0$
$q_3 = ₹\,300$ million $R_3 = 300$
$q = 600$ $R = 620$

If $q ₹ 400$ million

$q_1 = ₹\,300$ million $R_1 = 320$
$q_2 = 0$ $R_2 = 0$
$q_3 = ₹\,300$ million $R_3 = 120$
$q = ₹\,400$ $R = 440$

Example 4.6: *In an irrigation project, 6 million m^3 of water is to be allured to 3 irrigation districts. The net returns depending upon the quantity of water supplied are given below. Using dynamic programming;*

(a) Determine the allotment of water to each district so that the return maximum.

Quantity of Water in Million m^3	Returns from Districts		
	1	2	3
0	0	0	0
1	5	6	4
2	9	11	9
3	14	15	13
4	17	19	18
5	21	22	20
6	25	26	23

[Nov. 2012]

Solution: To begin with we can select any two districts (say 1 and 2) allocate/available supplied quantity of water between the two districts. There can be seven combinations as under.

Combinations No.	Allocation of water to	
	1	2
1	0	6
2	1	5
3	2	4
4	3	3
5	4	2
6	5	1
7	6	0

Estimate increase in net return for each seven combination can be found out adding the increase of the return for districts.

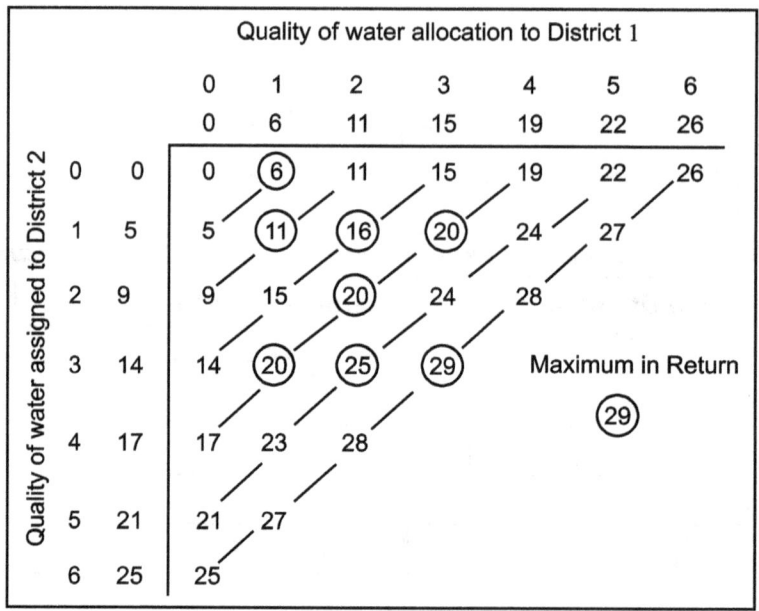

Fig. 4.16

For different allocation of water the circled Figs. 4.16 and 4.17 along the diagonal line indicate maximum return. The circled Figs. 4.16 and 4.17 in the above table have following signification.

Quantity of Water to be Allocated to District (1 and 2) Outer the no of Six	Circled Figs. 4.16 and 4.17 along the Diagonal of Water Supplied Line		Best Possible Combination of Water Supplied between the District	
	Diagonal of Water Supplied	Circled Fig. 4.17	1	2
6	6 – 6	29	3	3
5	5 – 5	25	2	3
4	4 – 4	20	2	2
			1	3
			3	1
3	3 – 3	16	2	1
2	2 – 2	11	1	1
1	1 – 1	06	1	0

Having found the maximum return for different values of combined supplied (allocation) of water thin district con be consisted. Another table similar to above. Can be prepared for combined (optimal) value of water supplied to district 1 and 2 and quantity of water supplied to district 3).

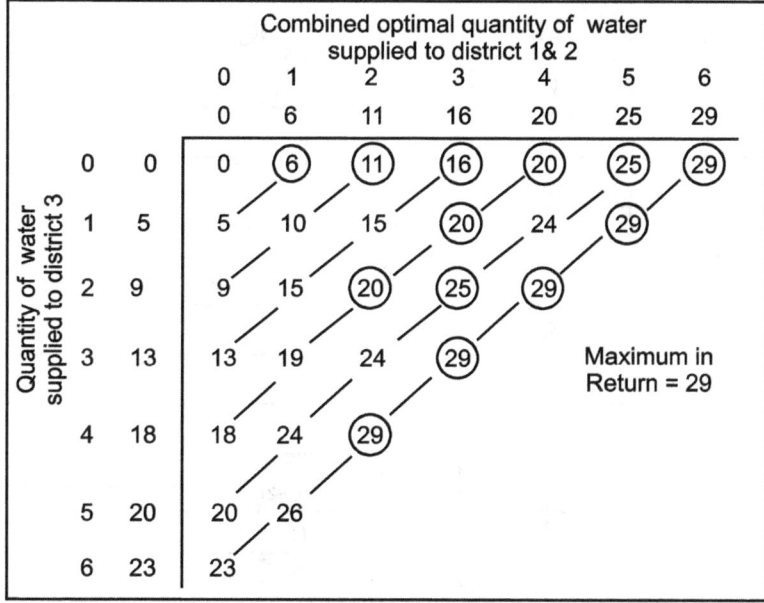

Fig. 4.17

From above table maximum return is 29 can be achieved by allocation/supplying water to district 3 and 5 m^3 water to district 1 and 2 OR 2 m^3 to district 3 and 4 m^3 to district 1 and 2, OR 3 m^3 to district 3 and 3 m^3 to district 1 and 2 OR 2 m^3 district 3 and 4 m^3 to district 1 and 2.

Recursive equation for 1st

$$f_3 = [r_3 + f_2^*]^*$$

Optimal output = [29 + 0] = 29

Thus the optimal allocation / supply of water to three district maximum return is.

District	Quantity of Water Supply in m^3	Maximum Return
1	3	15
2	3	14
3	0	0
	6	29

Max. Return = 29 ⇒ 0 m^3 $q_3 = 0$ $R_1 = 29$

$q_2 + q_3 = q - q_1 = 6 - 0 = 6$

$q_1 = 3$ $q_2 = 3$ $q_3 = 0$

$R_1 = 15$ $R_2 = 14$ $R_3 = 0$

$R_{max} = 29$

Method: 2

Step 1:

q	q_3	R_3	$R_3^*(q_3)$	q_3^*
0	0	0	0	0
1	1	4	4	1
2	2	9	9	2
3	3	13	13	3
4	4	18	18	4
5	5	20	20	5
6	6	23	23	6

Step 2:

q	q_3	q_3^*	$R_2(q_2)$	$R_3(q_3)$	R_2+R_3
0	0	0	0	0	0
1	0	0	0	4	4
	1	1	6	0	6
2	0	2	0	9	9
	1	1	6	4	10
	2	0	11	0	11

... contd.

3	0	3	0	13	13
	1	2	6	9	15
	2	1	11	4	15
	3	0	15	0	15
4	0	4	0	18	18
	1	3	6	13	19
	2	2	11	9	20
	3	1	15	4	19
	4	0	19	0	19
5	0	5	0	20	20
	1	4	6	18	24
	2	3	11	13	24
	3	2	15	9	24
	4	1	19	4	22
	5	0	22	0	22
6	0	6	0	23	23
	1	5	6	20	26
	2	4	11	18	29
	3	3	15	13	28
	4	2	19	9	28
	5	1	22	4	26
	6	0	26	0	26

$$f_2^*(q_2) = \underset{q_2}{\text{Max}} [R_2(q_2) + f_3(q - q_2)]$$

$$= \underset{q}{\text{Max}} (R_2 + R_3)$$

q_1 \ q_2	$f_2(q_2) = R_2 + R_3$							$f_2^*(q_2)$	q_2^*
	0	1	2	3	4	5	6		
0	0	–	–	–	–	–	–	0	0
1	4	6	–	–	–	–	–	6	1
2	9	10	11	–	–	–	–	11	2
3	13	15	15	15	–	–	–	15	2
4	18	10	20	19	19	–	–	20	2
5	20	22	24	24	23	22	–	24	2
6	23	26	29	28	28	26	26	29	4

q	q_1	$q - q_1 =$ $q_2 - q_3$	R_1	$R_1 + R_3$	$R_1 + R_2 + R_3$
0	0	0	0	0	0
1	0	1	0	6	6
	1	0	5	0	5
2	0	2	0	11	11
	1	1	5	6	11
	2	0	9	0	9
3	0	3	0	15	15
	1	2	5	11	16
	2	1	9	6	15
	3	0	14	0	14
4	0	4	0	20	20
	1	3	5	15	20
	2	2	9	11	20
	3	1	14	6	20
	4	0	17	0	17
5	0	5	0	24	24
	1	4	5	20	25
	2	3	9	15	24
	3	2	14	11	26
	4	1	17	6	23
	5	0	21	0	21
6	0	6	0	29	29
	1	5	5	24	29
	2	4	9	20	29
	3	3	14	15	29
	4	2	17	11	28
	5	1	21	6	27
	6	0	25	0	25

Stage 1: Max. return = 29 when q_1 = 0, 1, 2, 3

$Q_1 = 0 \Rightarrow q_2 + q_3 = q - q_1 = 6 - 0 = 6, 5, 4, 3$

Stage 2: $q_2 + q_3 = 29$

Max. return = 29

$q_3 = 2 \quad q_2 = 4 \quad q_1 = 0$

$R_1 = 15 \quad R_2 = 14 \quad R_3 = 0$

SYSTEMS APPROACH IN CIVIL ENGG. (B.E. Civil Sem. – I)   DYNAMIC PROGRAMMING

Example 4.7: *A member of certain political party is making plans for an upcoming presidential election. He has received the services of six volunteer workers for precinct work and he wishes to assign them to three precincts in such a way as to maximise their effectiveness. He feels that it would be inefficient to assign a worker to more than one precincts if they can accomplish more in other precincts.*

The following table gives the estimated increase in popularity of the party's candidate if it were allocated various number of workmen.

No. of Workers	Precinct		
	I	II	III
0	0	0	0
1	25	22	33
2	42	33	43
3	55	54	47
4	63	65	50
5	69	73	42
6	74	80	53

How many workers should be assigned to each of the tree precincts in order to maximise total estimated increase in the popularity of the party's candidate?

Solution: To begin with, we can select any two precincts (say I and 11) and allocate the available volunteers between the two precincts. There can be seven combinations as under:

Combination No.	Allocation of Volunteers to Precincts	
	I	II
1	0	6
2	1	5
3	2	4
4	3	3
5	4	2
6	5	1
7	6	0

Estimated increase in popularity for each of the seven combinations can be found out by adding the increases of the precincts. This is shown in Table.

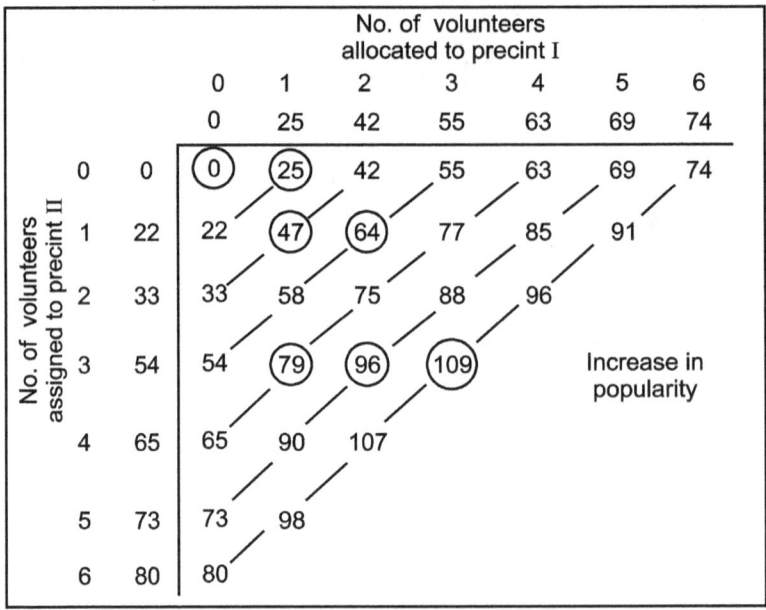

Fig. 4.18

For different allocation of volunteers the circled Figs. 4.18 and 4.19 along the diagonal line indicate the maximum percentage increase in popularity. The circled Figs. in the above table have following significance.

No. of Volunteers Decided to be Allocated to the Precincts (I and II) Out of the no. of Six	Circled Figs. 4.18 and 4.19 along the Diagonal of Volunteers Line		Best possible Combination of Volunteers Allocation between the Precincts	
	Diagonal of Volunteers	Circled Fig. 4.19	I	II
6	6 – 6	109	3	3
5	5 – 5	96	2	3
4	4 – 4	79	1	3
3	3 – 3	64	2	1
2	2 – 2	47	1	1
1	1 – 1	25	1	0

Maximum percentage popularity for different values of combined allocation of volunteers third prescient can be considered. Another table is proposed for combined (optimal) various of volunteers. Assigned to prescient I and II and number of volunteers to be assigned to prescient III.

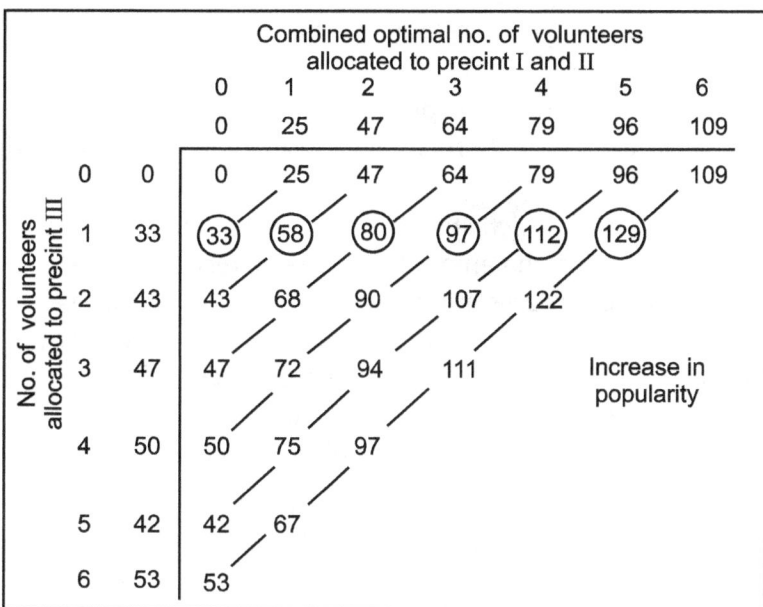

Fig. 4.19

From this tablet it's observed that highest % increase in popularity of 129% (circle Fig. 4.19 along 6–6 diagonal) and can be achieved by allocation 1 valuators to prescient III and 5 volunteers to prescient I and II.

Prescient	No. of volunteers	% increase in popularity
I	2	42
II	3	54
III	1	33
	6	129

Thus, the optimal allocation among three prescient and % increase in popularity is 129

4.11 APPLICATION OF DYNAMIC PROGRAMMING TO LPP

Consider a Linear Programming Problem (LPP) as follows:

$$\text{Max. } z = c_1 x_1 + c_2 x_2 + c_3 x_3 + \dots + c_n x_n$$

Subject to:
$$a_{11} x_1 + a_{12} x_2 + a_{13} x_3 + \dots + a_{1n} x_n \leq b_1$$
$$a_{21} x_1 + a_{22} x_2 + a_{23} x_3 + \dots + a_{2n} x_n \leq b_2$$
$$a_{31} x_1 + a_{32} x_2 + a_{33} x_3 + \dots + a_{3n} x_n \leq b_3$$

$$a_{m1} x_1 + a_{m2} x_2 + a_{m3} x_3 + \dots + a_{mn} x_n \leq b_m$$

Where $x_1 \geq 0, x_2 \geq 0, x_3 \geq 0$

The above problems consists of 'm' resources end 'n' decision variables. This problem can be expressed as dynamic problem as follows:

Each activity j (j = 1, 2, 3, ... n) is expressed as stage. Then the problem can be expressed as 'n' stage problem and alternatives (decision variables) are the level of activities x_j (≥ 0) as stage j.

If x_j is continuous, there each activities has infinite number of values of x_j (alternative) within the feasible location. Here, the amount of available resources are $b_1, b_2, b_3,$ ...... b_m. The state of problem at any stage is represented by the amount of allocated at that stage and left for the rest in stages. Thus, the state would be an 'm' dimensional vector $(b_1, b_2, b_3, ... b_m)$. Consider $f_n (b_1, b_2, b_3, ... b_n)$ as the optimal value of objective function defined above for stages $x_1, x_2, x_3, ... x_n$ for stages $b_1, b_2, b_3, ... b_m$.

By forward computational technique, the recursive equation can be written as:

$$f(b_1, b_2, b_3, ... b_m) = \max. [c_j x_j + f_{j-1} (b_1 - a_{1j}) x_j, b_2 - a_{2j} x_j ... b_m - a_{mj} x_j]$$
$$0 \leq x_j \leq b$$

The maximum value of b that x_j can assume is expressed as follows:

$$b = \min. \left[\frac{b_1}{a_{1j}} \frac{b_2}{a_{2j}} \frac{b_3}{a_{3j}} .... \frac{b_m}{a_{mj}} \right]$$

Example 4.8: *Apply dynamic programming to solve the following LPP.*

$$Max. \ z = 2x_1 + 5x_2$$
$$Subject \ to = 2x_1 + x_2 \leq 430$$
$$2x_2 \leq 460$$
$$x_1 \geq 0, \quad x_2 \geq 0$$

Solution: This is two variable problems.

Let x_1, and x_2 be decision variable and b, and b_2 be the two resources. Here, the state of equivalent dynamic programming problem are $b_1 = 430, b_2 = 460$.

Stage 1: $\qquad f_1(b_1, b_2) = \max. (2x_1)$
$$0 \leq x_1 \leq b$$

The maximum value of b that x_1 can assume is expressed as follows:

$$b = \min. \left[\frac{430}{2} \frac{460}{0} \right]$$
$$= \min. [215, \infty]$$
$$b = 215$$

$\therefore \qquad f_1(430,460) = \max. [2x_1] = 2 \min. \left[\frac{430-x_1}{z}, \infty \right]$
$$0 \leq x_1 \leq 215$$

and $\qquad x_1^0 = 215$

Stage 2: The recursive equation is expressed as [By forward computational technique]

$$f_2(b_1, b_2) = \max.(5x_1 + 2x_2)$$

$$0 \leq x_2 \leq b$$

OR

$$f_2(430, 460) = \max.\left[5x_2 + 2\min.\left[\frac{430-x_1}{2}, \infty\right]\right]$$

$$0 \leq x_2 \leq b$$

But the maximum value of b that x_2 can assume is expressed as follows:

$$b = \min.\left[\frac{430}{1}, \frac{460}{2}\right]$$

$$= \min. [430, 230]$$

$$b = 230$$

thus,
$$f_2(430,460) = \max.\left[5x_2 + 2\min.\left[\frac{430-x_2}{2}, \infty\right]\right]$$

$$0 \leq x_2 \leq 230$$

Now,
$$\min.\left[\frac{430-x_2}{2}, \infty\right] = \frac{430-x_2}{2}$$

$$= 100 \quad 0 \leq x_2 \leq 230$$

Thus
$$5x_2 + 2\min.\left[\frac{430-x_2}{2}, \infty\right] = 5x_2 + 200 \quad 0 \leq x_2 \leq 230$$

Hence,
$$f_2(430, 460) = 5x_2 + 200$$

$$= 5 \times 230 + 200$$

$$= 1350$$

$$x_2^* = 230$$

Thus,
$$z_{max.} = 1350$$

$$x_2^* = \frac{430 - 230}{2}$$

$$x_1^* = 100$$

THEORETICAL QUESTIONS

1. Explain Forward Recursion and Backward Recursion.
2. What is Bellman's principle of optimality?
3. State Bellman's principle of optimality. What is a recursive equation?
4. What are the applications of D.P. in Civil Engineering?
5. Explains the relationship between stages and stags in dynamic programming.
6. Define the following terms in connection with dynamic programming.
   (i) Stage
   (ii) State variable
   (iii) Decision variable
   (iv) Immediate returns
   (v) Optimal return
   (vi) Recursive relations
7. **Example:** Construction equipment is to be transported from place 1 to place 11. The equipment call be transported along different routes. The travel distances along different routes from place i to j are given below:

Place i–j	Distance in Km	Place i – j	Distance in Km
1 – 2	30	5 – 8	21
1 – 3	34	5 – 9	33
1 – 4	36	5 – 10	33
2 – 5	29	6 – 8	22
2 – 6	27	6 – 9	24
2 – 7	30	6 – 10	29
3 – 5	31	7 – 8	33
3 – 6	25	7 – 9	32
3 – 7	23	7 – 10	34
4 – 5	28	8 – 11	37
4 – 6	27	9 – 11	28
4 – 7	26	10 – 11	36

   (a) Use dynamic programming to determine the shortest route between place I and place 11.
   (b) Write the recursive equation for each stage.

8. **Example:** Equipment is to be transported from destination X to destination Y. Various routes are available for this transport. The tray al distance along various routes, between nodes is given below, in Km. Use dynamic programming to determine the shortest route between X and Y.

Form	To	Distance
X	A	9
X	B	7
X	C	13
X	D	14
A	E	11
A	F	5
B	E	7
B	G	11
C	F	12
C	G	1
C	F	5
C	G	8
E	I	2
E	J	14
F	H	7
F	I	3
F	K	14
G	I	14
G	J	8
H	Y	15
I	Y	5
J	Y	9
K	Y	1

9. **Example:** A pipeline is to laid from point 1 to point 8. The unit cost of laying the pipeline considering various route from place i to place j are given below. Use Dynamic programming to find the route which will be cheapest.

From i to j	1–2	1–3	1–4	2–5	2–6	3–6	3–7	4–7	5–8	6–8	7–8
Unit Cost in Thousand of ₹	7	5	6	8	4	9	6	7	6	3	5

10. **Example:** An earn moving equipment is to be transported from place 1 to place 10. The equipment can be transported along the different routes. The cost C_{ij} of transporting it along different possible route from place i to place j are given below.

C_{1-2}	4	C_{4-6}	5
C_{1-3}	6	C_{4-7}	7
C_{1-4}	6	C_{5-8}	6
C_{2-5}	6	C_{5-9}	8
C_{2-6}	8	C_{6-8}	4
C_{2-7}	9	C_{6-9}	9
C_{3-5}	5	C_{7-8}	3
C_{3-6}	4	C_{7-9}	7
C_{3-7}	6	C_{8-10}	9
C_{4-5}	5	C_{9-10}	6

Use dynamic programming to determine the minimum cost of transportation and the corresponding route. Write recursive equation at each stage.

11. **Example:** A promoter builder has 3 money units which he wishes to utilize in developing 3 projects. Depending upon the amount invested, the resulting profits expected are given below. Determine the optimal allocation to each of the projects which will maximize the total amount expected returns.

Investment	Projects		
	1	2	3
0	0	0	0
1	4	2	6
2	8	10	10
3	12	12	12

12. **Example:** Six units of water are to be distributed among three regions designated as A, B and C. The expected returns from each region depending upon the number of units of power supplied are given below. Use Dynamic programming to determine an optimal power allocation as to maximize the return.

Power Supplied (in units)	Return from Regions (in Money Units)		
	A	B	C
0	0	0	0
1	10	30	24
2	20	40	48
3	60	44	50
4	62	46	52
5	64	48	54
6	66	50	56

13. **Example:** A promoter builder intends 6 money units in three projects. The returns depending upon the level of investment are given in the following table.

Investment	Return from Regions		
	A	B	C
0	0	0	0
1	25	20	33
2	42	38	43
3	55	54	47
4	63	65	50
5	69	73	52
6	74	80	53

14. **Example:** Solve the following problem using dynamic programming

$$\text{Max } Z = 36x_1 + 9x_1^2 - 6x_1^3 + 36x_2 - 3x_2^3$$

Subject to $\quad x_1 + x_2 = 3$

$\quad\quad\quad\quad\quad X_{ij}\ x_2 \geq 0$

■■■

Unit 5
LINEAR PROGRAMMING (A)

5.1 FORMULATION OF LINEAR PROGRAMMING MODEL

The usefulness of LP as a tool for optimal decision making on resource allocation based on its applicability to many decision problems. The effective use and application require as a first step, the mathematical formulation of LP model.

Step of LP Model Formulation:
1. Define decision variables which optimise the objective function.
2. Formulate the constraints imposed by the resource availability and express them as linear equality or inequality in terms of decision variables defined in step1. The constraints define range within which values of decision variables can lie.
3. Formulate the objective function: Determine whether the objective function is to be maximized or minimized. Then express it as a linear function of decision variables multiplied by their profit or cost contributions.

SOLVED EXAMPLES

Example 5.1: *A firm uses three different machines A, B and C to produce two products following table gives the machine time for each product. The maximum time available on different machine of the profit on each product is also given,*

Type of Machine	Time Required for each Product		Maximum Time Available
	I	II	
A	3	4	1200
B	4	5	1500
C	2	1	600
Profit per unit	20,000	50,000	

Formulate the mathematical model to maximize the profit.

Solution:
1. Let x_1, x_2 be the products I and II manufactured respectively. Then, the key decision is to determine the number of products to be manufactured so as to maximize the profit.

2. Objective function is to maximize profit
   Max. $Z = 20{,}000\, x_1 + 50{,}000\, x_2$
3. Constraints are on the time available on each machine A, B and C.

$$3x_1 + 4x_2 \leq 1200$$
$$4x_1 + 5x_2 \leq 1500$$
$$2x_1 + x_2 \leq 600$$

Where, $x_1, x_2 \geq 0$

Example 5.2: *A furniture manufacturer makes two products chair and tables. These products are processed using two machines A and B. A chair requires 2 hrs on machine A and 6 hrs on machine B. A table require 5 hrs on machine A and no time on machine B. There are 16 hrs per day available on machine A and 30 hrs on machine B. The profit gained by selling each chair is Rs. 200 and from each table is Rs. 100. Formulate this problem as L.P. stating variables, objective function and constraints.*

Solution:
1. Let x be no. of chairs to be manufactured and y be no. of tables to be manufactured.
2. Objective function:
   Maximum $Z = 200\, x + 100\, y$
3. Constraints,

$$2x + 5y \leq 16$$
$$6x + 0y \leq 30$$
$$x, y \geq 0$$

5.2 GRAPHICAL METHOD

Graphical method to solve *Linear Programming Problem (LPP)* helps to visualize the procedure explicitly. It also helps to understand the different terminologies associated with the solution of LPP. In this class, these aspects will be discussed with the help of an example. However, this visualization is possible for a maximum of two decision variables. Thus, a LPP with two decision variables is opted for discussion. However, the basic principle remains the same for more than two decision variables also, even though the visualization beyond two-dimensional case is not easily possible.

Let us consider the same LPP (general form) discussed in previous class, stated here once again for convenience.

Maximize $\quad Z = 6x + 5y$
Subject to $\quad 2x - 3y \leq 5 \qquad$ (C – 1)
$\qquad\qquad\; x + 3y \leq 11 \qquad$ (C – 2)
$\qquad\qquad\; 4x + y \leq 15 \qquad$ (C – 3)
$\qquad\qquad\; x, y \geq 0 \qquad\qquad$ (C– 4) and (C – 5)

First step to solve above LPP by graphical method is to plot the inequality constraints one-by-one on a graph paper. Fig. 5.1 (a) shows one such plotted constraint.

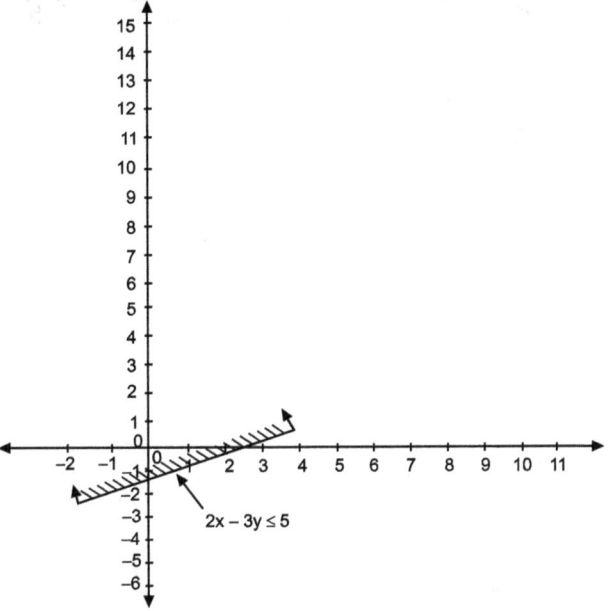

Fig. 5.1 (a)

Fig. 5.1 (b) shows all the constraints including the non negativity of the decision variables (i.e., $x \geq 0$ and $y \geq 0$).

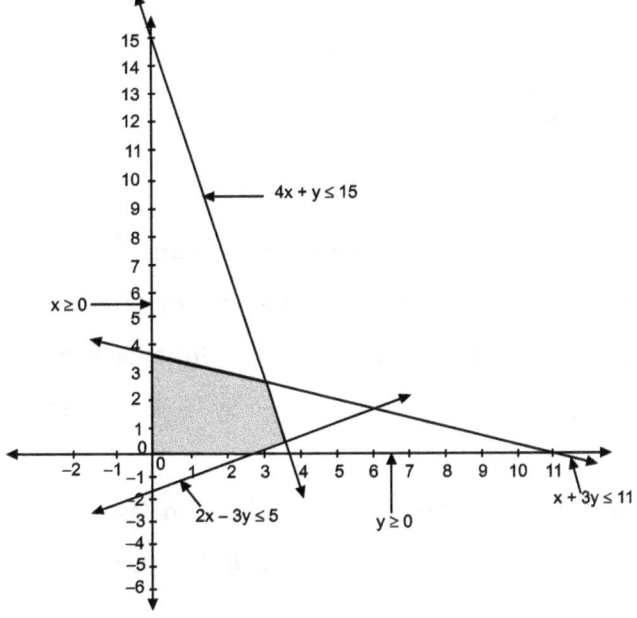

Fig. 5.1 (b)

Common region of all these constraints is known as feasible region [Fig. 5.1 (c)]. Feasible region implies that each and every point in this region satisfies all the constraints involved in the LPP.

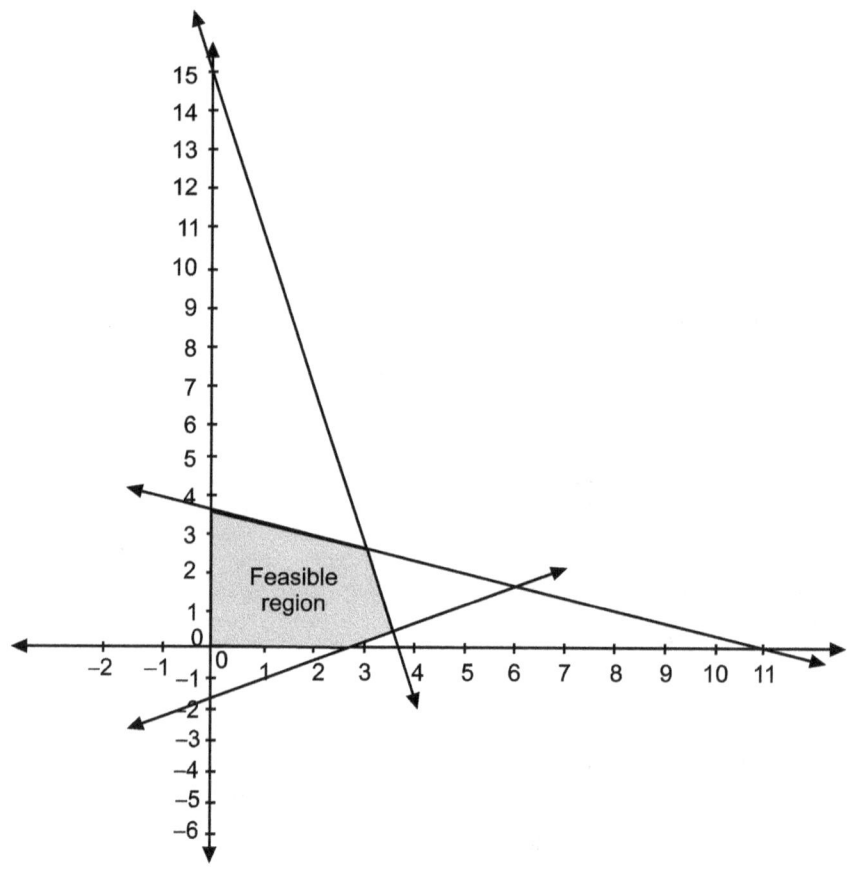

Fig. 5.1 (c) Feasible region

Once the feasible region is identified, objective function (Z = 6x + 5y) is to be plotted on it. As the (optimum) value of Z is not known objective function is plotted by considering any constant, k [Fig. 5.1 (d)]. The Straight line, 6x + 5y = k (constant), is known as *Z line* [Fig. 5.1 (d)].

This line can be shifted in its perpendicular direction (as shown in the Fig. 5.1 (d)) by changing the value of k. Note that, position of *Z line* shown in Fig. 5.1 (d), showing the intercept, c, on the

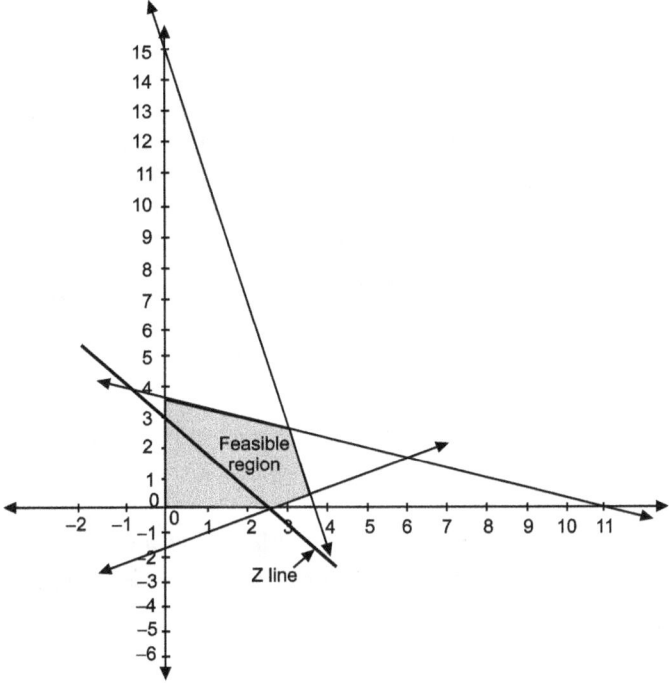

Fig. 5.1 (d) Plot of Z line and Feasible region

And

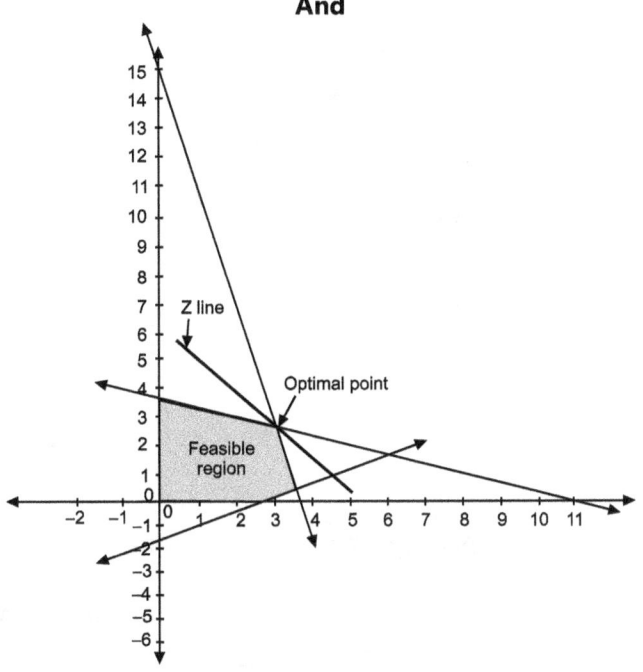

Fig. 5.1 (e) Location of optimal point

Now it can be visually noticed that value of the objective function will be maximum when it passes through the intersection of $x + 3y = 11$ and $4x + y = 15$ (straight lines associated with the second and third inequality constraints). This is known as optimal point [Fig. 5.1 (e)]. Thus the optimal point of the present problem is $x^* - 3.091$ and y^* 2.636 and the optimal solution is = $6x^* + 5y^* = 31.727$.

Visual Representation of Different Cases of Solution of LPP:

A linear programming problem may have (i) a unique, finite solution, (ii) an unbounded solution (iii) multiple (or infinite) number of optimal solutions, (iv) infeasible solution and (v) a unique feasible point. In the context of graphical method it is easy to visually demonstrate the different situations which may result in different types of solutions.

Unique, Finite Solution

The example demonstrated above is an example of LPP having a unique, finite solution. In such cases, optimum value occurs at an extreme point or vertex of the feasible region.

Unbounded Solution

If the feasible region is not bounded, it is possible that the value of the objective function goes on increasing without leaving the feasible region. This is known as unbounded solution (Fig. 5.2).

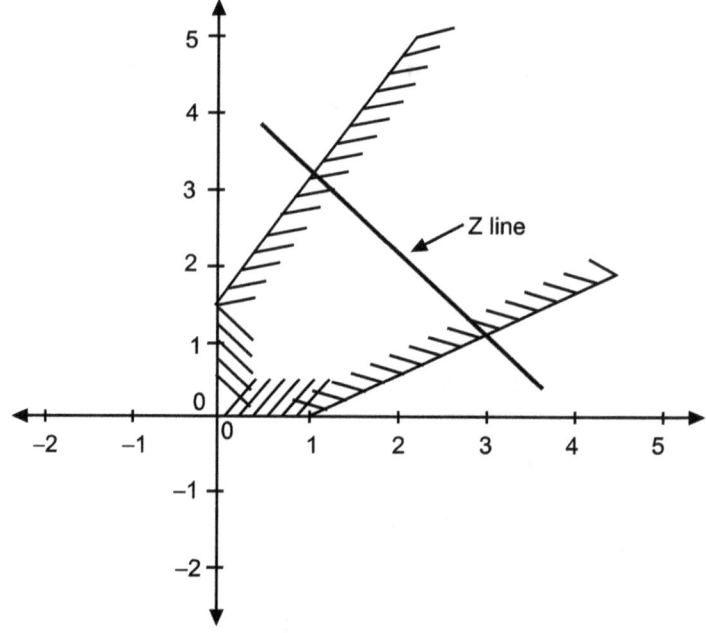

Fig. 5.2: Unbounded Solution

Multiple (Infinite) Solutions

If the Z line is parallel to any side of the feasible region all the points lying on that side constitute optimal solutions as shown in Fig. 5.3.

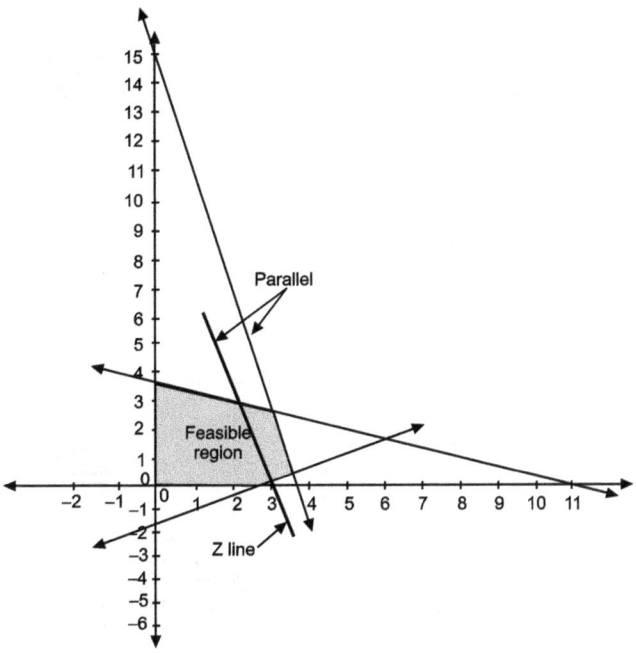

Fig. 5.3: Multiple in fine solution

Infeasible Solution

Sometimes, the set of constraints does not form a feasible region at all due to inconsistency in the constraints. In such situation the LPP is said to have infeasible solution. Fig. 5.4 illustrate such a situation.

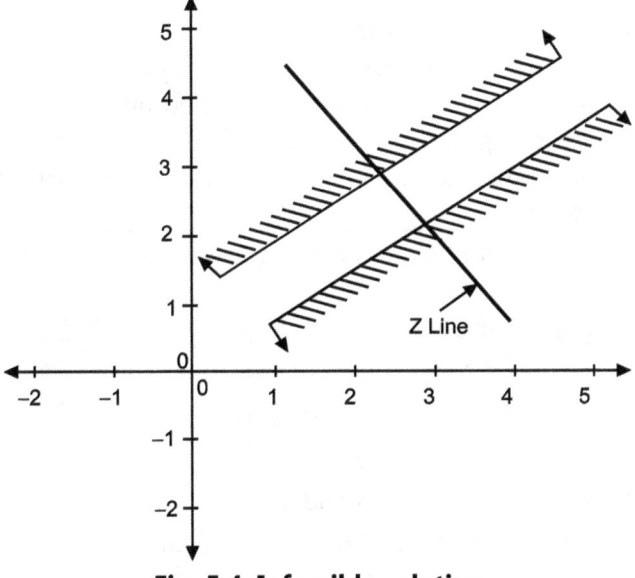

Fig. 5.4: Infeasible solution

Unique Feasible Point:

This situation arises when feasible region consist of a single point. This situation may occur only when number of constraints is at least equal to the number of decision variables. An example is shown in Fig. 5.5. In this case, there is no need for optimization as there is only one solution.

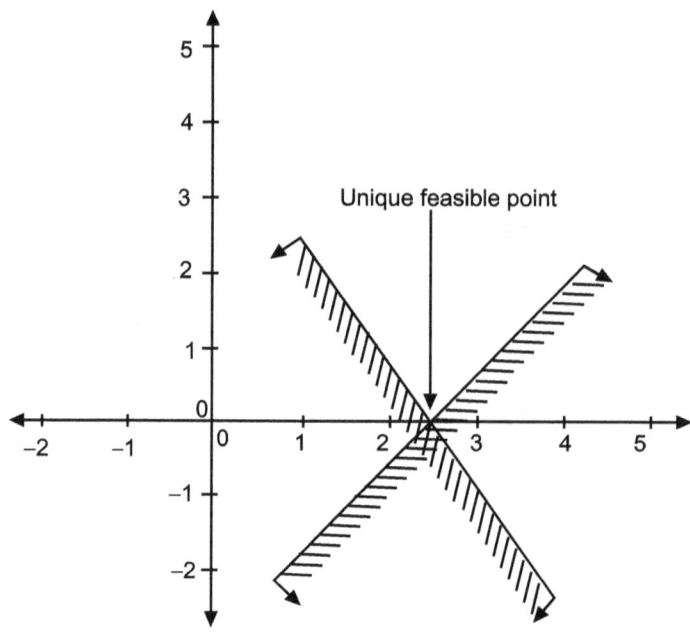

Fig. 5.5

Graphical Solution Methods of LP Problem:

1. Extreme Point Solution Method: In this method, the co-ordinates of all corner (or extreme) points of the feasible region are determined and then values of the objective function these points are computed and compared because the mathematical theory of LP states that an optimal solution to any LP problem always lie at one of the corners points of the feasible solution space.

Example 5.3: *Use graphical method to solve the following LP problem.*

Maximize $\quad Z = 15x_1 + 10x_2$

Subject to the constraints $\quad 4x_1 + 6x_2 \leq 360$

$\qquad\qquad\qquad\qquad\qquad 3x_1 + 0x_2 \leq 180$

$\qquad\qquad\qquad\qquad\qquad 0x_1 + 5x_2 \leq 200$

And $\qquad\qquad\qquad\qquad x_1, x_2 \geq 0$

Solution: Consider x_1 as horizontal axis and x_2 as the vertical axis.

Now, consider the first constraint $4x_1 + 6x_2 \leq 360$, take it as equality equation i.e.

$$4x_1 + 6x_2 = 360$$

Now take $x_1 = 0$

∴ $x_2 = 60$. Similarly take $x_2 = 0$

∴ $x_1 = 90$

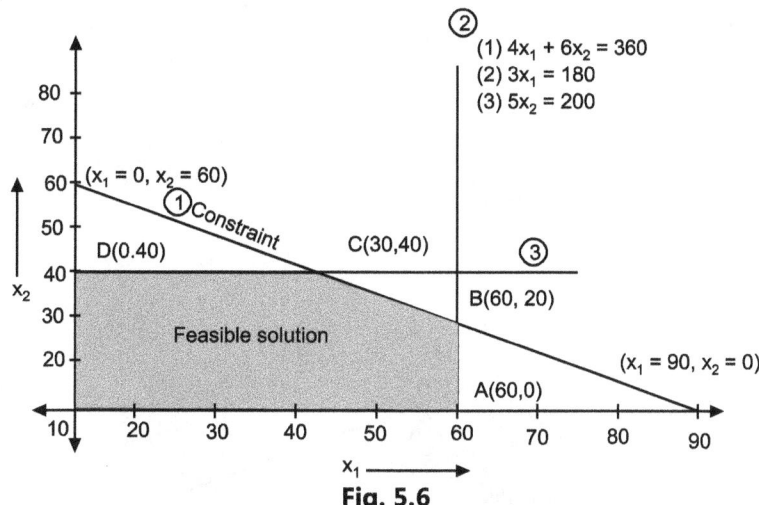

Fig. 5.6

Now, $3x_1 \leq 180$ and $5x_2 \leq 200$

∴ $x_1 = 60$ for 2nd constraint.

∴ $x_2 = 40$ for 3rd constraint.

The co-ordinate of extreme points of the feasible region are 0(0,0), A(60, 0), B(60, 20), C(30,40), D(0, 40).

Now evaluate objective function values at each extreme co-ordinates / points.

Extreme Point	Co-ordinates	Objective Function $Z = 15x_1 + 10x_2$
0	0, 0	Z = 0
A	60, 0	Z = 900
B	60, 20	Z = 1100
C	30, 40	Z = 850
D	0, 40	Z = 400

Here we see that Z is maximum for B point where the co-ordinates are (60, 20) and Maximum Z = 1100

Example 5.4: *Use graphical method to solve the following LP problem.*

Maximize $Z = 10x_1 + 15x_2$

Subject to
$2x_1 + x_2 \leq 25$
$2x_1 + 4x_2 \leq 56$
$-x_1 + x_2 \leq 5$

And $x_1 \geq 0, x_2 \geq 0$

Solution:
1. To draw the graph.
   (a) $2x_1 + x_2 = 26$
   (b) $2x_1 + 4x_2 = 56$
   (c) $-x_1 + x_2 = 5$

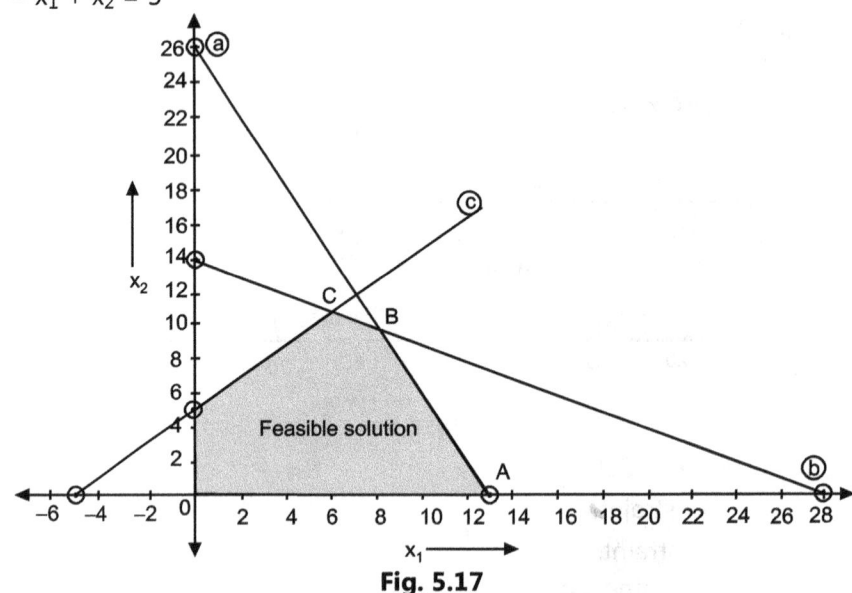

Fig. 5.17

(a) $2x_1 + x_2 = 26$
   Let $x_1 = 0 \therefore x_2 = 26$
   Let $x_2 = 0 \therefore x_1 = 13$
(b) $2x_1 + 4x_2 = 56$
   Let $x_1 = 0 \therefore x_2 = 14$
   Let $x_2 = 0 \therefore x_1 = 28$
(c) $-x_1 + x_2 = 5$
   Let $x_1 = 0 \therefore x_2 = 5$
   Let $x_2 = 0 \therefore x_1 = -5$

2. Extreme points and their co-ordinates.

Point	Co-ordinate	$Z = 10x_1 + 15x_2$
O	(0,0)	Z = 0
A	(13, 0)	Z = 130
B	(8, 10)	Z = 230
C	(6, 11)	Z = 225
D	(0, 5)	Z = 75

3. Maximum Z = 230 at co-ordinate B (8, 10) on the extreme point. B, where $x_1 = 8$ and $x_2 = 10$.

5.3 SIMPLEX METHOD

When the real life problems are formulated as an LP model which has two variables and are too large for the graphical method. Then we need an efficient method for determing an optimal solution for such problems. So simplex method can be used to find out the optimal solution. Simplex method, which is also known as simplex technique or simplex algorithm. It is a universal method which can be used to solve the linear model for which the solutions exist.

The simplex method examines the extreme points in a systematic manner, repeating the same set of steps of the algorithm until an optimal solution is reached. It is also known as iterative method.

As the number of extreme points of feasible solution space are finite, this method give an improved value of objective function as we move from one iteration to another and we get an optimal solution in finite no. of steps. This method also indicates when an unbounded solution is reached.

Standard form of an LP Model:

To solve an LP problem by simplex method, it is first converted into standard form. Characteristics of standard form of the LP problem are;
1. The objective function should be of maximization type.
2. All the constraints should be expressed as an equation by adding Slack, surplus and artificial variable.
3. RHS of the constraints should be non-negative.

The General LP Problem:

Optimize (Maximum) $Z = C_1x_1 + C_2x_2 + \ldots\ldots\ldots C_n X_n$

Subjected to,

$\quad a_{11}x_1 + a_{12}x_2 + \ldots\ldots\ldots + a_{1n}x_n \leq b_1$

$\quad a_{21}x_1 + a_{22}x_2 + \ldots\ldots\ldots + a_{2n}x_n \leq b_2$

$\quad a_{m1}x_1 + a_{m2}x_2 + \ldots\ldots\ldots + a_{mn}x_n \leq b_n$

$\quad x_1, x_2 \ldots\ldots\ldots\ldots x_n \geq 0$

Standard form of LP:

Optimize $Z = C_1x_2 + C_2x_2 + C_nx_n + OS_1 + OS_2 + \ldots\ldots\ldots + OS_m$

Subject to,

$\quad a_{11}x_1 + a_{12}x_2 + \ldots\ldots\ldots + a_{1n}x_n + S_1 = b_1$

$\quad a_{21}x_1 + a_{22}x_2 + \ldots\ldots\ldots + a_{2n}x_n + S_2 = b_2$

$\quad a_{m1}x_1 + a_{m2}x_2 + \ldots\ldots\ldots + a_{mn}x_n + S_m = b_m$

and $x_1, x_2 \ldots\ldots\ldots\ldots x_n, S_1, S_2 \ldots\ldots\ldots S_m \geq 0$

Important Definitions in Simplex Method:

1. **Slack Variable:** This variable is added in the constraint equation to make it equality from ≤ unequality equation.
2. **Surplus Variable:** This variable is subtracted from the constraint equation to convert the inequality ≥ to equality.
3. **Basic Variable:** The variable in LP is said to be basic when it appears with a unit coefficient in that equation and zero in all other equations.

Example 5.5: Maximize $Z = 5x_1 + 3x_2$
Subject to
$$x_1 + x_2 \leq 2$$
$$5x_1 + 2x_2 \leq 10$$
$$3x_1 + 8x_2 \leq 12$$
and $x_1, x_2 \geq 0$

Solution: Step 1: Introducing slack variables S_1, S_2, and S_3 to convert inequality constraints to equality. Then the LP problem becomes.

Maximize $Z = 5x_1 + 3x_2 + 0S_1 + 0S_2 + 0S_3$
Subject to constraints
$$x_1 + x_2 + S_1 = 2$$
$$5x_1 + 2x_2 + S_2 = 10$$
$$3x_1 + 8x_2 + S_3 = 12$$
And $x_1, x_2, S_1, S_2, S_3 \geq 0$

Step 2: Since all RHS values are > 0 so we choose initial feasible solution as $x_1 = x_2 = 0$, $S_1 = 2$, $S_2 = 10$, $S_3 = 12$ and maximum $Z = 0$.

Step 3: To see whether the current solution is optimal or not.

Table 5.1: Initial Solution

Co-eff	Basic Variable	$C_j \rightarrow$ $b_i \downarrow$	5 x_1	3 x_2	0 S_1	0 S_2	0 S_3	Exchange Ration b_i/a_{ij}
0	S_1	2	1	1	1	0	0	2
0	S_2	10	5	2	0	1	0	2
0	S_3	12	3	8	0	0	1	4
		Z_j	0*	0	0	0	0	
		$C_j - Z_j$	5	3	0	0	0	
			↑					

*$Z_j = (1 \times 0) + (5 \times 0) + (3 \times 0) = 0$

Here x_1 is chosen to enter into the basic as $C_j - Z_j = 5$ is the largest positive number in the x_1 column. The x_1 – column is the key column.

Here $a_{ij} = x_1$ column.

$b_i/a_{ij} = \dfrac{2}{1} = 2, \dfrac{10}{5} = 2, \dfrac{12}{3} = 4$

Now, selecting $\dfrac{b_i}{a_{ij}} = 2$ as minimum ratio and the corresponding row is known as key row. Now x_1 is entering as the basic variable and slack variable S_1 is removed (i.e.) S_1 is replaced by x_1. The element at the intersection of the key column and row is made unity and remaining elements in the column are made zero.

Step 4: Iteration 1

Table 5.2: Improved Solution

Coefficient	Basic Variable	C_j	5	3	0	0	0
		b_i	x_1	x_2	S_1	S_2	S_3
5	x_1	2	1	1	1	0	0
0	S_2	0	0	–3	–5	1	0
0	S_3	6	0	5	–3	0	1
		Z_j	5	5	5	0	0
		$C_j - Z_j$	0	–2	–5	0	0

R_2 new = R_2 old – $5R_1$ new

$0 = 5 - 5 \times 1$
$-3 = 2 - 5 \times 1$
$-5 = 0 - 5 \times 1$
$1 = 1 - 5 \times 0$
$0 = 10 - 5 \times 2$

R_3 new = R_3 old – $3R_1$ new

$0 = 3 - 3 \times 1$
$5 = 8 - 3 \times 1$
$-3 = 0 - 3 \times 1$
$1 = 0 - 3 \times 0$
$0 = 1 - 3 \times 0$
$6 = 12 - 3 \times 2$

In the above table all $C_j - Z_j \leq 0$. There for the optimal solution is reached,

Where
$$x_1 = 2$$
$$x_2 = 0$$
$$S_1 = 0$$
$$S_2 = 0$$
$$S_3 = 6$$

Put these values in,

Maximize $Z = 5x_1 + 3x_2 + 0S_1 + 0S_2 + 0S_3$

$\therefore \quad Z = 10$

Example 5.6: Maximize $Z = 2x_1 + 3x_2$

Subject to constraints $\quad x_1 \leq 6$

$$x_1 + 2x_2 \leq 10$$
$$x_1 + x_2 \geq 2$$

and $\quad x_1, x_2 \geq 0$

Solution:

Step 1: Introduction slack and surplus variable S_1, S_2 and S_3 to convert inequality to equality. Then the LP problem becomes:

Maximize $\quad Z = 2x_1 + 3x_2 + 0S_1 + 0S_2 + 0S_3$

Subject to constraints $\quad x_1 + S_1 = 6$

$$x_1 + 2x_2 + S_2 = 10$$
$$x_1 + x_2 - S_3 = 2$$

and $\quad x_1, x_2, S_1, S_2, S_3 \geq 0$

Step 2: Since all RHS values are > 0 so we choose initial feasible solution as $x_1 = x_2 = 0$, $S_1 = 6$, $S_2 = 10$, $S_3 = -2$ and maximum $Z = 0$.

Step 3: To see whether the current solution is optimal or not,

Table 5.3: Initial Solution

Coeffi-cient	Basic Variable	C_j b_i	2 x_1	3 x_2	0 S_1	0 S_2	0 S_3	Exchange Ratio b_i/a_{ij}
0	S_1	6	1	0	1	0	0	0
0	S_2	10	1	2	0	1	0	5 ←
0	S_3	−2	1	1	0	0	1	−2
		Z_j	0*	0	0	0	0	
		$C_j - Z_j$	2	3	0	0	0	
				↑				

*$Z_j = (1 \times 0) + (1 \times 0) + (1 \times 0)$

Here x_2 is chosen to enter the basic variable as $C_j - Z_j = 3$, which is largest positive number in the x_2 column. The x_2 column is the key column and here $a_{ij} = x_2$ column.

$$\frac{b_i}{a_{ij}} = \frac{6}{0} = 0, \frac{10}{2} = 5, \frac{-2}{1} = -2$$

Now selecting $\frac{b_i}{a_{ij}} = 5$ as minimum ratio and the corresponding row is known as key row.

Now x_2 is entering as the basic variable and slack variable S_2 is removed. i.e. S_2 is replaced by x_2. The element at the intersection of the key column and row is made unity and remaining elements in the column are made zero.

Step 4: Iteration 1:

Table 5.4: Improved Solution

Coefficient	Basic Variable	C_j b_i	2 x_1	3 x_2	0 S_1	0 S_2	0 S_3	Exchange Ratio b_i/a_{ij}
0	S_1	6	1	0	1	0	0	6 ←
3	x_2	5	0.5	1	0	0.5	0	10
0	S_3	−3	1	0	1	−1	0	0
		Z_j	1.5	3	0	1.5	0	
		$C_j - Z_j$	0.5	0	0	−1.5	0	
			↑					

$$R_2 \text{ new} = \frac{R_2 \text{ old}}{2}$$

R_1 new = R_1 old
R_3 new = R_3 old − R_2 new
= 1 − 1
= −2 − 1
= 1 − 1
= 0 − 1

Here x_1 is choose to enter the basic variable as $C_j - Z_j = 0.5$, which is largest positive number in the x_1 column. The x_1 column is the key column and here $a_{ij} = x_1$ column.

$$\frac{b_i}{a_{ij}} = \frac{6}{1} = 6, \frac{5}{0.5} = 10, \frac{-3}{0} = 0$$

Now selecting $\frac{b_i}{a_{ij}} = 6$ as minimum ratio and the corresponding row is called key row.

Now x_1 is entering as the basic variable and slack variable S_1 is removed. i.e. The element at the intersection of the key row and column is made unity and remaining elements in the column are made zero.

Step 5: Iteration 2:

Table 5.5: Improved Solution

Coefficient	Basic Variable	C_j b_i	2 x_1	3 x_2	0 S_1	0 S_2	0 S_3
2	x_1	6	1	0	1	0	0
3	x_2	2	0	1	− 0.5	0.5	0
0	S_3	− 3	0	0	− 1	− 1	0
		Z_j	*2	3	0.5	1.5	0
		$C_j - Z_j$	0	0	− 0.5	− 1.5	0

R_2 new = R_2 old − 0.5 R_1 new

0 = 0.5 − 0.5
2 = 5 − 0.5 × 6
1 = 1 − 0.5 × 0
− 0.5 = 0 − 0.5 × 1
0.5 = 0.5 − 0.5 × 0
0 = 0 − 0.5 × 0

R_3 new = R_3 old.

$^*Z_j$ = (1 × 2) + (0 × 3) + (0 × 0) = 2
= (0 × 2) + (1 × 3) + (0 × 0) = 3
= (1 × 2) + (0.5 × 3) + (− 1 × 0) = 0.5
= (0 × 2) + (0.5 × 3) + (− 1 × 0) = 1.5

In the above table all $C_j - Z_j \le 0$. Therefore the optimal solution is reached.

Where,
$x_1 = 6$
$x_2 = 2$
$S_1 = 0$
$S_2 = 0$
$S_3 = -3$

Put all these values in,

Maximize $Z = 2x_1 + 3x_2 + OS_1 + OS_2 + OS_3$

∴ $Z = 12 + 6 + 0 + 0 + 0$

∴ $Z = 18$

Example 5.7: Use simplex method to solve the following L.P.

Maximize $\quad Z = 3x_1 + 5x_2 + 4x_3$

Subject to constraints
$$2x_1 + 3x_2 \le 8$$
$$2x_2 + 5x_3 \le 10$$
$$3x_1 + 2x_2 + 4x_3 \le 15$$

and $\quad x_1, x_2, x_3 \ge 0$

Solution: Step 1: Introducing slack variable S_1, S_2 and S_3 to convert inequality to equality.

Maximize $\quad Z = 3x_1 + 5x_2 + 4x_3 + OS_1 + OS_2 + OS_3$

Subject to constraints $\quad 2x_1 + 3x_2 + S_1 = 8$
$$2x_2 + 5x_2 + S_2 = 10$$
$$3x_1 + 2x_2 + 4x_3 + S_3 = 15$$

And here $\quad x_1, x_2, x_3, S_1, S_2, S_3 \ge 0$

Step 2: Since all the RHS values are >0 so we choose initial feasible solution as $x_1 = x_2 = x_3 = 0$, $\therefore S_1 = 8$, $S_2 = 10$ and $S_3 = 15$ and maximum $Z = 0$.

Step 3: To see whether the current solution is optimal or not.

Table 5.6: Initial Solution

Coefficient	Basic Variable	C_j b_i	3 x_1	5 x_2	4 x_3	0 S_1	0 S_2	0 S_3	Exchange Ratio b_i/a_{ij}
5	x_2	2.7	0.66	1	0	0.33	0	0	2.7/0 = ∞/ –
0	S_2	4.6	– 1.32	0	5	– 0.66	1	0	$\boxed{0.92}$ ←
0	S_3	9.6	1.68	0	4	– 0.66	0	1	2.4
		Z_j	3.3	5	0	1.65	0	0	
		$C_j – Z_j$	– 0.3	0	$\boxed{4}$	– 1.65	0	0	
					↑				

R_2 new = R_2 old – 2 (R_1 new)
$$0 = 2 - 2(1)$$
$$4.6 = 10 - (2 \times 2.7)$$
$$-1.32 = 0 - (2 \times 0.66)$$
$$5 = 5 - (2 \times 0)$$
$$-0.66 = 0 - (2 \times 0.33)$$
$$1 = 1 - (2 \times 0)$$

$$R_3 \text{ new} = R_3 \text{ old} - 2(R_1 \text{ new})$$
$$9.6 = 15 - (2 \times 2.7)$$
$$1.68 = 3 - (2 \times 0.66)$$
$$0 = 2 - (2 \times 1)$$
$$4 = 4 - (2 \times 0)$$
$$-0.66 = 0 - (2 \times 0.33)$$
$$0 = 0 - (2 \times 0)$$
$$1 = 1 - (2 \times 0)$$

Step 4: Iteration 1:

Table 5.7: Improved Solution

Coeffi-cient	Basic Variable	C_j b_i	3 x_1	5 x_2	4 x_3	0 S_1	0 S_2	0 S_3	Exchange Ratio b_i/a_{ij}
0	S_1	8	2	3	0	1	0	0	8/3 = 2.7 ←
0	S_2	10	0	2	5	0	1	0	10/2 = 5
0	S_3	15	3	2	4	0	0	1	15/2 = 7.5
		Z_j	0	0	0	0	0	0	
		$C_j - Z_j$	3	5	4	0	0	0	
				↑					

Here x_2 is chosen to enter the basic variable as $C_j - Z_j = 5$, which is largest positive number. The x_2 column. The x_2 column is the key column and here $a_{ij} = x_2$ column.

Now selecting $\dfrac{b_i}{a_{ij}} = 2.7$ which is minimum ratio and the corresponding row is known as key row, now x_2 is entering as the basic variable and slack variable S_1 is removed S_1 is replaced by x_2 and the element at the intersection of the key row and column is made unity and remaining elements in the column are made zero.

Here x_3 is chosen to enter the basic variable as $C_j - Z_j = 4$, which is largest positive number. The x_3 column is the key column and here $a_{ij} = x_3$ column.

Now selecting $\dfrac{b_i}{a_{ij}} = 0.92$ as minimum ratio and the corresponding row is known as key row.

Now x_3 is entering as the basic variable by replacing S_2. Here the intersection of the key row and column is made unity and remaining elements in the column are made zero.

Step 5: Iteration 2:

Table 5.8: Improved Solution

Coefficient	Basic Variable	C_j b_i	3 x_1	5 x_2	4 x_3	0 S_1	0 S_2	0 S_3	Exchange Ratio b_i/a_{ij}
5	x_2	2.7	0.66	1	0	0.33	0	0	4.09
4	x_3	0.92	– 0.264	0	1	– 0.132	0.2	0	– 3.49
0	S_3	5.92	2.736	0	0	– 0.132	– 0.8	1	2.164 ←
		Z_j	2.244	5	4	1.122	0.8	0	
		C_j–Z_j	0.756	0	0	– 1.122	– 0.8	0	
			↑						

R_2 new = R_2 old / 5
R_1 new = R_1 old
R_3 new = R_3 old – 4 (R_2 new)

$$0 = 4 - (4 \times 1)$$
$$5.92 = 9.6 - (4 \times 0.92)$$
$$2.736 = 1.68 - (4 \times -0.264)$$
$$0 = 0 - (4 \times 0)$$
$$-0.132 = -0.66 - (4 \times -0.132)$$
$$-0.8 = 0 - (4 \times 0.2)$$
$$1 = 1 - (4 \times 0)$$

Here x_1 is choose to enter the basic variable and will replace S_3 as $C_j - Z_j$ = 0.756 is maximum positive value and $\dfrac{b_i}{a_{ij}}$ = 2.164 is minimum positive value.

Step 6: Iteration 3:

Table 5.9: Improved Solution

Coefficient	Basic Variable	C_j b_i	3 x_1	5 x_2	4 x_3	0 S_1	0 S_2	0 S_3
5	x_2	1.272	0	1	0	0.363	0.198	0.2442
4	x_3	1.49	0	0	1	– 0.119	0.121	0.980
3	x_1	2.164	1	0	0	– 0.05	0.30	0.37
		Z_j	3	5	4	1.189	2.374	6.25
		C_j–Z_j	0	0	0	– 1.189	– 2.374	– 6.25

$$R_3 \text{ new} = R_3 \text{ old} / 2.736$$
$$R_1 \text{ new} = R_1 \text{old} - 0.66 \, (R_3 \text{ new})$$
$$0 = 0.66 - 0.66 \, (1)$$
$$1.272 = 2.7 - (0.66 \times 2.164)$$
$$1 = 1 - (0.66 \times 0)$$
$$0 = 0 - (0.66 \times 0)$$
$$0.363 = 0.33 - (0.66 \times -0.05)$$
$$0.198 = 0 - (0.66 \times -0.30)$$
$$0.2442 = 0 - (0.66 \times 0.37)$$
$$R_2 \text{ new} = R_2 \text{ old} + 0.264 \, (R_2 \text{ new})$$
$$1.49 = 0.92 + (0.264 \times 2.164)$$
$$0 = -0.264 + (0.264 \, (1))$$
$$0 = 0 + (0.264 \times 0)$$
$$1 = 1 + (0.264 \times 0)$$
$$-0.1188 = -0.132 + (10.264 \times -0.05)$$
$$0.1208 = 0.2 + (0.264 \times -0.30)$$
$$0.98 = 0 + (0.264 \times 0.37)$$

As there is no $C_j - Z_j > 0$, therefore this solution is optimal.

Where,
$$x_1 = 2.164$$
$$x_2 = 1.272$$
$$x_3 = 1.49$$
$$S_1 = 0$$
$$S_2 = 0$$
$$S_3 = 0$$
$$\therefore \text{Max. } Z = 18.812$$

Example 5.8: Maximize $Z = 7x_1 + 3x_2 + 5x_3$
Subject to constraints
$$x_1 + 2x_2 + 3x_3 \leq 26$$
$$x_1 + x_2 + x_3 \leq 18$$
$$2x_1 + x_2 + x_3 \leq 22$$
and
$$x_1, x_2, x_3 \geq 0$$
Solve by simplex method.

Solution: Step 1: Introducing slack variable S_1, S_2, S_3 to convert inequality to equality.
Maximize $Z = 7x_1 + 3x_2 + 5x_3 + OS_1 + OS_2 + OS_3$
Subject to the constraints
$$x_1 + 2x_2 + 3x_3 + S_1 = 26$$
$$x_1 + x_2 + x_3 + S_2 = 18$$
$$2x_1 + x_2 + x_3 + S_3 = 22$$
And
$$x_1, x_2, x_3, S_1, S_2, S_3 \geq 0$$

Step 2: Since all the RHS values are > 0, so we choose initial feasible solution as $x_1 = x_2 = x_3 = 0$ ∴ $S_1 = 26$, $S_2 = 18$, and $S_3 = 22$ and maximum Z = 0.

Step 3: To see whether the current solution is optimal or not,

Table 5.10: Initial Solution

Co-eff.	Basic Variable	C_j b_i	7 x_1	3 x_2	5 x_3	0 S_1	0 S_2	0 S_3	Exchange Ratio
0	S_1	26	1	2	3	1	0	0	26
0	S_2	18	1	1	1	0	1	0	18
0	S_3	22	2	1	1	0	0	1	11 ←
		Z_j	0	0	0	0	0	0	
		$C_j - Z_j$	7	3	5	0	0	0	
			↑						

As $C_j - Z_j = 7$ is maximum positive number so selected x_1 is the basic variable now and all the element of x_1 are a_{ij}. $\dfrac{b_i}{a_{ij}} = 11$ is the minimum positive number so it is selected.

Now S_3 is replaced by x_1

Step 4: Iteration 1:

Table 5.11: Improved Solution

Co-eff	Basic Variable	C_j b_i	7 x_1	3 x_2	5 x_3	0 S_1	0 S_2	0 S_3	Exchange Ration b_i/a_{ij}
0	S_1	15	0	1.5	2.5	1	0	− 0.5	15/2.5 = 6 ←
0	S_2	7	0	0.5	0.5	0	1	− 0.5	7/0.5 = 14
7	x_1	11	1	0.5	0.5	0	0	0.5	11/0.5 = 22
		Z_j	7	3.5	3.5	0	0	3.5	
		$C_j - Z_j$	0	− 0.5	1.5	0	0	− 3.5	
					↑				

R_3 new = R_3 old/2
R_2 new = R_2 old − R_3 new
0 = 1 − 1
7 = 18 − 11
0.5 = 1 − 0.5
0.5 = 1 − 0.5
0 = 0 − 0
1 = 1 − 0
− 0.5 = 0 − 0.5

R_2 new $= R_2$ old $- R_3$ new
$$15 = 26 - 11$$
$$0 = 1 - 1$$
$$1.5 = 2 - 0.5$$
$$2.5 = 3 - 0.5$$
$$1 = 1 - 0$$
$$0 = 0 - 0$$
$$-0.5 = 0 - 0.5$$

Placing S_1 by x_3

Step 5: Iteration 2:

Table 5.12: Improved Solution

Co-eff	Basic Variable	C_j b_i	7 x_1	3 x_2	5 x_3	0 S_1	0 S_2	0 S_3
5	x_3	6	0	0.6	1	0.4	0	-0.2
0	S_2	4	0	0.2	0	-0.2	1	-0.4
7	x_1	8	1	0.2	0	-0.2	0	0.6
		Z_j	7	4.4	5	0.6	0	3.2
		$C_j - Z_j$	0	-1.4	0	-0.6	0	-3.2

R_1 new $= R_1$ old $/ 2.5$
R_2 new $= R_2$ old $- 0.5$ (R_1 new)
$$0 = 0.5 \quad -0.5 \times 1$$
R_3 new $= R_3$ old $- 0.5$ R_1 new

As all $C_j - Z_j$ are negative and zero, so the current solution is optimal,

Where,
$$x_1 = 8$$
$$x_2 = 0$$
$$x_3 = 6$$
$$S_1 = 0$$
$$S_2 = 4$$
$$S_3 = 0$$

∴ Maximum $Z = 86$

5.4 TWO PHASE METHOD

When artificial variables are add to the constraints to obtain an initial basic feasible solution to an LP problem. If this problem is to be solved, then this add artificial variables must be driven to zero. The two phase method is another method to handle these artificial variable.

Here the LP problem is solved in two phases. In the first phase, the sum of the artificial variables is minimized subject to the given constraints to get a basic feasible solution. Then in the second phase, the original objective function is minimized, starting with the basic feasible solution obtained at the end of the first phase. As the optimal solution is achieved in two phases, therefore this method is known as two phase method.

Example 5.9: Use two phase simplex method to solve the following LP problem.
Maximize $Z = 5x_1 + 3x_2$
Subject to constraints
$$2x_1 + x_2 \leq 1$$
$$x_1 + 4x_2 \geq 6$$
And $x_1, x_2 \geq 0$

Solution: Phase I: It consist of the following steps.

Step 1: Set up the problem in the standard form,

The original objective function $Z = 5x_1 + 3x_2$ is temporarily set aside during this phase. Add slack, surplus and artificial variables in the constraints.

So that it becomes,
$$2x_1 + x_2 + S_1 = 1$$
$$x_1 + 4x_2 - S_2 + A_1 = 6$$
And $x_1, x_2, S_1, S_2, A \geq 0$

Now, the new objective function is
Minimize $W = A_1$

Now, as earlier, the simplex method required that a variable which appears in one equation must appear in all the equations. This is done by placing zero coefficient.

∴ The standard form for phase 1 becomes,
Minimize $W = 0x_1 + 0x_2 + 0S_1 + 0S_2 + A_1$

Step 2: Find an initial basic feasible solution

Substituting $x_1 = x_2 = S_2 = 0$

∴ $S_1 = 1$ and $A_1 = 6$

Coeffi-cient	Basic Variable	C_j b_i	0 x_1	0 x_2	0 S_1	0 S_2	1 A_1	Exchange Ration b_i/a_{ij}
0	S_1	1	2	1	1	0	0	☐1 ←
1	A_1	6	1	4	0	−1	1	− 1.5
		Z_j	1	4	0	−1	1	
		$C_j - Z_j$	−1	☐−4	0	1	0	
				↑				

As minimization problem, so $C_j - Z_j = -4$ is selected.

∴ Replace S_1 by x_2

Coeffi-cient	Basic Variable	C_j b_j	0 x_1	0 x_2	0 S_1	0 S_2	1 A_1
0	x_2	1	2	1	1	0	0
1	A_1	2	−7	0	−4	−1	1
		Z_j	−7	0	−4	−1	1
		$C_j - Z_j$	7	0	4	1	0

R_1 new = R_1 old
R_2 new = R_2 old − 4 (R_1 new)
0 = 4 − 4 (1)

Since all $C_j - Z_j$ values are positive and zero, so optimal solution is obtained.
Where $A_1 = 2$, $x_2 = 1$

∴ Minimize W = 2 (> 0)

As A_1 appears in the basic at a positive level, the given problem does not have a feasible solution and hence the process in stopped.

Example 5.10: *Use the two phase simplex method to,*
Maximize $Z = 5x_1 - 4x_2 + 3x_3$
Subject to constraints $2x_1 + x_2 - 6x_3 = 20$
$6x_1 + 5x_2 + 10x_3 \le 76$
$8x_1 - 3x_2 + 6x_3 \le 50$
And $x_1, x_2, x_3, \ge 0$

Solution: Phase I:
Step 1: Set up the problem in the standard form.
Introduce slack, surplus and artificial variables.
$2x_1 + x_2 - 6x_3 + A_1 = 20$
$6x_1 + 5x_2 + 10x_3 + S_1 = 76$
$8x_1 - 3x_2 + 6x_3 + S_2 = 50$
And $x_1, x_2, x_3, A_1, S_1, S_2 \ge 0$

The new objective function
Minimize W = A_1

This objective function is also known as infeasibility form or dummy objective function.
Thus the problem for phase 1 in standard from is written as,
Minimize W = $0x_1 + 0x_2 + 0x_3 + 0S_1 + 0S_2 + A_1$

Step 2: Find an initial basic feasible solution
Substituting $x_1 = x_2 = x_3 = 0$
∴ $A_1 = 20$, $S_1 = 76$ and $S_2 = 50$

Coefficient	Basic Variable	C_j b_i	0 x_1	0 x_2	0 x_3	0 S_1	0 S_2	1 A_1	Exchange Ratio b_i/a_{ij}
1	A_1	20	2	1	−6	0	0	1	10
0	S_1	76	6	5	10	1	0	0	12.667
0	S_2	50	8	−3	6	0	1	0	6.25 ←
		Z_j	2	1	−6	0	0	1	
		C_j-Z_j	−2	−1	6	0	0	0	
			↑						

As minimization problem $C_j - Z_j = -2$ is selected.

Step 3: Perform optimality Test

Replace S_2 by x_1

Coefficient	Basic Variable	C_j b_i	0 x_1	0 x_2	0 x_3	0 S_1	0 S_2	1 A_1	Exchange Ratio b_i/a_{ij}
1	A_1	7.5	0	1.75	−7.5	0	−0.25	1	4.29 ←
0	S_1	38.5	0	7.25	5.5	1	−0.75	0	5.31
0	x_1	6.25	1	−0.375	0.75	0	0.125	0	−16.67
		Z_j	0	1.75	−7.5	0	−0.25	1	
		C_j-Z_j	0	−1.75	7.5	0	0.25	0	
				↑					

Key column → R_3 new = R_3 old / 8 = 1
R_2 new = R_2 old − 6(R_3 new)
0 = 6 − 6 (1)
R_1 new = R_1 old − 2 (R_2 new)
0 = 2 − 2 (1)

Step 4: Replacing A_1 by x_2

Coefficient	Basic Variable	C_j b_i	0 x_1	0 x_2	0 x_3	0 S_1	0 S_2	1 A_1
0	x_2	4.29	0	1	−4.29	0	−0.15	0.57
0	S_1	7.40	0	0	36.60	1	0.3325	−4.1325
0	x_1	7.86	1	0	−0.86	0	0.069	0.214
		Z_j	0	0	0	0	0	0
		C_j-Z_j	0	0	0	0	0	1
					↑			

Key column → R_1 new = R_1 old / 1.75
R_2 new = R_2 old − (R_1 new) 7.25
0 = 7.25 − 7.25 (1)
R_3 new = R_3 old + (R_1 new) 0.375
0 = − 0.375 + (1) 0.375

Since $C_j - Z_j$ is non negative under all columns, hence the above solution is optimal.

Here W_{min} = 0 and no artificial variable appears in the basic variable.

Phase II: In this phase, we will find optimal solution to the given problem. Objective function of this phase is same as the given problem. The remaining part of initial table for phase II is the last table for phase I, with the only difference that Z_j and $C_j - Z_j$ rows will change as the coefficients are going to change. Phase II table will not contain any artificial variable.

Coefficient	Basic variable	C_j	0	0	0	0	0
		b_i	x_1	x_2	x_3	S_1	S_2
− 4	x_2	4.29	0	1	− 4.29	0	− 0.15
0	S_1	7.40	0	0	36.60	1	0.3375
5	x_1	7.86	1	0	− 0.86	0	0.069
		Z_j	5	− 4	12.86	0	0.945
		$C_j - Z_j$	0	0	− 9.86	0	− 0.945

Since $C_j - Z_j$ is either negative or zero under all variable columns, so optimal solution is achieved.

Where,
x_1 = 7.86
x_2 = 4.29
x_3 = 0
S_1 = 7.40
S_2 = 0

∴ Maximum Z = 22.14

Example 5.11: *Use two phase simplex method to solve the following LP problem.*

Maximize $Z = x_1 + x_2$

Subject to constraints,
$2x_1 + x_2 \geq 4$
$x_1 + 7x_2 \leq 7$

And $x_1, x_2 \geq 0$

Note: It the objective function is of minimization, then convert it into one of maximization by using the following relationship,

Minimize Z = − Maximize Z^*
Where Z^* = −Z

Solution: Phase I:
Step 1: Set up the problem in standard form,
Introduce slack, surplus and artificial variables, to the constraints.

$$2x_1 + x_2 - S_1 + A_1 = 4$$
$$x_1 + 7x_2 - S_2 + A_2 = 7$$
And $x_1, x_2, S_1, S_2, A_1, A_2 \geq 0$

The new artificial objective function is

$$\text{Minimize } W = A_1 + A_2$$

So the problem for phase 1 in standard form is
Minimize $W = 0x_1 + 0x_2 + 0S_1 + 0S_2 + A_1 + A_2$

Step 2: Find on initial basic feasible solution.
Setting variable $x_1 = x_2 = S_1 = S_2 = 0$

$$\therefore A_1 = 4$$
$$A_2 = 7$$

Coefficient	Basic Variable	C_j b_i	0 x_1	0 x_2	0 S_1	0 S_2	1 A_1	1 A_2	Exchange Ratio b_i/a_{ij}
1	A_1	4	2	1	−1	0	1	0	4
1	A_2	7	1	7	0	−1	0	1	1 ←
		Z_j	3	8	−1	−1	1	1	
		C_j–Z_j	−3	−8	1	1	0	0	
				↑					

As minimization problem $C_j - Z_j = -8$ is selected.
Step 3: Perform Optimality Test

Replace A_2 by x_2

Coefficient	Basic Variable	C_j b_i	0 x_1	0 x_2	0 S_1	0 S_2	1 A_1	1 A_2	Exchange Ratio b_i/a_{ij}
1	A_1	3	1.857	0	−1	0.143	1	−0.143	20.97 ←
1	x_2	1	0.143	1	0	−0.143	0	0.143	−6.99
		Z_j	1.857	0	−1	0.143	1	−0.143	
		C_j–Z_j	−1.857	0	1	−0.143	0	0.143	
						↑			

R_2 new = R_2 old / 7
R_1 new = R_1 old − R_2 new
0 = 1 − 1

Step 4: Replace A_1 by S_2

Coefficient	Basic variable	C_j b_i	0 x_1	0 x_2	0 S_1	0 S_2	1 A_1	1 A_2
0	S_2	20.97	12.99	0	− 6.99	1	6.99	− 1
0	x_2	3.999	2.001	1	− 0.952	0	0.952	0
		Z_j	0	0	0	0	0	0
		$C_j - Z_j$	0	0	0	0	− 1	− 1

$$R_1 \text{ new} = R_1 \text{ old} / 0.143$$
$$R_2 \text{ new} = R_2 \text{ old} + (R_1 \text{ new}) \, 0.143$$
$$0 = -0.143 + (1) \, 0.143$$

Since $C_j - Z_j$ is non negative under all columns, so the above solution is optimal.

Here W min = 0 and no artificial variable appears in the basic variable.

Phase II:

Step 5: It this phase, we will find optimal function of this phase is same as the given problem. The remaining part of initial table for phase II is the last table for phase I, with the only difference in Z_j and $C_j - Z_j$ row which will change Phase II table will not contain any artificial variable.

Coefficient	Basic Variable	C_j b_i	0 x_1	0 x_2	0 S_1	0 S_2	Exchange Ratio b_i/a_{ij}
0	S_2	20.97	12.99	0	− 6.99	1	1.614 ←
1	x_2	3.999	2.001	1	− 0.952	0	1.999
		Z_j	2.001	1	− 0.952	0	
		$C_j - Z_j$	− 1.001	0	0.952	0	
			↑				

As minimization, so $C_j - Z_j = -1.001$

Step 6: Now replace S_2 by x_1

Coefficient	Basic Variable	C_j b_i	0 x_1	0 x_2	0 S_1	0 S_2
1	x_1	1.614	1	0	− 0.538	0.077
1	x_2	0.769	0	1	0.125	− 0.154
		Z_j	1	1	− 0.413	− 0.077
		$C_j - Z_j$	0	0	0.413	0.077

$$R_1 \text{ new} = R_1 \text{ old} / 12.99$$
$$R_2 \text{ new} = R_2 \text{ old} - R_1 \text{ new}$$
$$0 = 2.001 - (1) \, 2.001$$

∴ Optimal solution is achieved

$$x_1 = 1.614$$
$$x_2 = 0.769$$

∴ Minimize $Z = 2.383$

Example 5.12: *Minimize $Z = x_1 + x_2 + 3x_3$*
Subject to constraints $\quad 3x_1 + 2x_2 + x_3 \leq 3$
$$2x_1 + x_2 + 2x_3 \geq 2$$
And $\quad x_1, x_2, x_3, \geq 2$
Solve the problem by Two- Phase Method.

Solution: Phase I:

Step 1: Set up the problem in standard form:

Introduce slack, surplus and artificial variables to the constraints,

$$3x_1 + 2x_2 + x_3 + S_1 = 3$$
$$2x_1 + x_2 + 2x_3 - S_2 + A_1 = 2$$

And $\quad x_1, x_2, x_3, A_1, S_2, A_1 \geq 0$

The new artificial objective function is minimize $W = A_1$

So the problem for phase 1 in standard form is

Minimize $W = 0x_1 + 0x_2 + 0x_3 + 0S_1 + 0S_2 + A_1$

Step 2: Find the initial basic feasible solution substitution variable $x_1 = x_2 = x_3 = S_2 = 0$

∴ $S_1 = 3, A_1 = 2$

Coefficient	Basic Variable	C_j b_i	0 x_1	0 x_2	0 x_3	0 S_1	0 S_2	0 A_1	Exchange Ration b_i/a_{ij}
0	S_1	3	3	2	1	1	0	0	3
1	A_1	2	2	1	(2)	0	−1	1	1 ←
		Z_j	2	1	2	0	−1	1	
		C_j−Z_j	−2	−1	−2	0	1	0	
					↑				

As minimization problem $C_j - Z_j = -2$ is selected.

Step 3: Perform optimality test.
Replace A_1 by x_3

Coefficient	Basic Variable	C_j b_i	0 x_1	0 x_2	0 x_3	0 S_1	0 S_2	0 A_1
0	S_1	2	2	1.5	0	1	0.5	−0.5
1	x_3	1	1	0.5	1	0	−0.5	0.5
		Z_j	0	0	0	0	0	0
		$C_j−Z_j$	0	0	0	0	0	1

R_2 new = R_1 old / 2
R_1 new = R_1 old − R_2 new

Since all $C_j − Z_j$ are non negative under all columns, so the above solution is optimal. Here $W_{min} = 0$ and no artificial variable appears in the basic variable.

Phase II:

Step 5: Using initial objective function for optimality test.

Coefficient	Basic Variable	C_j b_i	0 x_1	0 x_2	0 x_3	0 S_1	0 S_2	Exchange Ration b_i/a_{ij}
0	S_1	2	2	1.5	0	1	0.5	1 ←
3	x_3	1	1	0.5	1	0	−0.5	1
		Z_j	3	1.5	3	0	−1.5	
		$C_j−Z_j$	−2	−0.5	0	0	1.5	
			↑					

Step 6: Replace S_1 by x_1

Coefficient	Basic Variable	C_j b_i	0 x_1	0 x_2	0 x_3	0 S_1	0 S_2
1	x_1	1	1	0.75	0	0.5	0.25
3	x_3	0	0	−0.25	1	−0.5	−0.75
		Z_j	1	0	3	−1	−2
		$C_j−Z_j$	0	1	0	1	2

R_2 new = R_1 old/2
R_1 new = R_1 old − R_1 new

∴ Optimal solution is achieved

$$x_1 = 1$$
$$x_2 = 0$$
$$x_3 = 0$$

∴ Minimize $Z = 1$

5.5 BIG M - METHOD

In this method, we assign a large unacceptable coefficient to artificial variables from the objective function Z is to minimize, and then a very large positive penalty is assigned to each of these artificial variables. Similarly if Z is to be maximized then a very large negative penalty is assigned to these variables. The penalty will be assigned as – M for maximization and + M for minimization problem, where M > 0.

The method consist of the following basic steps:

Step 1 : Express the linear programming problem is standard form by introducing slack variables, surplus variable and artificial variable.

Step 2 : Assign zero coefficient to both slack and surplus variable and a large positive or negative coefficient in case of maximization (+M) and minimization (–M) respectively, to the artificial variable in the objective function.

Step 3 : The initial basic feasible solution obtained by assigning zero value to non-basic variables.

Step 4 : Continue with the regular steps of simplex method. During operation, at any stage of simplex method, on artificial variable leaves the basis, it is dropped and all the entries in the column of this variable are omitted from the succeeding table. While doing various iterations one of the following cases may arrive:

(a) It at least one artificial variable is present in the basic with zero value and the coefficient of M in each $C_j - Z_j$ (j = 1,2,3 ..... n) value is non-negative, then the given LP problem has no solution. That is, the current basic feasible solution is degenerate.

(b) If at least one artificial variable is present in the basic with positive value and the coefficient of M in each $C_j - Z_j$ (j = 1,2,3 .... n) values is non-negative, then given LP problem has no optimum basic feasible solution.

Example 5.13: *Use big M method to solve the following LP problem.*
Minimize $\qquad Z = 12x_1 + 20x_2$
Subject to constraints $\qquad 6x_1 + 8x_2 \geq 100$
$\qquad\qquad\qquad\qquad\qquad 7x_1 + 12x_2 \geq 120$
And $\qquad\qquad\qquad\qquad x_1, x_2 \geq 0$

Solution: Step 1: Express the problem in standard form,

Slack variables are to be introduced in LHS of constraints to convert them form inequality to equality.

∴ The problem is written as follows.

Minimize $Z = 12x_1 + 20x_2 + OS_1 + OS_2$
Subject to $6x_1 + 8x_2 - S_1 = 100$
             $7x_1 + 12x_2 - S_2 = 120$
And $x_1, x_2, S_1, S_2 \geq 0$

Step 2: Find initial basic feasible solution:

Putting x_1 and $x_2 = 0$, we get $S_1 = -100$ and $S_2 = -120$, but this is not feasible as S_1 and S_2 are negative and that do not satisfy. Therefore we have to introduce artificial variables A_1 and A_2 in the constraints such that,

$$6x_1 + 8x_2 - S_1 + A_1 = 100$$
$$7x_1 + 12x_2 - S_2 + A_2 = 120$$

And $x_1, x_2, S_1, S_2, A_1, A_2 \geq 0$

Now artificial variables with values greater than zero violate the equality in constraints established in the previous step. So A_1 and A_2 should not appear in the final solution. So for this the artificial variables are assigned a large unity penalty in the objective function, which can be written as,

Minimize $Z = 12x_1 + 20x_2 + OS_1 + OS_2 + MA_1 + MA_2$

Here, we have six variable and two constraints. Four of the variables have to be equated to zero to get the initial feasible solution to the 'artificial system'.

Putting $x_1 = x_2 = S_1 = S_2 = 0$

We get, $A_1 = 100$, $A_2 = 120$ and $Z = 220$ M.

Step 3: Optimality test

Coefficient	Basic Variable	C_j b_i	12 x_1	20 x_2	0 S_1	0 S_2	M A_1	M A_2	Exchange Ratio b_i/a_{ij}
M	A_1	100	6	8	-1	0	1	0	100/8 = 12.5
M	A_2	120	7	12	0	-1	0	1	120/12 = $\boxed{10}$ ←
		Z_j	13M	20M	-M	-M	M	M	
		$C_j - Z_j$	12-13M	$\boxed{20-20M}$	M	M	0	0	
				↑					

Here $C_j - Z_j = 20 - 20M$ is the maximum, so x_2 column is selected as key column. The elements of x_2 column are a_{ij}.

∴ Exchange ratio $\dfrac{b_i}{a_{ij}} = \dfrac{100}{8} = 12.5$

$= \dfrac{120}{12} = 10$

Here 10 is selected as it is the minimum positive number and that row is selected as key row. This means that A_2 is not a basic variable and should be replaced by x_2. Since A_2 is the replacing variable column of A_2 is deleted form the next table.

Step 4: Iteration 1:

Coefficient	Basic Variable	C_j b_i	12 x_1	20 x_2	0 S_1	0 S_2	M A_1	Exchange Ratio b_i/a_{ij}
M	A_1	20	1.36	0	−1	0.64	1	14.70 ←
20	x_2	10	0.58	1	0	−0.08	0	17.24
		Z_j	1.36M +11.6	20	−M	0.64 M −1.6	M	
		$C_j - Z_j$	1.36 M−0.4	0	M	−0.64 M +1.6	0	
			↑					

R_2 new = R_2 old / 12

R_1 new = R_1 old − 8 R_2 new

0 = 8 − 8(1)

Here $C_j - Z_j$ = 1.36 M − 0.4 is maximum positive number so x_1 column is selected as key column. Element of x_1 column are a_{ij}.

∴ Exchange ratio $\dfrac{b_i}{a_{ij}} = \dfrac{20}{1.36} = 14.70$

$= \dfrac{10}{0.58} = 17.24$

So we select 14.70, as it is minimum positive number and the row is selected as key row.

This means that A_1 is not a basic variable and is to be replaced by x_2 and A_1 column is eliminated from the next iteration table.

Step 5: Iteration 2:

Coefficient	Basic Variable	C_j b_i	12 x_1	20 x_2	0 S_1	0 S_2	Exchange Ratio b_i/a_{ij}
12	x_1	14.70	1	0	– 0.735	0.470	31.28
20	x_2	1.474	0	1	0.426	– 0.353	– 4.176
		Z_j	12	20	– 0.3	– 1.42	
		$C_j - Z_j$	0	0	0.3	$\boxed{1.42}$	
						↑	

R_1 new = R_1 old / 1.36

R_2 new = R_2 old – 0.58 R_1 new

0 = 0.58 – 0.58(1)

∴ Optimal solution is reached.

Here
$$x_1 = 14.70$$
$$x_2 = 1.474$$
∴
$$Z \min = 205.88$$

Example 5.14: Minimize $Z = 40x_1 + 60x_2$

Subject to $x_1 + 2x_2 \geq 80$

$3x_1 + x_2 \geq 75$

and $x_1, x_2 \geq 0$

Solution: Step 1: Express the problems in standard form.

Slack variables are to be introduced in LHS of constraints to convert them form inequality to equality.

∴ The problem is written as follows

Minimize $Z = 40x_1 + 60x_2 + OS_1 + OS_2$

Subject to $x_1 + 2x_2 - S_1 = 80$

$3x_1 + x_2 - S_2 = 75$

And $x_1, x_2, S_1, S_2 \geq 0$

Step 2: Find initial basic feasible solution.

Putting x_1 and $x_2 = 0$, we get $S_1 = -80$ and $S_2 = -75$ but this is not feasible as S_1 and S_2 are negative and that do not satisfy.

Therefore we have to introduce artificial variable A_1 and A_2 in the constraints, such that,

$$x_1 + 2x_2 - S_1 + A_1 = 80$$
$$3x_1 + x_2 - S_2 + A_2 = 75$$

And $\quad x_1, x_2, S_1, S_2, A_1, A_2 \geq 0$

Now artificial variables with values greater than zero violate the equality in constraints established in the previous step. So A_1 and A_2 should not appear in final solution. So for this the artificial variables are assigned a large unity penalty in the objective function, which can be written as,

Minimize $Z = 40x_1 + 60x_2 + OS_1 + OS_2 + MA_1 + MA_2$

Now, we have six variables and two constraints.

Four variables have to be equated to zero to get the initial feasible solution to the artificial system.

Putting $x_1 = x_2 = S_1 = S_2 = 0$,

∴ We get. $A_1 = 80$ and $A_2 = 75$

Step 3: Optimality test

Coefficient	Basic variable	C_j b_i	40 x_1	60 x_2	0 S_1	0 S_2	M A_1	M A_2	Exchange Ratio b_i/a_{ij}
M	A_1	80	1	2	−1	0	1	0	80
M	A_2	75	3	1	0	−1	0	1	25 ←
		Z_j	4M	3M	−M	−M	M	M	
		$C_j - Z_j$	40−4M	60−3M	M	M	0	0	
			↑						

Here $C_j - Z_j = 40 - 4M$ is maximum, so x_1 column is selected as key column. The elements of x_2 column are a_{ij}.

∴ Exchange ratio $\quad \dfrac{b_i}{a_{ij}} = \dfrac{80}{1} = 80$

$$= \dfrac{75}{3} = 25$$

Here 25 is selected as it is the minimum positive no. and that row is selected as key row.

This means that A_2 is not a basic variable and should be replaced by x_1 since A_2 is the replacing variable, column of A_2 is deleted from the next table.

Step 4: Iteration 1:

Coefficient	Basic Variable	C_j b_i	40 x_1	60 x_2	0 S_1	0 S_2	M A_1	Exchange Ratio b_i/a_{ij}
M	A_1	55	0	1.67	−1	0.33	1	32.93 ←
40	x_1	25	1	0.33	0	−0.33	0	75.76
		Z_j	40	1.67M +13.2	−M	0.33 M −13.2	M	
		$C_j - Z_j$	0	46.8+1.67 M	M	−0.33M +13.2	0	
				↑				

$$R_2 \text{ new} = R_2 \text{ old} / 3$$
$$1 = 3/3$$
$$R_1 \text{ new} = R_1 \text{ old} - R_2 \text{ New}$$
$$0 = 1 - 1$$

As $C_j - Z_j = 46.8 + 1.67$ M is maximum positive number so x_2 column is selected as key column. Element of x_2 column are a_{ij}.

From the exchange ration 32.93 is selected as it is the minimum positive number and the row is selected as key row.

This means that A_1 is not a basic variable and is to be replaced by x_2 and A_1 column is eliminated from the next iteration table.

Step 5: Iteration 2:

Coefficient	Basic Variable	C_j b_i	40 x_1	60 x_2	0 S_1	0 S_2	Exchange Ratio b_i/a_{ij}
60	x_1	32.93	0	1	−0.598	0.198	−55.066
40	x_2	14.13	1	0	0.197	−0.395	71.065
		Z_j	40	60	−28	−3.92	
		$C_j - Z_j$	0	0	28	3.92	
					↑		

$$R_1 \text{ new} = R_1 \text{ old} / 1.67$$
$$R_2 \text{ new} = R_2 \text{ old} - 0.33 \, R_1 \text{ new}$$
$$0 = 0.33 - 0.33(1)$$

∴ Optimal solution is reached.
Here
$$x_1 = 14.13$$
$$x_2 = 32.93$$
∴ Minimize
$$Z \min = 40 x_1 + 60 x_2$$
$$= 2541$$

Example 5.15:

Minimize $\quad Z = x_1 + x_2 + 3x_3$

Subject to $\quad 3x_1 + 2x_2 + x_3 \leq 3$

$\quad\quad\quad\quad\quad 2x_1 + x_2 + 2x_3 \geq 2$

And $\quad\quad\quad x_1, x_2, x_3 \geq 0$

Use Big M method.

Solution: Step 1: Express the problem in standard form.

Slack and surplus variables are to be introduced in LHS of the constraints to convert them from inequality to equality.

∴ The problem is written as follows.

Minimize $\quad Z = x_1 + x_2 + 3x_3 + 0S_1 + 0S_2$

Subject to $\quad 3x_1 + 2x_2 + x_3 + S_1 = 3$

$\quad\quad\quad\quad\quad 2x_1 + x_2 + 2x_3 - S_2 = 2$

And $\quad\quad\quad x_1, x_2, x_3, S_1, S_2 \geq 0$

Step 2: Find initial basic feasible solution

Putting x_1, x_2 and $x_3 = 0$

∴ $S_1 = 3$ and $S_2 = -2$

But this is not feasible as S_2 is negative. Therefore we have to introduction artificial variable A_1 in the constraints, such that,

$$3x_1 + 2x_2 + x_3 + S_1 = 3$$
$$2x_1 + x_2 + 2x_3 - S_2 + A_1 = 2$$

And $\quad\quad\quad x_1, x_2, x_3, S_1, S_2, A_1 \geq 0$

Now artificial variables with values greater than zero violate the equality in constraints established in the previous step. So A_1 should not appear in final solution. So far this artificial variable are assigned a large unity penalty in the objective function, which can be written as,

Minimize $Z = x_1 + x_2 + 3x_3 + 0S_1 + 0S_2 + MA_1$

Now, we have six variables and two constraints four variables have to be equated to zero to get the initial feasible solution to the artificial system.

Putting $x_1 = x_2 = x_3 = S_2 = 0$

∴ We get $S_1 = 3$ and $A_1 = 2$

Step 3: Optimality test:

Coefficient	Basic Variable	C_j \\ b_j	1 \\ x_1	1 \\ x_2	3 \\ x_3	0 \\ S_1	0 \\ S_2	M \\ A_1	Exchange Ratio b_i/a_{ij}
0	S_1	3	3	2	1	1	0	0	3
M	A_1	2	2	1	2	0	−1	1	1 ←
		Z_j	2M	M	2m	0	−M	M	
		$C_j - Z_j$	1−2M	1−M	$\boxed{3-2M}$	0	M	0	
					↑				

Here $C_j - Z_j = 3 - 2M$ is maximum, so x_3 column is selected as key column. The elements of x_3 column are a_{ij}.

∴ Exchange ratio $\dfrac{b_i}{a_{ij}} = \dfrac{3}{1} = 3$

$= \dfrac{2}{2} = 1$

Here 1 is selected as it is the minimum positive number and that row is selected as key row. This means that A_1 is not a basic variable and should be replaced by x_3. Since A_1 is the replacing variable, column of A_1 is deleted from the next table.

Step 4: Iteration 1:

Coefficient	Basic Variable	C_j \\ b_i	1 \\ x_1	1 \\ x_2	3 \\ x_3	0 \\ S_1	0 \\ S_2	Exchange Ratio b_i/a_{ij}
0	S_1	2	2	1.5	0	1	0.5	$\boxed{4}$ ←
3	x_3	1	1	0.5	1	0	−0.5	−2
		Z_j	3	1.5	3	0	−1.5	
		$C_j - Z_j$	−2	−0.5	0	0	$\boxed{1.5}$	
							↑	

R_2 new = R_2 old / 2
R_1 new = R_1 old − (R_2 new)
0 = 1 − 1

As $C_j - Z_j = 1.5$ is maximum positive number so S_2 column is selected as key column. Element of S_2 column are a_{ij}.

From the exchange ratio 4 is selected as it is the minimum positive number and the row is selected as key row.

This means that S_1 is not a basic variable and is to be replaced by S_2.

Step 5: Iteration 2

Coefficient	Basic Variable	C_j b_i	1 x_1	1 x_2	3 x_3	0 S_1	0 S_2
0	S_2	4	4	3	0	2	1
3	x_3	3	3	2	1	1	0
		Z_j	9	6	3	3	0
		$C_j - Z_j$	−8	−5	0	−3	0

R_1 new = 2 (R_1 old)

1 = 2 (0.5)

R_2 new = R_2 old + 0.5 (R_1 new)

0 = −0.5 + 0.5(1)

3 = 1 + 0.5 (4)

2 = 0.5 + 0.5 × 3

1 = 1 + 0.5 × 0

1 = 0 + 0.5 × 2

∴ Optimal solution is reached.

Here $S_2 = 4$, x_1 $x_2 = 0$

$x_3 = 3$

∴ Minimize $Z = x_1 + x_2 + 3x_3 + OS_1 + OS_2$

$= 0 + 0 + 3 × 3 + 0 + 0$

$= 9$

Example 5.16: Maximize $Z = 3x_1 - x_2$

Subject to

$2x_1 + x_2 \leq 2$

$x_1 + 3x_2 \geq 3$

$x_2 \leq 4$

and $x_1, x_2, \geq 0$

Solution: Step 1: Set up the problems in standard form.

Introducing slack, surplus and artificial variables the problem is as follows,

Maximize $Z = 3x_1 - x_2 + OS_1 + OS_2 + OS_3 - MA_1$

Subject to $2x_1 + x_2 + S_1 = 2$

$x_1 + 3x_2 - S_2 + A_1 = 3$

$x_2 + S_3 = 4$

And $x_1, x_2, S_1, S_2, S_3, A_1 \geq 0$

Step 2: Find initial basic feasible solution

Substituting $x_1 = x_2 = S_2 = 0$, and the initial basic feasible solution is obtained

Where,
$$S_1 = 2$$
$$A_1 = 3$$
$$S_3 = 4$$

And
$$Z = -3M$$

Step 3: Perform optimality test

Coefficient	Basic Variable	C_j b_i	−1 x_1	−1 x_2	0 S_1	0 S_2	0 S_3	M A_1	Exchange Ratio b_i/a_{ij}
0	S_1	2	2	1	1	0	0	0	2
−M	A_1	3	1	3	0	−1	0	1	1←
0	S_3	4	0	1	0	0	1	0	4
		Z_j	−M	−3M	0	M	0	−M	
		C_j-Z_j	3+M	−1+3M	0	−M	0	0	
			↑						

Step 4: Iterate towards an optimal solution.

Coefficient	Basic Variable	C_j b_i	1 x_1	1 x_2	0 S_1	0 S_2	0 S_3	Exchange Ratio b_i/a_{ij}
0	S_1	1	1	0	0	−1	−1	1←
−1	x_2	1	0.33	1	0	−0.33	0	3.03
0	S_3	3	−1	0	−1	−1	0	−3
		Z_j	−0.33	−1	0	0.33	0	
		C_j-Z_j	3.33	0	0	−0.33	0	
			↑					

$$R_2 \text{ new} = R_2 \text{ old} / 3$$
$$R_1 \text{ new} = R_1 \text{ old} - R_2 \text{ new}$$
$$0 = 1 - 1$$
$$R_3 \text{ new} = R_3 \text{ old} - R_2 \text{ new}$$
$$0 = 1 - 1$$

Step 5: Iteration 2:

Coefficient	Basic Variable	C_j b_i	3 x_1	−1 x_2	0 S_1	0 S_2	0 S_3	Exchange Ratio b_i/a_{ij}
3	x_1	1	1	0	0	−1	−1	−1
1	x_2	0.67	0	1	0	0	0.33	0
0	S_3	4	0	0	−1	−2	−1	−2
		Z_j	3	1	0	−3	−2.67	
		C_j–Z_j	0	−2	0	⬜3	2.67	
						↑		

$$R_2 \text{ new} = R_2 \text{ old} - R_1 \text{ new}$$
$$0 = 0.33 - 0.33(1)$$
$$R_3 \text{ new} = R_3 \text{old} + R_1 \text{ new}$$
$$0 = -1 + 1$$

∴ Optimal solution is reached.

Here
$$x_1 = 1$$
$$x_2 = 0.67$$
$$S_1 = 0$$
$$S_2 = 0$$
$$S_3 = 4$$
∴ $$Z \max = 2.33$$

Example 5.17:

Maximize $\quad Z = 2x_1 + 3x_2$

Subject to
$$x_1 \leq 6$$
$$x_1 + 2x_2 \leq 10$$
$$x_1 + x_2 \geq 2$$

And $\quad x_1, x_2 \geq 0$

Solution: Step 1: Set up the problems in standard form.
Introducing slack, surplus and artificial variables the problem is as follows,

Step 1:

Maximize $\quad Z = 2x_1 + 3x_2 + OS_1 + OS_2 + OS_3 - MA_1$

Subject to
$$x_1 + S_1 = 6$$
$$x_1 + 2x_2 + S_2 = 10$$
$$x_1 + x_2 - S_3 + A_1 = 2$$

And $\quad x_1, x_2, S_1, S_2, S_3, A_1 = 0$

Step 2: Find initial basic feasible solution

Substituting $x_1 = x_2 = S_3 = 0$, and the initial basic feasible solution is obtained

We get
$$S_1 = 6$$
$$S_2 = 10$$
$$A_1 = 2$$

And
$$Z = -2M$$

Step 3: Perform optimality test

Coefficient	Basic Variable	C_j b_i	2 x_1	3 x_2	0 S_1	0 S_2	0 S_3	M A_1	Exchange Ration b_i/a_{ij}
0	S_1	6	1	0	1	0	0	0	0
0	S_2	10	1	2	0	1	0	0	5
–M	A_1	2	1	1	0	0	–1	1	2←
		Z_j	–M	–M	0	0	M	–M	
		C_j–Z_j	2+M	3+M	0	0	–M	0	
				↑					

Step 4: Iteration 1:

Coefficient	Basic Variable	C_j b_i	2 x_1	3 x_2	0 S_1	0 S_2	0 S_3	Exchange Ration b_i/a_{ij}
0	S_1	6	1	0	1	0	0	0
0	S_2	6	–1	0	0	1	2	3←
3	x_2	2	1	1	0	0	–1	–2
		Z_j	3	3	0	0	–3	
		C_j–Z_j	–1	0	0	0	3	
							↑	

$$R_2 \text{ new} = R_2 \text{ old} - 2 (R_3 \text{ new})$$
$$0 = 2 - 2(1)$$
$$R_1 \text{ new} = R_1 \text{ old}$$

Step 5: Iteration 2:

Coefficient	Basic Variable	C_j b_i	2 x_1	3 x_2	0 S_1	0 S_2	0 S_3
0	S_1	6	1	0	1	0	0
0	S_3	3	−5	0	0	0.5	1
3	x_2	3	2	2	1	1	0
		Z_j	6	6	3	3	0
		$C_j - Z_j$	−4	−3	−3	−3	0

R_2 new = R_2 old / 2
R_1 new = R_1 old
R_3 new = R_3 old + R_2 new
0 = −1 + 1

∴ Optimal solution is achieved.

∴
$$S_1 = 6$$
$$S_2 = 0$$
$$S_3 = 3$$
$$x_1 = 0$$
$$x_2 = 3$$

∴ Maximize $Z = 9$

5.6 DUALITY IN LINEAR PROGRAMMING

"Dual" means two or double. Duality in linear programming implies that every linear programming problem can be analyzed in two different ways but having equivalent solutions. Each LP problem (both maximization and minimization) stated in its original form has associated with another linear programming problem, which is known as dual linear programming problem. It is immaterial which of the two problems is called primal or dual.

As in LP problem for production planning, the production manager attempts to optimize resource allocation by determining qualities for each product to be produced that will maximize the profits. But in dual LP problem, he will try to make such a plan that optimizes resources allocation so that each product is produced at that quantity such that its marginal opportunity cost equals its marginal return. Therefore the main focus of dual is to find for each resource its best marginal value, it is dual price or shadow price.

Shadow price is defined as the rate of change in the optimal objectives function value with respect to the unit change in the availability of a resource.

$$\text{Shadow price} = \frac{\text{Change in optimal objective function value}}{\text{Unit change in the availability of resources}}$$

According to the type of problem, whether maximization or minimization LP problem, the interpretation of rate of change in the value of objective function depends. The shadow price for a less than or equal to type constraint will be greater than or equal to zero because increasing the right hand side resources value cannot make the value of objective function worse. Similarly, the shadow price for a greater less than or equal to type constraint will always be less than or equal to zero because increasing the right hand side resources value cannot improve the value of the objective function.

Formation of Dual Linear Programming Problem:

We have two important forms of primal and dual problems, namely the symmetrical form and standard form.

For Example

The primal L.P problem is given in the form

Maximize $Z_n = C_1x_1 + C_2x_2 + \ldots C_nx_n$

Subject to the constraints

$$a_{11}x_1 + a_{12}x_2 + \ldots + a_{1n}x_n \leq b_1$$
$$a_{21}x_1 + a_{22}x_2 + \ldots + a_{2n}x_n \leq b_2$$
$$\vdots \qquad \qquad \vdots$$
$$a_{m1}x_1 + a_{m2}x_2 + \ldots + a_{mn}x_n \leq b_m$$

and

$$x_1, x_2, \ldots x_n \leq 0$$

Here n is variables and m is constraints Then the corresponding dual LP problem is defined as:

Minimize $\quad Z_y = b_1y_1 + b_2y_2 + \ldots + b_my_m$

Subject to the constraints

$$a_{11}y_1 + a_{21}y_2 + \ldots + a_{m1}y_m \geq C_1$$
$$a_{12}y_1 + a_{22}y_2 + \ldots + a_{m2}y_m \geq C_2$$
$$\vdots \qquad \qquad \vdots$$
$$a_{1n}y_1 + a_{2n}y_2 + \ldots + a_{mn}y_m \leq C_n$$

and

$$y_1, y_2, \ldots y_m \geq 0$$

here m – variable and n – constraints

Let us see the general relationship between primal and dual LP problems:

- If the primal contains n variable and m constrains, the dual will contain m variable and n constraints.
- The maximization problem in the primal becomes the minimization problem in the dual and vice versa.

- The maximization problem has (≤) constraints while the minimization problem has (≥) constraints.
- Constraints of ≤ type in the primal become ≥ type in the dual of vice versa.
- The coefficient matrix of the constraints of the dual is the transpose of the primal.
- The new set of variables appears in the dual.
- The constants $C_1, C_2, C_3, \ldots C_n$ in the objective function of the primal appear in the constraints of the dual.
- The constants $b_1, b_2, b_3, \ldots b_m$ in the constraints of the primal appears in the objective function of the dual.
- The variables in both problems are non-negative.

Example 5.18

Construct the dual to the primal problem

Maximize $\quad Z = 3x_1 + 5x_2$

Subject to $\quad 2x_1 + 6x_2 \leq 50,$

$\quad\quad\quad\quad 3x_1 + 2x_2 \leq 35,$

$\quad\quad\quad\quad 5x_1 - 3x_2 \leq 10,$

where $x_1 \geq 0, x_2 \geq 0 \quad\quad x_2 \leq 20$

Solution:

Let y_1, y_2, y_3 and y_4 be the corresponding dual variables, then the dual problem is given by

Minimize $\quad W = 50y_1 + 35y_2 + 10y_3 + 20y_4$

Subject to $\quad 2y_1 + 3y_2 + 5y_3 \geq 3,$

$\quad\quad\quad\quad 6y_1 + 2y_2 - 3x_3 + y_4 \geq 5,$

where, $y_1, y_2, y_3, y_4 \geq 0$

Example 5.19

Construct the dual of the problem

Maximize $\quad Z = 3x_1 - 2x_2 + 4x_3,$

Subject to $\quad 3x_1 + 5x_2 + 4x_3 \geq 7,$

$\quad\quad\quad\quad 6x_1 + x_2 + 3x_3 \geq 4,$

$\quad\quad\quad\quad 7x_1 - 2x_2 - x_3 \leq 10,$

$\quad\quad\quad\quad x_1 - 2x_2 + 5x_3 \geq 3,$

$\quad\quad\quad\quad 4x_1 + 7x_2 - 2x_3 \geq 2,$

$\quad\quad\quad\quad x_1, x_2, x_3 \geq 0$

Solution:

As the given problem is of minimization, all the constraints should be of ≥ type

∴ Multiply the third constraint by −1 on both sides, we get

$$-7x_1 + 2x_2 + x_3 \geq -10,$$

The dual of the given problem will be,
Maximize $\quad W = 7y_1 + 4y_2 - 10y_3 + 3y_4 + 2y_5$
Subject to $\quad 3y_1 + 6y_2 - 7y_3 + y_4 + 4y_5 \leq 3$
$\quad\quad\quad\quad\quad 5y_1 + y_2 + 2y_3 - 2y_4 + 7y_5 \leq -2$
$\quad\quad\quad\quad\quad 4y_1 + 3y_2 + y_3 + 5y_4 - 2y_5 \leq 4$
$\quad\quad\quad\quad\quad y_1, y_2, y_3, y_4, y_5 \geq 0$

Example 5.20
Construct the dual of the problem
Maximize $\quad Z = 3x_1 + 10x_2 + 2x_3,$
Subject to $\quad 2x_1 + 3x_2 + 2x_3 \leq 7,$
$\quad\quad\quad\quad\quad 3x_1 - 2x_2 + 4x_3 = 3,$
$\quad\quad\quad\quad\quad x_1 \geq 0, x_2 \geq 0, x_3 \geq 0$

Solution:
As the given problem is of maximization, all the constraints should be of $\leq$ type. The equation $3x_1 - 2x_2 + 4x_3 = 3$ can be expressed as a pair of inequalities
$\therefore \quad 3x_1 - 2x_2 + 4x_3 \leq 3$ or $3x_1 - 2x_2 + 4x_3 \geq 3$
Or $3x_1 - 2x_2 + 4x_3 \leq 3$ or $-3x_1 + 2x_2 - 4x_3 \leq -3$

Let $y_1, y'_2,$ and y''_2 be the associated non-negative dual variables. Then the dual of the problem is
Minimize $\quad W = 7y_1 + 3(y'_2 - y''_2)$
Subjected to $\quad 2y_1 + 3(y'_2 - y''_2) \geq 3$
$\quad\quad\quad\quad\quad 3y_1 - 2(y'_2 - y''_2) \geq 10$
$\quad\quad\quad\quad\quad 2y_1 + 4(y'_2 - y''_2) \geq 2$
$\quad\quad\quad\quad\quad$ Where $y_1, y'_2, y''_2, \geq 0$

where $y_1, y'_2, y''_2 \geq 0$
Substituting $y'_2 - y''_2 = y_2,$ where y_2 is unrestricted in sign, the dual problem becomes
Minimize $\quad W = 7y_1 + 3y_2,$
Subjected to $\quad 2y_1 + 3y_2 \geq 3,$
$\quad\quad\quad\quad\quad 3y_1 - 2y_2 \geq 10,$
$\quad\quad\quad\quad\quad 2y_1 + 4y_2 \geq 2$
where, $y_1 \geq 0, y_2$ unrestricted in sign.

Example 5.21
Construct the dual of the problem
Maximize $\quad Z = x_2 + 3x_3,$
Subject to $\quad 2x_1 + x_2 \leq 3,$
$\quad\quad\quad\quad\quad x_1 + 2x_2 + 6x_3 \geq 5,$
$\quad\quad\quad\quad\quad -x_1 + x_2 + 2x_3 = 2$
$\quad\quad\quad\quad\quad x_1, x_2, x_3 \geq 0$

Solution:
As the given problem is of minimization, all constraints should be of $\geq$ type, Multiplying the first constraints by -1 on both sides we get,
$$-2x_1 - x_2 \geq -3$$
The equation $-x_1 + x_2 + 2x_3 = 2$ can be expressed as a pair of in equalities
$$-x_1 + x_2 + 2x_3 \geq 2 \text{ and } -x_1 + x_2 + 2x_3 \leq 2$$
Or
$$-x_1 + x_2 + 2x_3 \geq 2 \text{ and } -x_1 - x_2 - 2x_3 \geq -2$$
Therefore the given problem becomes

Minimize $\quad Z = 0x_1 + x_2 + 3x_3$
Subject to
$$-2x_1 - x_2 \geq -3,$$
$$x_1 + 2x_2 + 6x_3 \geq 5,$$
$$-x_1 + x_2 + 2x_3 \geq 2,$$
$$x_1 - x_2 - 2x_3 \geq -2,$$
$$x_1, x_2, x_3 \geq 0$$

Let y_1, y_2, y'_3, and y''_3 be the associated non-negative dual variables. Then the dual of the problem is

Maximize $\quad W = -3y_1 + 5y_2 + 2y'_3 - 2y''_3$
$$-2y_1 + y_2 - y'_3 + y''_3 \leq 0$$
$$-y_1 + 2y_2 + y'_3 - y''_3 \leq 1$$
$$6y_2 + 2y'_3 - 2y''_3 \leq 3$$

Here, $y_1, y_2, y'_3, y''_3, \geq 0$,
Substituting $\quad y'_3 - 2y''_3 = y_3$
Where y_3 is unrestricted in sign, the dual problem becomes,

Maximize $\quad W = -3y_1 + 5y_2 + 2y_3$
$$-2y_1 + y_2 - y_3 \leq 0$$
$$-y_1 + 2y_2 + y_3 \leq 1$$
$$6y_2 + 2y_3 \leq 3$$

$y_1, y_2 \geq 0$, y_3 unrestricted in sign.

THEORETICAL QUESTIONS

1. What are the application of system approach in Civil Engineering?
2. What is operations research?
3. State five engineering applications of optimization?
4. Define the following:
    1. Objective function
    2. Constraints
    3. Convex and Concave set
5. Explain convex and concave functions.
6. A firm manufactures two type of blocks A and B for any day it must produce 200 nos. of B. The maximum total requirement of blocks A and B is 1250 and minimum total is 500. Both blocks are to processed on machines m_1 and m_2 available are 5 each.

Processing times in hours for each shaft on machines m_1 and m_2 are as follows.

m_1	1.5	2
m_2	1.2	1.4
profit /unit (₹)	1.5	25

it the firm has 26 working days a month, each of 8 hours, formulate the mathematical model for the problem. **[May 2013]**

7. Solve the following problem using Big m method.

   Minimize $x_0 = x_1 - 3x_2 + 2x_3$

   Subject to $3x_1 - 3x_2 + 2x_3 \geq 7$

   $-2x_1 - 4x_2 \leq 12$

   $-4x_1 + 3x_2 + 8x_3 \leq 10$

   $x_1, x_2, x_3 \geq 0$ **[May 2013]**

8. Maximize $Z = 2x_1 + 3x_2 + 4x_3$

   Subject to: $3x_1 + x_2 + 4x_3 \leq 600$

   $2x_1 + 4x_2 + 2x_3 \geq 480$

   $2x_1 + 3x_2 + 3x_3 = 540$

   $x_1, x_2, x_3 \geq 0$ Use Big-M method **[Nov. 2012]**

9. Solve the problem in Q.1 above by Two-Phase Method. **[Nov. 2012]**

10. Minimize $Z = 4x_1 + x_2$

    Subject to $3x_1 + x_2 = 3$

    $4x_1 + 3x_2 \geq 6$

    $x_1 + 2x_2 \leq 3$

    $x_1, x_2 \geq 0$

    Use Big M method **[May 2012]**

11. Applying the principle of duality, solve the following LPP.

    Minimize $Z = 3x_1 + 2x_2$

    Subject to $x_1 + x_2 \geq 1$

    $x_1 + x_2 \leq 7$

    $x_1 + 2x_2 \leq 10$

    $x_2 \leq 3$

    $x_1, x_2 \geq 0$ **[May 2012]**

■■■

Unit 6

LINEAR PROGRAMMING (B)
TRANSPORTATION AND ASSIGNMENT PROBLEM / MODEL

TRANSPORTATION PROBLEM

6.1 INTRODUCTION

Transportation problem/model is a technique used to find 'Least cost route' of transportation of goods from the company's plants (source) to its ware houses (destinations).

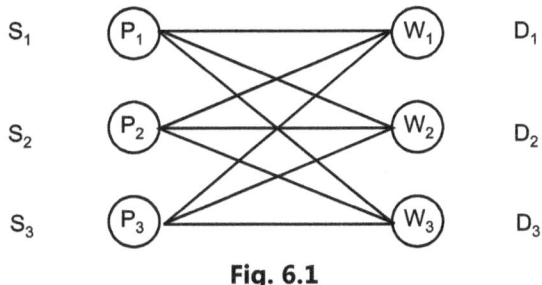

Fig. 6.1

6.2 APPLICATIONS

Transportation problem is used for the following applications:
- Scheduling of employee
- Assignment of resources such as men, machines etc.
- Inventory management
- Production and Investment analysis
- Location of factory.

6.3 MATHEMATICAL REPRESENTATION OF PROBLEM

The main characteristic of transportation problem is that sources (origins) and products must be expressed in term of only one kind of unit. Consider that there are 'm' origins and 'n' destinations. Let a_j be the number of supply item or unit available at source i (where, i = 1, 2, 3,... m) and b_j be the number of requirement units at destination j (where, j = 1, 2, 3, ... n).

Let c_{ij} represents the unit transportation cost for shipping units from origins (sources) i to destination j.

The main objective is to minimize total transportation cost for the number of units to be distributed from origin (source) i to destination j and the supply limits at the origins (sources) and demands at the distribution must be equal.

If x_{ij} ($x_{ij} \geq 0$) is the number of units distributed from source (origin) i to destination j then the equivalent linear programming problem will be as follows:

> Determine x_{ij} (i = 1, 2, 3, ...m, j = 1, 2, 3, ...n) in order minimize
>
> $$Z = \sum_{j=1}^{n} \sum_{i=1}^{m} x_{ij} c_{ij}$$
>
> Subject to $\sum_{i=1}^{m} x_{ij} = a_i, i = 1, 2, 3, ..., m$
>
> $\sum_{j=1}^{n} x_{ij} = 1, 2, 3, ..., n$
>
> Where, $x_{ij} \geq 0$
>
> The system will be in balance (The two sets of constrains will be consistent).
>
> If $\sum_{i=1}^{m} a_i = \sum_{j=1}^{n} b_j$

Generally the problem will have (m + n — 1) constituents and m x n unknowns for feasible solution of transportation problem the necessary as well as sufficient condition is

$$\sum_{i=1}^{m} a_i = \sum_{j=1}^{n} b_j$$

The transportation problem which satisfies this condition is referred as **balanced transportation problem or standard transportation problem.** The transportation problem which does not satisfy the above condition is referred as **unbalanced transportation problem.** The unbalanced transportation problem is converted to balanced transportation problem by adding dummy source (origin) or destination.

All the above discussion can be expressed in form of an effectiveness matrix as shown below in Table 6.1. In table 6.1, c_{ij} is the unit transportation cost from the jth source (origin) to j^{th} destination and x_{ij}, is quantity distributed from i^{th} source (origin) to j^{th} destination, a_i is the supply available at source (origin) and b_j is demand at destination j.

Table 6.1

	1	2	3	--	--	j	--	--	n	Supply
1	C_{11} X_{11}	C_{12} X_{12}	C_{13} X_{13}	--	--	C_{ij} X_{ij}	--	--	C_{in} X_{in}	a_1
2	C_{21} X_{21}	C_{22} X_{22}	C_{23} X_{23}	--	--	C_{2j} X_{2j}	--	--	C_{2n} X_{2n}	a_2
3	C_{31} X_{31}	C_{32} X_{32}	C_{33} X_{33}	--	--	C_{3j} X_{3j}	--	--	C_{i3n} X_{3n}	a_3
⋮	⋮	⋮	⋮	⋮	⋮	⋮	⋮	⋮	⋮	
⋮	⋮	⋮	⋮	⋮	⋮	⋮	⋮	⋮	⋮	
i	C_{i1} X_{i1}	C_{i2} X_{i2}	C_{i3} X_{i3}	--	--	C_{ij} X_{ij}	--	--	C_{in} X_{in}	a_i
⋮	⋮	⋮	⋮	--	∞-	--	--	--		⋮
⋮	⋮	⋮	⋮	--	--	--	--	--		⋮
m	C_{m1} X_{m1}	C_{m2} X_{m2}	C_{m3} X_{m3}	--	--	C_{mj} X_{mj}	C_{mj} X_{mj}	--	C_{mn} X_{mn}	a_m
Demand→	b_1	b_2	b_3	--	--	b_j	--	--	b_n	

(Origin (source) labels the rows)

6.4 BASIC TERMINOLOGY

1. **Balanced and Unbalanced Transportation Problem:** A transportation problem in which total capacity at the supply points equals the total demand at the destinations, if above condition is not satisfied then it's called unbalanced transportation problem.

2. **Dummy Source or Destination:** An extra row or column in a transportation tableau, with zero cost in each of its cells, used to balances an unbalanced problem.

3. **An Initial Feasible Solution:** A solution that satisfies supply and demand conditions and yet it may or may not be optimal.

4. **Optimal Solution:** A feasible solution is said to be optimal if it minimizes the total transportation cost.

5. **Degeneracy:** A feasible solution is said to degenerate if the number of occupied cells (called stone squares are less than (m + n- 1) where 'm' represent no. of supply points or plants and 'n' represent destinations.

Table 6.2

Plants	Warehouses		Supply
	1	2	
1	C_{11}, X_{11}	C_{12}, X_{12}	S_1
2	C_{21}, X_{21}	C_{22}, X_{22}	S_2
Demand	D_1	D_2	

C_{11}, C_{12} ---→ Unit cost of transportation

X_{11}, X_{12} ---→ Quantity of product transported

m = no of rows
n = no of col's

6.5 METHODS OF SOLUTION

Transportation problem can be solved by simplex method but it is not the most efficient method because there is a large number of variables and constraints. Most efficient method has been developed to get an optimal solution. The various steps in it are as follows:

1. Find an initial feasible solution, from the data regarding unit cost of transportation, supply and demand.
2. The initial feasible solution is basic if the number of positive allocations are (m + n – 1).
3. Test the solution for optimality.
4. If the solution is not optimal, get an improved transportation solution.
5. Repeat steps 3 and 4 till the solution becomes optimal and no further improvement is possible in the solution.

To find basic feasible solution, there are three different methods.

6.5.1 North-West Corner Method (NWCM)

According to this rule, maximum possible amount is allocated to the variable in the northwest corner (Variable X_{11}) without violating the constraint conditions. The satisfied row or column is deleted indicating that the remaining entries in that deleted row or column are zero. Then, again choose the next north-west corner entry for the remaining matrix and repeat the procedure till all the demands and supplies are satisfied.

SOLVED EXAMPLES

Example 6.1: *Water to be supplied from four sources to four different villages. The quantity and water required by each village, the quantity available at each sources and the unit cost of transport are given.*

Determine the transportation policy which will minimize the total cost of transportation. Solve by North West Corner method.

Table 6.3

Source	Village				Quantity available
	A	B	C	D	
1	6	8	10	9	60
2	5	7	11	10	70
3	3	5	14	12	110
4	2	6	10	8	150
Quantity Required	80	90	100	120	390

Solution:

Establishing an Initial Feasible Solution

The North West Corner Method (NWCM): Total quantity available at source = Total requirement at destinations. Therefore given problem is balanced transportation problem.

Source	Villages				Quantity available
	A	B	C	D	
1	(60) 6	× 8	× 10	× 9	60
2	(20) 5	(50) 7	× 11	× 10	70
3	× 3	(40) 5	(70) 14	× 12	110
4	× 2	× 6	(30) 10	(120) 8	150
Quantity required	80	90	100	120	390

Total cost of transport by NWCM method

= 60 × 6 + 20 × 5 + 50 × 7 + 40 × 5 + 70 × 14 + 30 × 10 + 120 × 8

= ₹ 3250/-

6.5.2 Least Cost Method (LCM)

1. Select the cell with the smallest unit cost in the entire transportation matrix and allocate as much as possible to this cell and eliminate that row or column in which either supply or demand is exhausted. If both a row and column are satisfied simultaneously one may be eliminated. In case the smallest unit cost cell is not unique, then select the cell where maximum allocation can be made.

2. After adjusting the supply and demand for all uncrossed-out rows and columns, repeat the procedure with the next smallest unit cost among the remaining all rows and columns and allocate as much as possible to this cell and eliminate that row and column in which either supply or demand exhausted.
3. Repeat the procedure until the entire available supply at various sources and demand at various destinations is satisfied

Example 6.2: *Solving previous problem by Least Cost Method (LCM).*

Solution: Least cost method (LCM)

Source	Villages				Quantity available
	A	B	C	D	
1	× 6	× 8	⑩ 10	㊿ 9	60
2	× 5	× 7	⑦⓪ 11	× 10	70
3	× 3	⑨⓪ 5	㉑ 14	× 12	110
4	⑧⓪ 2	× 6	× 10	⑦⓪ 8	150
Quantity required	80	90	100	120	390

1. Find least unit cost and allocate quantity satisfying row and column.
2. Find next least cost and allocate quantity.
3. In case of tie, make arbitrary selection.
4. Delete row/column which satisfied.

Total cost of transport by LCM = $80 \times 2 + 90 \times 5 + 10 \times 10 + 70 \times 11 + 20 \times 14 + 50 \times 9 + 70 \times 8$

= ₹ 2770/-

Above cost shows that LCM gives **better** solution as compared with NWCM.

6.5.3 Vogel's Approximation Method (VAM)

Step 1 : Calculate penalties for each row (column) by taking the difference between the smallest and second (next) smallest unit transportation cost in the same row (column). This difference indicates the penalty which has to be paid if one fails to allocate to the cell with the minimum unit transportation cost. These penalties in the column are written below the corresponding column and for rows to the right of the row.

Step 2 : Select the row or column with the largest penalty and allocate as much as possible in the cell having the least cost in the selected row or column satisfying the constraint conditions.

If there is a tie in the values of penalties, then select one arbitrarily. The corresponding totals of row and column are adjusted accordingly and the satisfied row or column is deleted from further calculations.

Step 3 : Check if all the rows and columns have been deleted or not. If deleted, the solution is obtained and the entire available supply at various sources and demand at various destinations are satisfied. If not go to step 4.

Step 4 : Calculate the row and column for the reduced matrix and goto step 2.

Example 6.3: *Solving same problem by Vogel's Approximation Method (VAM).*

Solution: Vogel's Approximation Method (VAM)

Source	Villages				Quantity available	Row difference					
	A	B	C	D		1	2	3	4	5	
1	× [6]	× [8]	30 [10]	30 [9]	60	2	1	1	1	1	B a l a n c e
2	× [5]	× [7]	70 [11]	× [10]	70	2	3	1	1	1	
3	× [3]	90 [5]	× [14]	20 [12]	110	2	7	2	2	—	
4	80 [2]	× [6]	× [10]	70 [8]	150	4	2	2	—	—	
Quantity required	80	80	100	120	390 / 390						
Column Diff. 1	1	1	0	1	Dash (–) indicates row or column is complete						
2	—	1	0	1							
3	—	—	0	1							
4	—	—	1	1							
5	—	—	1	1							
	B	a	l	a n c e							

Total cost of transportation by VAM
= $80 \times 2 + 90 \times 5 + 30 \times 10 + 70 \times 11 + 30 \times 9 + 20 \times 12 + 70 \times 8$
= ₹ 2750/-

This shows that VAM gives still better solution than LCM

Steps:
1. Calculate difference between two least unit cost elements for each row and each column.
2. Select the row or the column with largest difference.
3. Allocate maximum no of the units with minimum cost in selected row/column.
4. Cross out the row / column so completed by the assignment.
5. Re-determine row/ column difference for each row and each column except, the completed row(s) and column (s) ignoring the crossed out 'water square' (unfilled squares) and 'stone squares' (filled squares).
6. In case of tie for row/ column difference make arbitrary selection.

6.6 TEST FOR OPTIMALITY

Perform optimality test to find whether the obtained feasible solution is optimal or not. An optimality test can be performed only on that feasible solution in which:

(i) number of allocations is m + n – 1.

m – number of rows.

n – numbers of columns.

(ii) these (m + n – 1) allocations should be in independent positions.

An optimal solution is one in which there is not other set of transportation route that will reduce the total transportation cost. There are low methods to test optimality and improve upon.

6.6.1 Modified Distribution Method or MODI Method

MODI method saves time compared to stepping stone method. It is also applied for checking optimality. The steps involved are as follows:

Step 1 : Consider an effectiveness matrix having cost concerned with cell for which allocation have been made.

Step 2 : Consider dual variable (U_j, V_j) with respect to supply and demand constraints.

Step 3 : Write the empty cells with addition of U_j and V_j.

Step 4 : From the actual cost matrix, subtract the cell value of matrix of step (3).

Step 5 : The optimality of solution depends on signs of values in cell evaluation matrix. The significance of signs are as follows:

  (i) A negative value in vacant cell indicates that a better solution can be obtained by allocation units to the cell.

  (ii) A positive value in vacant cells shows that a poorer solution will result by allocating units of cell.

  (iii) A zero value in vacant cells indicates that another solution of same total value can be obtained by allocation units to this cell.

Checking initial feasible solution obtained by VAM for optimality

(A) Testing Initial Feasible solution for Acceptability (Feasibility) Condition.

No. of allocation (no. of stone squares) = m + n -1

Here   7 = 4 + 4 – 1

              7 = 7

SYSTEMS APPROACH IN CIVIL ENGG. (B.E. Civil Sem. - I) — LINEAR PROGRAMMING (B)

(B) Test for Optimality - By MODI Method

Source	Villages				Quantity available
	A	B	C	D	
1	6	8	10 / 30	9 / 30	60
2	5	7 / 70	11	10	70
3	3 +	5 / 90	14	12 / 20	110
4	2 / 80	6	10	8 / 70 +	150
Quantity required	80	90	100	120	390 / 390

Initial / 1st feasible solution

Step 1: Compute row and column (r and k) values from stone squares (filled square)

$$r_i + k_j = C_{ij}$$

Where, $r_i = i^{th}$ row, $k_j = j^{th}$ column, C_{ij} = Cost value in sub-square

Stone Squares	Equation $r_i + k_j = C_{ij}$	Value of r and k If $r_1 = 0$
1 C	$r_1 + k_3 = 10$	$k_3 = 10$
1 D	$r_1 + k_4 = 9$	$k_4 = 9$
2 C	$r_2 + k_3 = 11$	$r_2 = 1$
3 B	$r_3 + k_2 = 5$	$k_2 = 2$
3 D	$r_3 + k_4 = 12$	$r_3 = 3$
4 A	$r_4 + k_1 = 2$	$k_1 = 3$
4 D	$r_4 + k_4 = 8$	$r_4 = -1$

Step 2: Net cost change of water square (un-filled square)

Water Squares	Net Cost Change = $C_{ij} - (r_i + k_j)$	Scope for Improvement
1 A	$6 - (0 + 3) = 3$	No
1 B	$8 - (0 + 2) = 6$	No
2 A	$5 - (1 + 3) = 1$	No
2 B	$7 - (1 + 2) = 4$	No
2 D	$10 - (1 + 9) = 0$	No
3 A	$3 - (3 + 3) = -3$	Yes
3 C	$14 - (3 + 10) = 1$	No
4 B	$6 - (-1 + 2) = 5$	No
4 C	$10 - (-1 + 10) = 1$	No

(**Note:** If we solve above problem by stepping stone method it will give same net cost change value as that of MODI method. Therefore final allocations and total cost remains same in both method)

1. The negative value of net cost change indicates that a better solution can be obtained in next iteration. Select largest negative value i.e. -3, water square '3 A' and closed path is established making right angle turn at stone square only.
2. Alternate '+' and '-'signs are assigned on this path starting with positive sign at selected water square and determine no. of units to be shifted which equal the smallest of the values at the negative sign squares in the closed path.
3. Smallest no. at negative sign is 20, so shift it and prepare new tableau.

Source	Villages				Quantity available
	A	B	C	D	
1	6	8	10 30	9 30	60
2	5	7 70	11	10	70
3	3 20	5 90	14	12	110
4	2 60	6	10	8 90	150
Quantity required	80	90	100	120	390 / 390

Step 1: Row and Column (r and k) Values from Stone Squares

Stone squares	Equation $r_i + k_j = C_{ij}$	Value of r and k If $r_1 = 0$
1 C	$r_1 + k_3 = 10$	$k_3 = 10$
1 D	$r_1 + k_4 = 9$	$k_4 = 9$
2 C	$r_2 + k_3 = 11$	$r_2 = 1$
3 A	$r_3 + k_1 = 3$	$r_3 = 0$
3 B	$r_3 + k_2 = 5$	$k_2 = 3$
4 A	$r_4 + k_1 = 2$	$k_1 = 3$
4 D	$r_4 + k_4 = 8$	$r_4 = -1$

Step 2: Net Cost Change of Water Squares:

Water Squares	Net Cost Change = $C_{ij} - (r_i + k_j)$	Scope for Improvement
1 A	6 – (0 + 3) = 3	No
1 B	8 – (0 + 5) = 6	No
2 A	5 – (1 + 3) = 1	No
2 B	7 – (1 + 5) = 1	No
2 D	10 – (1 + 9) = 0	No
3 C	14 – (0 + 10) = 4	No
3 D	12 – (0 + 9) = 3	No
4 B	6 – (-1 + 5) = 2	No
4 C	10 – (-1 + 10) = 1	No

∴ Total cost of transportation = $30 \times 10 + 30 \times 9 + 70 \times 11 + 20 \times 3 + 90 \times 5 + 60 \times 2 + 90 \times 8$

= ₹ 2690/-

Ans.:

Minimum cost of transportation = ₹ 2690/- Optimal solution

Initial feasible solution by

∴   VAM = ₹ 2750/-

∴   LCM = ₹ 2770/-

∴   NWCM = ₹ 3250/-

VAM gives absolute minimum total cost.

6.6.2 Stepping Stone Method

Since, optimality includes checking of each empty cell (vacant cells) to determine whether or not making an allocation in it minimizes the total cost of transportation, in this method, procedure start with empty cell (vacant cell). The steps involved are as follows:

Step 1 : Choose the empty cell (vacant cell) (i.e. cell without allocation) arbitrarily.

Step 2 : Draw a path in the matrix consisting of a series of alternate horizontal and vertical line such that path begin and ends in the chosen empty cell (vacant cell) and cell corner of path lie in the cell for which allocation have been made. The path may skip over any number of allocated vacant cell.

Step 3 : Consider the corner of path in the chosen vacant cell as positive and other corner of path alternately negative, positive and so on.

Step 4 : Allocate 1 unit to chosen vacant cell, subtract and add 1 unit from cell at the corner of path, without disturbing the row and column requirement.

Step 5 : Evaluate the chosen vacant cell (i.e. the net change in cost of transportation).

(**Note:** This method is inefficient for large transportation problem since $(m-1)(n-1)$ cell evaluation should be made).

Example 6.4: *The unit cost of transporting precast units from 4 factories to 3 sites is given the following table along with the availability at each factory and the requirement of each site. Obtain the optimal solution to minimize the total cost of transportation. Use VAM to find the initial feasible solution.*

Factories	Sites			Supply
	1	2	3	
1	2	7	4	5
2	3	3	7	8
3	5	4	1	7
4	1	6	2	14
Demand	7	9	18	

Solution: 1. Initial solution by VAM

Factories	Sites			Supply	Row difference			
	1	2	3		1	2	3	4
1	5 [2]	× [7]	× [4]	5	2	2	2	—
2	× [3]	8 [3]	× [7]	8	0	0	—	—
3	× [5]	× [4]	7 [1]	7	3	—	—	—
4	2 [1]	1 [6]	11 [2]	14	1	1	1	1
Demand	7	9	18	34 / 34				
Column Diff. 1	1	1	1					
2	1	3↑	2					
3	1	1	2					
4	—	—	—					

2. Check the initial solution for feasibility
   No. of allocation (No. of stone squares) = $m + n - 1$
   $$6 = 4 + 3 - 1$$
   $$6 = 6$$

3. Check solution for optimality-**stepping stone method**
   (a) Proceed row by row and select water square
   (b) Establish a closed path, assign '+' and '-'sign
   (c) Calculate net cost change for each water square and water square with largest negative net cost change is selected for quicker or better solution a suggest, scope for improvement.

Factories	Sites			Supply
	1	2	3	
1	5 [2] −	+ [7]	+ [4]	5
2	[3]	8 [3]	[7]	8
3	[5]	+ [4]	7 [1] −	7
4	+/− 2 [1]	1 [6] +	−11 [2]	14
Demand	7	9	18	34

Select smallest of the value of negative sign square is closed path and shift it.

4. Net cost change of water square

Water square	Closed Path	Net Cost Change
12	12 → 11 → 41 → 42 → 12	7 − 2 + 1 − 6 = 0
13	13 → 11 → 41 → 43 → 13	4 − 2 + 1 − 2 = 1
21	21 → 41 → 42 → 22 → 21	3 − 1 + 6 − 3 = 5
23	23 → 22 → 42 → 43 → 23	7 − 3 + 6 − 2 = 8
31	31 → 41 → 43 → 33 → 31	5 − 1 + 2 − 1 = 5
32	32 → 42 → 43 → 33 → 32	4 − 6 + 2 − 1 = − 1 ←

5. Transportation table an with improved solution/ 2nd feasible solution

Factories	Sites			Supply
	1	2	3	
1	5− [2]	+ [7]	[4]	5
2		[3] 8	[3]	[7]	8
3		[5] −1	[4] +6	[1]	7
4	2+ [1]	[6]	−12 [2]	14
Demand	7	9	18	34

Select smallest of the value at negative sign square in closed path and shift it.

6. Net cost change of water square:

Water Square	Closed Path	Net Cost Change
12	12 → 11 → 41 → 43 → 33 → 32 → 12	7 − 2 + 1 − 2 + 1 − 4 = 1
13	13 → 11 → 41 → 43	4 − 2 + 1 − 2 = 1
21	21 → 41 → 43 → 33 → 32 → 22 → 21	3 − 1 + 2 − 1 + 4 − 3 = 4
23	23 → 22 → 32 → 33 → 23	7 − 3 + 4 − 1 = 7
31	31 → 41 → 43 → 33 → 31	5 − 1 + 2 − 1 = 5
42	42 → 43 → 33 → 32 → 42	6 − 2 + 1 − 4 = 1

As the net cost change of all water squares are positive, the optimal solution has reached.
Total cost of improved solution

= 5 × 2 + 8 × 3 + 1 × 4 + 6 × 1 + 2 × 1 + 12 × 2

= ₹ 70/-

6.7 SPECIAL CASES IN TRANSPORTATION PROBLEM

6.7.1 Unbalanced Transportation Problems → Supply ≠ Demand

Example 6.5: *A company has three warehouse W_1, W_2 and W_3 and four consumption centres C_1, C_2, C_3 and C_4. Determine the transportation policy which will minimize the total cost of transportation.*

Warehouses	Consumption Centres			
	C_1	C_2	C_3	C_4
W_1	100	120	90	20
W_2	70	30	70	70
W_3	60	60	90	110

The warehouses have all together 2200 units of a given commodity in stock detailed as under:

Warehouse	Units in Stock
W_1	700
W_2	600
W_3	900

The four consumption centres altogether used 1800 units of the commodity. Individual requirement of the consumption centre are:

Consumption	Centre Requirement
C_1	600
C_2	400
C_3	600
C_4	200

The cost of shipping one unit of the commodity from each warehouse to each consumption centre is given in the matrix table.

Solution: As combined capacity of warehouse (2200 units) is greater than the combined requirement (1800 units), one additional column, designated as dummy consumption centre (C_5) has been entered, which requiring (2220 − 1800 = 400) units and zero cell costs. (If demand exceeds the capacity, then one additional row called dummy plant equal demand and zero cell cost is inserted)

Solution by VAM:

Ware houses	Consumption centres					Capacity	Row difference				
	C_1	C_2	C_3	C_4	C_5		1	2	3	4	5
1	× [100]	× [120]	100 [90]	200 [60]	400 [0]	700	60	30	30	10	Balance
2	× [70]	400 [30]	200 [70]	× [70]	× [0]	600	30	40	0	0	
3	600 [60]	× [60]	300 [90]	× [110]	× [0]	900	60	0	30	30	
Demand	600	400	600	200	400	2200/2200					
Column Diff. 1	10	30	20	10	0						
2	10	30	20	10	—						
3	10	—	20	10	—						
4	10	—	20	—	—						
5	Balance										

1. **Check for Feasibility:**

   No. of stone squares = m + n − 1

   7 = 3 + 5 − 1

   7 = 7

2. Check for Optimality (MODI Method)

(a) Row and Column (r and k) values for Stone Square

Stone Square	Relation $r_i + k_j = C_{ij}$	r and k Values if $r_1 = 0$
$W_1 C_3$	$r_1 + k_3 = 90$	$k_3 = 90$
$W_1 C_4$	$r_1 + k_4 = 60$	$k_4 = 60$
$W_1 C_5$	$r_1 + k_5 = 0$	$k_5 = 0$
$W_2 C_2$	$r_2 + k_2 = 30$	$k_2 = 50$
$W_2 C_3$	$r_2 + k_3 = 70$	$r_2 = -20$
$W_3 C_1$	$r_3 + k_1 = 60$	$k_1 = 60$
$W_3 C_3$	$r_3 + k_3 = 90$	$r_3 = 0$

(b) Net Cost Change of Water Square

Water Square	Net Cost Change of Water Squares	
	Relation $C_{ij} - (r_i + k_j)$	Net Cost Change
W_1C_1	$C_{11} - (r_1 + k_1)$	$100 - (0 + 60) = 40$
W_1C_2	$C_{12} - (r_1 + k_2)$	$120 - (0 + 50) = 70$
W_2C_1	$C_{21} - (r_2 + k_1)$	$70 - (-20 + 60) = 30$
W_2C_4	$C_{24} - (r_2 + k_4)$	$70 - (-20 + 60) = 30$
W_2C_5	$C_{25} - (r_2 + k_5)$	$0 - (-20 + 0) = 20$
W_3C_2	$C_{32} - (r_3 + k_2)$	$60 - (0 + 50) = 10$
W_3C_4	$C_{34} - (r_3 + k_4)$	$110 - (0 + 60) = 50$
W_3C_5	$C_{35} - (r_3 + k_5)$	$0 - (0 + 0) = 0$

As net cost change of all the water squares are positive. The optimal solution has reached.

∴ Total transportation cost = $100 \times 90 + 200 \times 60 + 400 \times 30 + 200 \times 70$
$+ 600 \times 60 + 300 \times 90$
= 1,10,000/-

6.7.2 Degenerate Solution

When No. of Stone Squares ≠ or < m + n – 1

The table gives the cost of transporting drinking water from 3 sources to 5 different villages, along with availability and demand units. Determine the distribution policy for minimum cost of transport. Use VAM to find initial feasible solution.

Source	Villages					Supply
	A	B	C	D	E	
1	5	2	3	7	10	110
2	7	5	4	6	8	120
3	6	3	7	5	9	130
Demand	40	60	70	90	100	360

(a) Initial Feasible Solution by VAM:

Source	Villages					Supply	Row difference			
	A	B	C	D	E		1	2	3	4
1	40 [5]	× [2]	70 [3]	× [7]	× [10]	110	1	2	2	—
2	× [7]	× [5]	× [4]	20 [6]	100 [8]	120	1	2	1	2
3	× [6]	60 [3]	× [7]	70 [5]	× [9]	130	2	1	1	4
Demand	40	60	70	90	100	360				
Column Diff 1	1	1	1	1	1					
Column Diff 2	1	—	1	1	1					
Column Diff 3	1	—	—	1	1					
Column Diff 4	—	—	—	1	1					

Total cost = $40 \times 5 + 70 \times 3 + 20 \times 6 + 100 \times 8 + 60 \times 3 + 70 \times 5$
= ₹ 1860/-

(b) Test of Feasibility:

No. of allocation (No. of stone square) = $m + n - 1$
Here No. of stone squares = 6 and
$m + n - 1 = 3 + 5 - 1 = 7$

∴ No. of stone square ≠ $m + n - 1$ or < $m + n - 1$, Hence it is a case of degeneracy. This difficulty can overcome by placing ε (negligible quantity) in water square having least cost i.e. 1B

Source	Villages					Supply
	A	B	C	D	E	
1	40 [5]	ε+ [2]	−70 [3]	[7]	[10]	110
2	[7]	[5] +	[4]	−20 [6]	100 [8]	120
3	[6]	60 [3]	[7]	+70 [5]	[9]	130
Demand	40	60	70	90	100	360

(c) Optimum Solution by MODI Method

1. Row and Column Values of Stone Squares:

Stone square	Equation $C_{ij} = r_i + k_j$	Value of r_i and k_j If $r_1 = 0$
1 A	$r_1 + k_1 = 5$	$k_1 = 5$
1 B	$r_1 + k_2 = 2$	$k_2 = 2$
1 C	$r_1 + k_3 = 3$	$k_3 = 3$
2 D	$r_2 + k_4 = 6$	$r_2 = 2$
2 E	$r_2 + k_5 = 8$	$k_5 = 6$
3 B	$r_3 + k_2 = 3$	$r_3 = 1$
3 D	$r_3 + k_4 = 5$	$k_4 = 4$

2. Net Cost Change of Water Square:

Water Square	Net Cost Change $C_{ij} - (r_i + k_j)$	Scope for Improvement
1 D	$7 - (0+4) = 3$	No
1 E	$10 - (0+6) = 4$	No
2 A	$7 - (2+5) = 0$	No
2 B	$5 - (2+2) = 1$	No
2 C	$4 - (2+3) = -1$	YES
3 A	$6 - (1+5) = 0$	No

3. 2nd Feasible Solution:

Source	Villages					Supply
	A	B	C	D	E	
1	40 [5]	20 [2]	50 [3]	[7]	[10]	110
2	[7]	[5]	20 [4]	[6]	100 [8]	120
3	[6]	40 [3]	[7]	90 [5]	[9]	130
Demand	40	60	70	90	100	360

Degeneracy is removed

No. of stone squares = m + n - 1

4. **Row and Column Values for Stone Squares:**

Stone Square	Equation $C_{ij} = r_i + k_j$	Value of r_i and k_j If $r_1 = 0$
1 A	$r_1 + k_1 = 5$	$k_1 = 5$
1 B	$r_1 + k_2 = 2$	$k_2 = 2$
1 C	$r_1 + k_3 = 3$	$k_3 = 3$
2 C	$r_2 + k_3 = 4$	$r_2 = 1$
2 E	$r_2 + k_5 = 8$	$k_5 = 7$
3 B	$r_3 + k_2 = 3$	$r_3 = 1$
3 D	$r_3 + k_4 = 5$	$k_4 = 4$

5. **Net Cost Change of Water Squares:**

Water Square	Net Cost Change $C_{ij} - (r_i + k_j)$	Scope for Improvement
1 D	7 – (0 + 1) = 6	No
1 E	10 – (0 + 7) = 3	No
2 A	7 – (1 + 5) = 1	No
2 B	5 – (1 + 2) = 2	No
2 D	6 – (1 + 4) = 1	No
3 A	6 – (1 + 5) = 0	No
3 C	7 – (1 + 3) = 3	No
3 E	9 – (1 + 7) = 1	No

As net cost changes for all water square are positive, optimal solution has reached.

$$\text{Total cost} = 40 \times 5 + 20 \times 2 + 50 \times 3 + 20 \times 4 + 100 \times 8 + 40 \times 3 + 90 \times 5$$
$$= ₹ 1840/\text{-}$$

i.e. Minimum total cost = ₹ 1840/-

6.7.3 Maximization Objective

Transportation model technique is essentially a minimization technique. The conversion of a 'maximization' problem into a 'minimization' problem can be done by subtracting each of the profit element form the largest profit element. This difference is known as opportunity cost. Minimization of these opportunity costs thus maximizes profits.

Example 6.6: *A company manufacturing concrete pipes has plants at Mumbai, Kolkata and Kanpur. Supplies are made to three shops situated at Ranchi, Delhi and Lucknow. Each manufacturing plant has capacity of 200 units per month. The monthly requirements of shops are 150, 300 and 150 Nos. respectively. Due to difference in raw material cost and transportation cost the profit per unit is different for each shop as given below:*

	Ranchi	Delhi	Lucknow
Mumbai	290	280	300
Kolkata	250	270	230
Kanpur	350	370	380

Decide the shipping schedule to **maximize** profit.

Solution: Largest profit figure = 380

1. Equivalent minimization problems:

	Ranchi	Delhi	Lucknow
Mumbai	90	100	80
Kolkata	130	110	150
Kanpur	30	10	0

2. Initial feasible solution by VAM, using opportunity costs.

Plants	Shops			Capacity	Row difference			
	Ranchi	Delhi	Lucknow		1	2	3	4
Mumbai	50 [90]	× [100]	150 [80]	200	10	10	10	B A L A N C E
Kolkatta	100 [130]	100 [110]	× [150]	200	20	20	20	
Kanpur	× [30]	200 [10]	× [0]	200	10	–	–	
Demand	150	300	150	600				
Column Diff. 1	60	90↑	80					
2	40	10	70↑					
3	40↑	10	–					
4	BALANCE							

3. Test for feasibility

   No. of stone square = m + n – 1, 5 = 3 + 3 – 1, 5 = 5

4. Test for optimality ⇒ using MODI method
   (a) Row and column values from stone squares

Stone Square	$r_i + k_j = C_{ij}$	Value of r and k if $r_1 = 0$
Mumbai – Ranchi	$r_1 + k_1 = 90$	$k_1 = 90$
Mumbai – Lucknow	$r_1 + k_3 = 80$	$k_3 = 80$
Kolkata – Ranchi	$r_2 + k_1 = 130$	$r_2 = 40$
Kolkata – Delhi	$r_2 + k_2 = 110$	$k_2 = 70$
Kanpur - Delhi	$r_3 + k_2 = 10$	$r_3 = -60$

   (b) Net cost change of water squares

Water Square	Net Cost Change = $C_{ij} - (r_i + k_j)$	Scope for Improvement
Mumbai – Delhi	$C_{12} - (r_1 + k_2) = 100 - (0 + 70) = 30$	No
Kolkata – Lucknow	$C_{23} - (r_2 + k_3) = 150 - (40 + 80) = 30$	No
Kanpur – Ranchi	$C_{31} - (r_3 + k_1) = 30 - (-60 + 90) = 0$	No
Kanpur – Lucknow	$C_{33} - (r_3 + k_3) = 30 - (-60 + 80) = 10$	No

All net cost value are positive, optimal solution has reached.

   (c) Maximum profit

   Total max. Profit = 50 × 290 + 150 × 300 + 100 × 250 +

   100 × 270 + 200 × 370

   = ₹ 1,85,500/-

ASSIGNMENT PROBLEM

6.8 INTRODUCTION

It is a special case of transportation problem with all supplies equal to 1 and all demands equal to 1.

It was developed by D. Konig, a Hungarian mathematician, therefore is also known as Hungarian method of assignment problem.

The objective of this type of problem is to determine which source should supply one unit to which destination (i.e. which task should be assigned to which facility) so that total cost is minimum.

6.9 THE ASSIGNMENT PROBLEM IS USED FOR ASSIGNMENT OF

- Jobs to machines
- Project engineers to project
- Buildings to sites
- Contracts to bidders
- Vehicle to routes

6.10 MATHEMATICAL REPRESENTATION OF ASSIGNMENT PROBLEMS

Let x_{ij} expresses the assignment of ith workmen to j^{th} destination (item).

$$x_{ij} = \begin{bmatrix} 1, \text{ if the } i^{th} \text{ workmen is assigned to } j^{th} \text{ destination (item)} \\ 0, \text{ if the } i^{th} \text{ workmen is not assigned to } j^{th} \text{ destination (item)} \end{bmatrix}$$

This problem is given by

Minimize $z = \sum_{i=1}^{n} \sum_{j=1}^{n} C_{ij} X_{ij}$

Subject to constraints:

$\sum_{j=1}^{n} X_{ij} = 1$ for $i = 1, 2, 3,\ldots n$ (one destination (item) is assigned to i^{th} workmen)

$\sum_{i=1}^{n} X_{ij} = 1$, for $j = 1, 2, 3,\ldots n$ (one workmen is assigned to j^{th} destination (item))

and $x_{ij} = 0$ or 1 $\left(\text{or } x_{ij} = x_{ij}^2\right)$

From above, we observe that if the last condition as replaced by $x_{ij} \geq 0$, we have transportation problem with all requirement and available resources equal to 1.

6.11 SOLUTION STEPS OF ASSIGNMENT PROBLEM

1. Check the given problem for n × n matrix (i.e. No. of rows = no. of columns)
2. Subtract algebraically smallest element in each row from every element in its row similarly subtract column also. (Row operation, Column operation)
3. Connect all zeros by minimum number of horizontal and or vertical lines and check No. of straight lines = No. of rows/ columns ⇒ if satisfied then optimal solution is said to be reached.
4. Job assignment – Examine the rows one by one starting with the first row unit a row with an exclusive zero.(i.e. row with exactly one zero) is found. Mark the zero as or Δ. Similarly examine next the column for any mutual exclusive zero, make as above. After marking in row or column, cross the remaining zeros.

Example 6.7: *A departmental head has four subordinates and four tasks for completion. The subordinates differ in their capabilities and tasks differ in their work contents. His estimate of time for each subordinate and each task is given in the matrix below.*

Tasks	Subordinates Processing Time (Hrs.)			
	I	II	III	IV
A	17	25	26	20
B	28	27	23	25
C	20	18	17	14
D	28	25	23	19

How should the tasks be assigned to minimize requirements of man-hours?

Solution:

Step 1 : Check the matrix for n × n (i.e. No. of row = No. of column)

Step 2 : Subtract smallest row element (row operation.)

Tasks	Subordinates Processing Time (Hrs.)			
	I	II	III	IV
A	0	8	9	3
B	5	4	0	2
C	6	4	3	0
D	9	6	4	0

Step 3 : Subtract smallest column element (column operation)

Tasks	Subordinates Processing Time (Hrs.)			
	I	II	III	IV
A	0	4	9	3
B	5	0	0	2
C	6	0	3	0
D	9	2	4	0

Step 4 : Connect all rows by min no. of straight lines (Horizontal or vertical)

Tasks	Subordinates Processing time (Hrs.)			
	I	II	III	IV
A	~~0~~	~~4~~	~~9~~	~~3~~
B	~~5~~	~~0~~	~~0~~	~~2~~
C	6	~~0~~	3	~~0~~
D	9	~~2~~	4	~~0~~

OR

~~0 4 9 3~~
~~5 0 0 2~~   no. of. st.
~~6 0 0 0~~   lines = 4
~~9 2 4 0~~

OR

~~0~~ 4 9 ~~3~~
~~5~~ 0 0 ~~2~~   no. of. st.
~~6~~ 0 3 ~~0~~   lines = 4
~~9~~ 2 4 ~~0~~

Here, No. of straight lines (4) = No. of rows/column, the optimal solution has reached.

Step 5 : Assignment of task to subordinate (Assign one zero to, each row and column).

Tasks	Subordinates Processing time (Hrs.)			
	I	II	III	IV
A	[0]	4	9	3
B	5	✗	[0]	2
C	6	[0]	3	✗
D	9	2	4	[0]

Step 6 : Summary of allocation and processing time

Tasks	Assigned to Subordinate	Processing Time (Hrs)
A	I	17
B	III	23
C	II	18
D	IV	19

Total processing time = 77 Hrs.

Example 6.8: *The table gives the costs of employing different types of earth moving equipment in different types of jobs. Find the assignment of the equipment to various jobs such that the overall cost is minimum.*

Solution:

Equipment	Jobs				
	1	2	3	4	5
A	14	12	15	9	11
B	17	9	13	15	4
C	9	11	16	14	13
D	12	8	14	4	15
E	5	7	9	10	2

Step 1 : Check the given problem for n × n matrix.

Here no. of row (s) = no. of column (s) i.e. 5 = 5.

Step 2 : Row operation

Equip-ment	Jobs				
	1	2	3	4	5
A	5	3	6	0	2
B	13	5	9	11	0
C	0	2	7	5	4
D	8	4	10	0	11
E	3	5	7	8	0

Step 3 : Column operation

Equip-ment	Jobs				
	1	2	3	4	5
A	5	1	0	0	2
B	13	3	3	11	0
C	0	0	1	5	4
D	8	2	4	0	11
E	3	3	1	8	0

Here, no. of straight lines (4) ≠ no. of row /columns, Hence solution is not optimal.

Step 4 : Select the smallest uncovered element and subtract it from all uncovered elements including itself, add it to the elements covered twice or element at intersection of lines and reproduce other element as they are.

Step 4

Equip-ment	Jobs				
	1	2	3	4	5
A	5	1	0	1	3
B	12	2	2	11	0
C	0	0	1	6	5
D	7	1	3	0	11
E	2	2	0	8	0

Step 5 : Repeat step 4

Equip-ment	Jobs				
	1	2	3	4	5
A	4	0	0	1	3
B	11	1	2	11	0
C	0	0	2	7	6
D	6	0	3	0	11
E	1	1	0	8	0

Step 5 : Now no. of stone lines (5) = No. of rows/column, optimal solution has reached.

Step 6 : Assignment

Equip-ment	Jobs				
	1	2	3	4	5
A	4	[0]	✗	1	3
B	11	1	2	11	[0]
C	[0]	✗	2	7	6
D	6	✗	3	[0]	11
E	1	1	[0]	8	✗

Answer:

Equipment	Jobs	Cost (₹)
A	2	12
B	5	4
C	1	9
D	4	4
E	3	9

Total minimum cost = 12 + 4 + 9 + 4 + 9
= ₹ 38/-

6.12 SPECIAL CASES IN ASSIGNMENT PROBLEM

6.12.1 Maximization Objective

Assignment model is essentially a minimization technique. To solve a problem of maximization, all elements in the matrix are subtracted from the largest element in the matrix or all elements in the matrix are multiplied by – 1

Example 6.9: *A large construction company has to assign four of its sub-contractors to four projects which it has taken up for execution. The profits that can accrue to the company based on the estimates, as per the capabilities of each sub-contractor, in respect of each project, are given below in money units. Find the assignment which will maximize the company's profit.*

Contractor	Projects			
	1	2	3	4
A	25	27	28	37
B	28	34	29	40
C	35	24	32	33
D	24	32	25	28

Solution:

Step 1 : Check the given problem for n × n matrix, 4 = 4.

Step 2 : Select maximum no. (40) Subtract it from all elements or multiply by-1. Equivalent minimization problem.

Contractor	Projects			
	1	2	3	4
A	15	13	12	3
B	12	6	11	0
C	5	16	8	7
D	16	8	15	12

OR

Contractor	Projects			
	1	2	3	4
A	-25	-27	-28	-37
B	-28	-34	-29	-40
C	-35	-24	-32	-33
D	-24	-32	-25	-28

Step 3 : Row operation.

Contractor	Projects					Contractor	Projects			
	1	2	3	4			1	2	3	4
A	12	10	9	0	OR	A	12	10	9	0
B	12	6	11	0		B	12	6	11	0
C	0	11	3	2		C	0	11	3	2
D	8	0	7	4		D	8	0	7	4

e.g. $-25 - (-37) = 12$
$-27 - (-37) = 10$

Step 4 : After row operation

Contractor	Projects			
	1	2	3	4
A	12	10	9	0
B	12	6	11	0
C	0	11	3	2
D	8	0	7	4

Step 5 : Column operation

Contractor	Projects			
	1	2	3	4
A	12	10	6	0
B	12	6	8	0
C	0	11	0	2
D	8	0	4	4

No. of st lines ≠ no. of rows/column

Step 6 : Smallest element = 6

Contractor	Projects			
	1	2	3	4
A	6	4	0	0
B	6	0	2	0
C	0	11	0	8
D	8	0	4	10

Step 7 : Assignment

Contractor	Projects			
	1	2	3	4
A	6	4	[0]	✗
B	6	✗	2	[0]
C	[0]	11	✗	8
D	8	[0]	4	10

No. of straight line = No. of rows, solution is optimal

Step 8 : Solution / Answer

Contractor	Projects	Profit
A	3	28
B	4	40
C	1	35
D	2	32
Total max. Profit		135

6.12.2 Unbalanced Assignment Problems

No. of rows ≠ No. of columns

In such situations, dummy row (s)/ column (s) are inserted with zero costs.

Example 6.10: *With the performance matrix given below, which three of the four tasks should be assigned to the subordinates?*

Tasks	Subordinates		
	I	II	III
A	9	12	11
B	8	13	17
C	20	12	13
D	21	15	17

Solution: As given matrix is not squared one, we need to add a dummy subordinate / column with zero costs.

Tasks	Subordinates			
	I	II	III	IV
A	9	12	11	0
B	8	13	17	0
C	20	12	13	0
D	21	15	17	0

By applying usual procedure, the optimal solution obtained is given below.

Tasks	Subordinates			
	I	II	III	IV
A	0			
B			0	
C		0		
D				0

The final and optimum allocation is

Assign task A to - Subordinate I
Assign task B to - Subordinate III
Assign task c to - Subordinate II

6.12.3 Restrictions in Assignment

Due to the restrictions an space, size of job, process capability of machine, technical difficulties, etc do not permit the assignment of a particular job to a particular facility. This difficulty can be cover come by assigning a very high value (∞) to the corresponding cell. Allocation of this high value gives least preference to job to allocate to facility.

6.12.4 Multiple Optimal Solutions

Sometimes, a final assignment matrix contains more than required no. of independent zero elements. This shows that there is more than one optimal solution with the same total cost assignment.

Example 6.11: *Consider the problem of assigning 5 operators to 5 machines. The assignment cost are given in the following table.*

Operators	Machines				
	M_1	M_2	M_3	M_4	M_5
A	7	7	-	4	8
B	9	6	4	5	6
C	11	5	7	-	5
D	9	4	8	9	4
E	8	7	9	11	3

Operator 'A' cannot be assigned to Machine 'M_3' and Operator 'C' cannot be assigned to machine 'M_4'. Find the optimal assignment schedule.

Solution:

Step 1 : Assign a extremely high value (∞) to restricted cell

Operators	Machines				
	M_1	M_2	M_3	M_4	M_5
A	7	7	∞	4	8
B	9	6	4	5	6
C	11	5	7	∞	5
D	9	4	8	9	4
E	8	7	9	11	3

Step 2 : Row operation

Operators	Machines				
	M_1	M_2	M_3	M_4	M_5
A	3	3	∞	0	4
B	5	2	0	1	2
C	6	0	2	∞	0
D	5	0	4	5	0
E	5	4	6	8	0

Step 3 : Column operation

Operators	Machine				
	M_1	M_2	M_3	M_4	M_5
A	~~0~~	~~3~~	∞	~~0~~	~~4~~
B	~~2~~	~~2~~	~~0~~	~~1~~	~~2~~
C	3	0	2	∞	0
D	2	0	4	5	0
E	2	4	6	8	0

No. of St. Lines ≠ No. of Rows
4 ≠ 5

Step 4 :

Operators	Machine				
	M_1	M_2	M_3	M_4	M_5
A	~~0~~	~~5~~	∞	~~0~~	~~6~~
B	2	4	0	1	4
C	1	0	0	∞	0
D	0	0	2	3	0
E	0	4	4	6	0

No. of St. Lines = 5

Step 5 : Assignment Multiple optimal solution

1st Solution

Operators	Machine				
	M_1	M_2	M_3	M_4	M_5
A	✗	5	∞	[0]	6
B	2	4	[0]	1	4
C	1	[0]	✗	∞	✗
D	[0]	✗	2	3	✗
E	✗	4	4	6	[0]

B – M_3, A – M_4, C = M_2, D = M_1, E = M_5
$Z_{min} = 4 + 4 + 5 + 9 + 3 = 25$

2nd Solution

Operators	Machine				
	M_1	M_2	M_3	M_4	M_5
A	✗	5	∞	[0]	6
B	2	4	[0]	1	4
C	1	✗	✗	∞	[0]
D	✗	[0]	2	3	✗
E	[0]	4	4	6	✗

B = M_3, A = M_4, C = M_5, E = M_1, D = M_2
$Z_{min} = 4 + 4 + 5 + 4 + 8 = 25$

3rd Solution

Operators	Machine				
	M_1	M_2	M_3	M_4	M_5
A	✗	5	∞	[0]	6
B	2	4	[0]	1	4
C	1	[0]	✗	∞	✗
D	✗	✗	2	3	[0]
E	[0]	4	4	6	0

A – M_4, B – M_3, C – M_2, D – M_5, E – M_1
$Z_{min} = 4 + 4 + 5 + 4 + 8 = 25$

THEORETICAL QUESTIONS

1. How will you formulate a transportation problem as on L.P. Model? Explain how you will solve an assignment problem where a particular assignment is restricted.
2. Give mathematical formulation of the transportation and simplex method. What are difference in the nature of problem that can be solved by these methods?

3. How will you use assignment model for solving a maximisation problem? **[May 12]**
4. How will you solve a transportation problems if it is degenerate? **[May 12]**
5. What is degeneracy in transportation problem. How is it resolved? **[Nov. 12]**
6. Write a short note on:
   (i) Assignment mode? **[May 13]**
   (ii) Transportation mode?
   (iii) Advantages of assignment and transportation model in civil engineering.
7. Water is to be transported from 3 reservoirs to 5 different distribution centres. The unit cost of transportation from the various reservoirs to each of the distribution centres and the quantities available at the reservoirs and those required at the distribution centres are given in the following table:

Reservoir	Distribution Centres					Quantity Available
	1	2	3	4	5	
A	15	10	7	9	12	50
B	14	17	11	6	18	70
C	22	23	21	13	20	80
Quantity required	20	30	40	50	50	200

   (i) Find initial feasible solution by VAM.
   (ii) Find the optimal solution which will minimize the distribution policy.

8. Solve following transportation problem for which origin availabilities destination requirements are given below : **[Nov. 2011]**

	D_1	D_2	D_3	D_4	D_5	D_6	a_i
O_1	1	2	1	4	5	2	30
O_2	3	3	2	1	4	3	50
O_3	4	2	5	9	6	2	75
O_4	3	1	7	3	4	6	20
	20	40	30	10	50	25	175 Total

Solve the example by :
(i) North West Corner method
(ii) Row minima method
(iii) Column minima method

9. A construction material is to be transported from 4 sources to 5 sites. The quantity available at sources and quantities required at sites are given below. The unit transportation costs are also given in the table below : **[May 2012]**

Sources	Sites					Quantity Available
	1	2	3	4	5	
A	9	10	11	2	21	20
B	7	14	9	3	7	40
C	22	11	17	9	14	120
D	12	15	6	16	5	120
Demand	20	40	60	80	100	300 / 300

10. Solve the following transportation problem using
    (i) North West corner method
    (ii) Row minima method
    (iii) Column minima method
    (iv) Least cost method

	D_1	D_2	D_3	D_4	D_5	D_6	
01	8	10	12	16	14	10	100
02	6	8	10	12	12	18	100
03	10	6	10	11	15	13	100
04	15	12	9	14	12	16	100
05	20	9	8	13	15	12	100
	75	50	150	25	75	125	

Give transportation cost by each method by specifying the allocations. **[May 2013]**

11. The following table gives the unit cost of transporting coarse aggregates from three crushing plants to four sites. The quantity of aggregates available at the plants and that required at the work sites are indicated below.

Plants	Sites				Quantity Available
	1	2	3	4	
A	13	7	19	0	200
B	17	18	15	7	500
C	11	22	14	5	300
Demand	180	320	100	500	

(a) Find initial feasible solution by VAM
(b) Find the optimal solution which will minimize the distribution policy.

12. Find the optimal assignment for the following assignment problem with the following cost matrix **[May 2011]**

	I	II	III	IV	V	VI
A	25	23	28	12	16	25
B	52	20	27	16	15	15
C	60	36	40	55	28	17
D	16	27	12	24	25	19
E	18	19	28	17	56	70
F	29	15	20	30	40	55

13. A company has to assign five jobs to five employees such that each employee is assigned to one job. The time in hours each employee may take to perform each job is given in the table below. How should the job be assigned to the employees to minimize the total man hours?

Jobs	Employees				
	1	2	3	4	5
A	10	5	13	15	16
B	3	9	18	13	6
C	10	7	2	2	2
D	7	11	9	7	12
E	7	9	10	4	12

[May 2012]

14. A Consider the problem of assigning 5 operators to 5 machines. The assignment cost are as given below

	m_1	m_2	m_3	m_4	m_5
A	6	8	-	7	9
B	5	4	8	9	6
C	10	11	8	-	9
D	9	4	6	5	8
E	7	8	9	10	3

Operator A cannot be assigned to machines M_3 & C cannot be assigned to m_4.

Find the optimum assignment schedule. **[May 2013]**

15. Solve the following assignment problem to give minimum cost. **[May 2013]**

	A	B	C	D
1	8	9	7	15
2	18	12	17	10
3	8	10	5	16
4	12	11	8	14
5	13	7	15	9

16. Five contractors have submitted their bids for 5 projects. Contractor A and C has not bid for project 3 and 4 respectively. Find the optimal assignment for minimum cost, if the cost bid by each contractor for the projects is given below in crore rupees.

[May 2012]

Contractors	Projects				
	1	2	3	4	5
A	7	7	-	4	6
B	9	6	4	5	6
C	11	5	11	-	5
D	9	4	8	9	4
E	8	7	9	11	3

■■■

Sample Question Paper For
In-Semester Examination (30 Marks)

Time : 1 Hour Marks: 30

Q.1 (a) What are the application of Optimization technique in Civil Engineering ? **[5 M]**

(b) Explain local and Global optima, Saddle point with figure. **[5 M]**

OR

Q.2 (a) Explain convex and concave function. **[5 M]**

(b) Check whether the given set is convex or otherwise. **[5 M]**

(i) $x_1^2 + x_2 \leq 9$

(ii) $x_2 - 4x_1^2 \geq 16$

Q.3 (a) Minimize $Z = x^3 - 108x$ within an accuracy of 0.1% in the range of 0 to 1. Carry out first three iterations. Use Fibonacci method. **[5 M]**

(b) Use method of Lagrangian multiplier to **[5 M]**

Maximize $\quad Z = 6x_1 + 8x_2 - x^2{}_1 - x^2{}_2$

$\quad\quad\quad\quad\quad 4x_1 + 3x_2 = 16$

Subject to $\quad 3x_1 + 5x_2 = 15,$

Where $-x_1, x_2, \geq 0$

OR

Q.4 (a) Solve the following problem by Golden section method. **[5 M]**

Maximize $f(x) = 48x - 60x^2 + 3x^2$ with n=4 and within the range (0 to 1)

(b) Maximize $f(x) = 6x_1 + 4x_2 - 2x^2{}_1 - 2x_1 x_2 - 2x^2{}_2$ Take $x_0 = (1, 1)$ and carry out first two iterations only. Using Steepest gradient technique. **[5 M]**

Q.5 (a) In a factory, there are six jobs to perform, each of which should go through two machines A and B in the order AB. The processing timings (in hrs.) for the jobs are given below. Determine the sequence for performing the jobs so as to minimize the total elapsed time. **[5 M]**

Job	1	2	3	4	5	6
Machine A	7	4	2	5	9	8
Machine B	3	8	6	6	4	1

(b) What are the main components of a waiting line model/ queuing. Explain Kendall-Lee notation. **[5 M]**

OR

Q.6 The inter arrival time and the service time in a waiting line problem have the following frequency distribution based on 10 such arrivals. **[10 M]**

Inter Arrival Time (hrs)	1	2	3	4	5	6	7
Frequency	18	10	20	20	16	10	6
Service time (hrs)	2		3	4	5		6
Frequency	7		10	46	32		5

Calculate the average waiting time and percentage waiting time of an arrival, average idle time and percentage idle time of the server, by simulating 10 such arrivals.

Use the following random numbers

Arrivals	60	48	64	65	83	31	40	80	55	15
Service	43	24	12	72	75	10	9	42	88	18

■■■

Sample Question Paper for End-Semester Examination (70 Marks)
Paper - I

Time : 2.30 Hours   Marks: 70

Q.1 (a) Explain convex and concave Function. **[6 M]**

(b) Use Newton's method to minimize **[6 M]**
$$f(x) = 2x_1^2 + 2x_2^2 + 2x_1x_2 - 3x_1 - 2x_2$$
Take the starting points as (0, 0)

(c) Explain in brief the various components of a queueing system. What is Kendall-Lee notation ? **[6 M]**

OR

Q.2 (a) Explain Term
  (i) Local Optima
  (ii) Global Optima
  (iii) Unimodal Function **[6 M]**

(b) Give the algorithm for Steepest Gradient method. What are the advantages of Newton's method over Steepest Gradient method ? **[6 M]**

(c) Find the sequence that minimizes the total time required for performing the following jobs on three machines in the order A-B-C **[8 M]**

Job	Processing Times In Minutes		
	A	B	C
1	8	3	8
2	3	4	7
3	7	5	6
4	2	5	9
5	5	1	10
6	1	6	9

Q.3 (a) What is the definition of Dynamic Programming ? What are the main characteristics of DP ? **[8 M]**

(b) Solve following DP problem : **[8 M]**

A firm has divided its marketing area into 3 zones A, B, and C. The amount of sales depends upon the number of salesman in each zone. The firm has been collecting the data regarding sales and salesman in each area over a number of past years. The information is summarised as follows:

Areas → No. of Salesman ↓	A	B	C
0	32	36	45
1	47	48	50
2	65	72	65
3	75	72	70
4	82	80	74
5	95	90	86
6	98	95	92
7	100	105	108
8	100	108	110
9	90	110	115

Allocate the salesman to the zones so that the total sales are maximum.

OR

Q.4 (a) Explain the following in the context of DP : [6 M]
(i) Principle of optimality (ii) State (iii) Stage

(b) Find the shortest path from 1 to 14 with the durations given as [10 M]

Act	1-2	1-3	1-4	2-6	3-6	4-7	2-5	5-9	6-9	7-9	5-8	7-10	10-13	13-14	8-11	11-14	9-12	12-14
du	5	4	6	3	9	8	2	4	5	3	6	5	5	4	8	4	7	7

Q.5 (a) Minimize $Z = 4x_1 + x_2$
Subject to
$3x_1 + x_2 = 3$
$4x_1 + 3x_2 \geq 6$
$x_1 + 2x_2 \leq 6$
$x_1, x_2 \geq 0$

Use Big M method. [12 M]

(b) What is degeneracy in LPP ? How is it resolved ? [4 M]

OR

Q.6 (a) Solve following problem : [10 M]
Maximize $Z = 4x_1 + 10x_2$
Subject to
$x_1 + x_2 + \leq 2$
$5x_1 + 2x_2 \leq 10$
$-2x_1 - 8x_2 \geq -12$
$x_1, x_2 \geq 0$

(b) How will you solve a LPP graphically ? What are its limitations ? Explain with example an LP problem which has [6 M]
(i) Infinite solution
(ii) No feasible solution

SYSTEMS APPROACH IN CIVIL ENGG. (B.E. Civil Sem. - I)   SAMPLE QUESTION PAPERS

Q.7 (a) Solve the following maximization assignment problem. The estimated sales per month in four different cities by 5 different managers are as follows : **[8 M]**

	A	B	C	D
P	13	15	12	14
Q	12	14	10	12
R	16	18	14	14
S	15	15	13	13
T	14	15	14	12

Find out the assignment of managers to cities in order to maximize sales.

(b) Solve following transportation problem and optimize the transportation cost using least cost method. **[10 M]**

	E	F	G	H	J	Supply
A	15	10	8	14	13	50
B	9	13	10	20	19	75
C	13	20	12	6	7	125
D	12	19	17	10	6	100
Demand	50	75	75	100	50	

OR

Q.8 (a) Cement is to be transported from 4 warehouses to 3 sites. The quantity available at each warehouse and that required at each site and the unit cost of transport are given below. Determine the transportation policy which will minimize the total cost of transportation. Use the solution obtained by least cost method as the initial basic feasible solution, to find the optimal solution. **[10 M]**

Warehouse	Sites			Quantity Available
	1	2	3	
1	2	7	4	5
2	3	3	1	8
3	5	4	7	7
4	1	6	2	14
Quantity Required	7	9	18	

(b) Explain degeneracy in a Transportation Problem. How is it resolved ? **[8 M]**

Sample Question Paper For
End-Semester Examination (70 Marks)
Paper - 2

Time : 2.30 Hours   **Marks: 70**

Q.1 (a) Verify whether the following function are convex or concave   **[6 M]**

(i) $f(x) = 2x_1^3 - 8x_2^2$

(ii) $f(x) = 2x^4 + 8x^2 + 5x$

(b) Give the steps to solve problems using one dimensional search technique: Dichotomous search, Fibonocci method and Golden rule section.   **[6 M]**

(c) Solve the following sequencing problem if the order of processing in C-A-B. Find the idle time of the machines and jobs   **[8 M]**

		1	2	3	4	5	6	7	8
Jobs	A	4	6	7	4	5	3	6	3
Machine	B	5	10	7	8	11	8	13	13
	C	5	6	3	4	4	9	15	11

OR

Q.2 (a) What is linear programming? Discuss the application of LP in Civil Engineering. **[6 M]**

(b) Use the method of Lagrangian multiplier to   **[8 M]**

Maximize $Z = 6x_1 + 8x_1 - x_1^2 - x_2^2$

Subject to $4x_1 + 3x_2 = 16$

                $3x_1 + 5x_2 = 15$

where, $x_1, x_2 \geq 0$

(c) How will you solve a sequencing problem of 2-jobs through m machines? **[6 M]**

Q.3 (a) Explain the following terms used in dynamic programming: **[6 M]**

(i) Bellman's principle of optimality

(ii) Stages and states.

(b) The management of a construction company is considering allocation of 80 lakh among three of its sites. The level of investment and the expected profits are given below. Using dynamic programming determine the investment policy which will maximize the total profits: **[10 M]**

Investment (In Lakhs of Rs.)	Profit (in Lakhs of Rs.)		
	Site A	Site B	Site C
0	0	0	0
20	4	6	8
40	10	12	18
60	30	24	22
80	28	30	32

OR

Q.4 (a) Explain forward recursion and backward recursion in dynamic programming. **[4 M]**

(b) State any four different application of dynamic programming. **[4 M]**

(c) Solve the following problems using DP **[8 M]**

$$\text{Maximize } Z = 36x_1 + 8x_1^2 - 6x_1^3 + 36x_2 - 3x_2^3$$

Subject to $x_1 + x_2 = 3$

$x_1, x_2 \geq 0$

Q.5 (a) Minimize $Z = 4x_1 + 12x_2 + 18x_3$ **[12 M]**

Subject to

$x_1 + 3x_3 \geq 3$

$2x_2 + 2x_3 \geq 5$

$x_1, x_2, x_3 \geq 0$

Use Big M method.

(b) Explain what is an **[4 M]**

(i) Unbound solution

(ii) Infeasible solution

OR

Q.6 (a) Explain the procedure of solving a linear programming problem by Two-Phase method. What is its advantages over Big M method? **[4 M]**

(b) Maximize $Z = 3x_2 + 3x_2 + 4x_3$

Subject to: $3x_1 + x_2 + 4x_3 \leq 600$ **[12 M]**

$2x_1 + 4x_2 + 2x_3 \geq 480$

$2x_1 + 3x_2 + 3x_3 = 540$

$x_1, x_2, x_3 \geq 0$

Use Two-Phase method.

Q.7 (a) Solve following transportation problem for which origin availabilities and destination requirements are given below: **[12 M]**

	D_1	D_2	D_3	D_4	D_5	D_6	a
O_1	1	2	1	4	5	2	30
O_2	3	3	2	1	4	3	50
O_3	4	2	5	9	6	2	75
O_4	3	1	7	3	4	6	20
	20	40	30	10	50	25	175 Total

Solve the example by
(i) North West Corner method
(ii) Row minima method
(iii) Column minima method

(b) Give mathematical formulation of the transportation and simplex method. What are differences in the nature of problem that can be solved by these methods? **[6 M]**

OR

Q.8 (a) Find the optimal assignment for the following assignment problem with the following cost matrix. **[12 M]**

	I	II	III	IV	V	VI
A	25	23	28	12	16	25
B	52	20	27	16	15	15
C	60	36	40	55	28	17
D	16	27	12	24	25	19
E	18	19	28	17	56	70
F	29	15	20	30	40	55

(b) Explain when degeneracy occurs in a Transportation problem. **[2 M]**
(c) Explain how a transportation mode is a linear programming model. **[4 M]**

www.ingramcontent.com/pod-product-compliance
Lightning Source LLC
Chambersburg PA
CBHW080243170426
43192CB00014BA/2542